AN ILLUSTRATED HISTORY OF

World War II

Crisis and Courage: Humanity on the Brink

gartenlokal

AN ILLUSTRATED HISTORY OF

World War II

Crisis and Courage: Humanity on the Brink

Foreword by Senator Bob Dole

BARNES & NOBLE
NEW YORK

This 2006 edition published by Barnes & Noble, Inc.
by arrangement with Direct Holdings Americas Inc.

2006 Barnes & Noble

ISBN-13: 978-0-7607-8412-9

ISBN-10: 0-7607-8412-4

Printed and bound in China

3 5 7 9 10 8 6 4 2

Editorial Director: Morin Bishop
Design Director: Barbara Chilenskas
Project Editor: Jeff Labrecque
Photography Editor: Alan Gottlieb
Managing Editor: Theresa Deal
Copyreader: A. Lee Fjordbotten

Writing by Harris Andrews, John Bolster, Steve Hyslop, *and* Jim Lynch

Designers: Jia Baek, Vincent Mejia, Ralph Groom

Historical Consultant: Professor Loyd Lee, SUNY–New Paltz

Researchers: Andrew Blais, Kate Brash, Ward Calhoun

Photo Researchers: Christine Hinze (London), Angelika Lemmer (Bonn), Martin Baldessari (Washington, DC)

Cartography by Alex Reardon

Table of Contents

Foreword

World War II was the most significant event of the 20th century, and those of us who encountered it firsthand had no choice but to be defined by it. The war was a life-altering experience, and everyone who lived through the war—whether as a soldier or a civilian—has his or her own story. For many people, the euphoria of peace in 1945 was tempered by the loss of loved ones on distant battlefields. Although the wounds heal, the scars never disappear.

There is nothing glorious about war. Approximately 60 million lives were lost during World War II, but that unfathomable number can't begin to measure the war's actual costs. History remembers who fired the first shot and who eventually won but often forgets the destructive impact of war on individual lives. Women and children die. Families are ripped apart indiscriminately and, in some cases, simply erased.

The American war experience was unique. With the exception of Pearl Harbor, our borders were never seriously threatened. Our women never had to fear occupying armies, and our children never had to sleep among the bombed-out ruins of their homes. Our war was not one of conquest or annihilation but one of liberation. We were sent to Europe and the Pacific to do nothing less than free the world. Ordinary Americans, raised in the poverty of the Great Depression, were saddled with the extraordinary task of fighting for the dignity of every life, the possibility of every mind, and the divinity of every soul. And we succeeded.

Time has a way of oversimplifying the past, often at the expense of the truth. In

the 21st century, World War II is commonly portrayed as an epic collision between good and evil. The undeniable evil of the Holocaust encourages this point of view. But this broad-brush approach to history overlooks America's treatment of Japanese Americans and ignores communism as a postwar threat to freedom. The truth is that battlefields are devoid of every ideological "ism" except heroism. Heroes are made by every soldier's desire to return home and live in peace. The promise of home inspired American soldiers to bravely charge the guns of Omaha Beach, just as it spurred thousands of Japanese soldiers to defend Okinawa to their last breaths. Maybe the inherent strengths of freedom did guide the Allies to ultimate victory, and maybe divine providence played a hand in our success, but heroism was never a monopolized virtue.

War is hell, and it is the responsibility of those who are spared its wrath to make sure that future generations never forget this fact. As you enjoy this book, I hope you'll see war for what it really is. It isn't only Winston Churchill charming the camera with his Victory salute or Douglas MacArthur triumphantly wading ashore in the Philippines. War is also the look of terror on an elderly woman's face after her home is bombed. It is also the mass graves of the German death camps, and it is the searing burns on the skins of Hiroshima children. The one undeniable lesson of World War II is that there must never be a World War III. We must remember what Albert Einstein said when he was asked how World War III would be fought: "I don't know, but World War IV will be fought with sticks and stones." Civilization could not survive a third global catastrophe. My generation's greatest accomplishment was not winning the war but sustaining the peace.

SENATOR BOB DOLE

Senator Bob Dole is a decorated World War II veteran and the national chairman of the World War II Memorial Campaign. To learn more about the Memorial, call 1-800-639-4WW2 or visit www.wwiimemorial.com.

The Road to War: 1918-1939

The Road to War: 1918-1939

On November 10, 1918, at a hospital near Berlin, Lance Corporal Adolf Hitler learned that the great war in which he had twice been seriously wounded had ended in utter defeat for Germany. Hitler had only recently recovered his eyesight after being gassed by advancing Allied forces in Belgium. Now he would have to cope with an injury of another sort—a blinding blow to his national pride. "Again everything went black before my eyes," he wrote of that day when he confronted defeat. "I tottered and groped my way back to the dormitory, threw myself on my bunk, and dug my burning head into my blanket and pillow."

The 29-year-old Hitler would spend the next two decades nursing his grievances and working to restore German might. In the process, he would ignite a conflict even greater and more terrible than the fearful struggle he had experienced as a soldier—a second world war born of the bitter consequences of the first.

Various factors conspired to transform Hitler from an obscure war veteran into the firebrand Germans would come to hail as their Führer, or leader. The victorious Allies unwittingly aided Hitler's cause by imposing harsh terms at the Versailles Peace Conference that stripped Germany of its colonies and transferred sizable chunks of the German homeland to France, Denmark, Poland, and the new nation of Czechoslovakia. The Rhineland, Germany's industrial core, was demilitarized, and the Allies demanded steep financial reparations that contributed to runaway inflation and destabilized the fledgling German Weimar Republic.

The war's end came as a profound shock to most Germans, who had been assured by their leaders until the last months of the war that victory was near. Hitler and other right-wing nationalists claimed that German troops had been stabbed in the back by leftists, blaming Germany's humiliation on what Hitler called the "Jewish doctrine of Marxism." As early as 1921 Hitler vowed to "prevent the Jewish subversion of our people, if necessary by securing its instigating virus in

Timeline: 1918-1939

1918
November 11
World War I ends.

1919
June 28
The Treaty of Versailles is signed.

1922
October 28
Benito Mussolini becomes premier of Italy.

1923
November 8/9
Beer Hall Putsch: Adolf Hitler tries to seize control of Bavaria. He fails, is captured, and is imprisoned.

1925
July 18
Publication of Hitler's Mein Kampf.

1929
October 29
The U.S. stock market crashes; investors lose $30 billion in a matter of days.

STAGE BROADWAY SCREEN
VARIETY
WALL ST. LAYS AN EGG

concentration camps." By fusing anticommunism with anti-Semitism he transformed his campaign for German supremacy into a venomous racial and ideological crusade.

Hitler found a vehicle for his ambitions in 1921, when he took charge of the obscure German Workers' Party. He would later rename the party the National Socialist, or Nazi, party—a deceptive name for an organization led by a man who despised both democracy and socialism. He gained notoriety two years later when he landed in prison after he tried in vain to overthrow the Bavarian government. Released after serving just nine months of a five-year sentence, he rededicated himself to achieving his goals within the political system. The depression that descended on Germany in 1929 increased the appeal of his radical rhetoric and brought the Nazis success at the polls. By 1932 he had the support of nearly one-third of the electorate and controlled Germany's largest political party. In January 1933, Hitler became chancellor and moved quickly to dismantle the democratic institutions that had brought him to power.

Once dictator, Hitler was free to pursue his long-term goal of forging a greater German Reich—an empire embracing all the territory lost in 1919 and more, including Alsace-Lorraine, Austria, and portions of Czechoslovakia and Poland. Most German-speakers in those areas would be welcomed into the Reich. Jews, Slavs, Gypsies, and others the Nazis considered undesirable, however, would be displaced, deported, or confined to ghettos or concentration camps to provide *Lebensraum*—or living space—for people Hitler deemed racially pure.

To secure this greater Reich, Hitler renounced restrictions on German rearmament in 1935 and launched a rapid buildup of his Wehrmacht—or armed forces—in direct violation of the Treaty of Versailles. Within a few years he had a war machine that struck fear into the hearts of rival powers. Few doubted his willingness to use it in his crusade to expand the Reich. The great question was which nations would oppose him and which would join him in defying the rules of international aggression laid out in 1919 in the charter for the League of Nations.

One likely source of support for Hitler lay to the south, where Benito Mussolini and his black-shirted fascists had ruled Italy with an iron fist since 1922. Hitler admired the Duce, and in the late 1920s and early 1930s, it was Mussolini who was inspiring the growing legions of dedicated fascists. Although fascists flexed their muscles throughout Europe in the interwar years, the fascist movement lacked

1931

September 18

The Japanese invade Manchuria.

1932

November 8

Franklin Roosevelt is elected president of the United States.

1933

January 30

Hitler is named chancellor of Germany.

February 27

The German Reichstag burns, enabling Hitler to suspend basic liberties.

1935

October 3

Italy invades Ethiopia

a coherent political philosophy. Taking its name from the Latin word *Fasces*, the ceremonial bundle of rods and ax that symbolized the strength and unity of ancient Rome, fascism promoted totalitarian leadership, fanatical nationalism, and a total subserviance of the individual to the well-being of the state. Unlike communism or democracy, which were driven by ideology, fascism fed on fear and hatred. Fascists like Mussolini and Hitler offered their people a radical vision for rebuilding the world through strength and violence.

Despite the marked similarities between the regimes, however, Italy had opposed Germany in the previous war and the two dictators were wary of each other. Ultimately, Mussolini sided with Hitler because he longed for an empire in North Africa. In Mussolini's words, the western nations were divided into the "haves"—the established imperial powers—and "have nots," like the Germans and Italians who aspired to empire and saw French and British imperialists as "our rivals, our competitors, our enemies."

A similar yearning for empire would lead Japan to seek an alliance with Germany and Italy. The booming population and industries of Japan had outstripped the finite resources of its home islands. One tempting avenue of expansion lay to the west in China, a nation convulsed by the struggle of its Nationalist leadership to suppress a Communist revolution. China alone stood little chance of resisting Japanese aggression. But if the western powers responded by cutting off shipments of vital resources to Japan, Tokyo would have to knuckle under or widen its offensive to include the resource-rich Asian colonies of the British, French, and Dutch. An alliance with Germany offered Japan the attractive prospect of picking off the Asian possessions of those European powers while they reckoned with the more immediate threat from Berlin.

Britain and France indeed feared losing control of their distant colonies if war erupted, and that may have been one reason they failed to challenge Hitler when he first violated the Versailles Treaty. But the root cause of their reluctance to oppose the Führer when he was most vulnerable was the memory of the unimaginable carnage of World War I, in which Britain and France each had lost a million men. The specter of renewed conflict on that scale left them eager for peace at almost any price.

In France sharp political divisions between left and right—intensified by the bitter civil war in neighboring Spain between left-wing Republicans and right-wing Nationalists—made it that much harder for elected leaders to build a consensus and meet Hitler's challenge. But even in Britain, where ideological differences were less pronounced, politicians found little public support for efforts to thwart German expansionism. Neville Chamberlain, who became prime min-

1936

March 7

German troops occupy the Rhineland.

July 17

Spanish Civil War begins; Italy and Germany send military aid to Franco's Nationalists

TODAS LAS MILICIAS FUNDIDAS EN EL EJERCITO POPULAR

1937

July 7

Sino-Japanese war begins.

1938

March 12/13

Germany annexes Austria.

September 29

Munich Conference: The leaders of Britain, France, Germany, and Italy meet to decide the fate of Czechoslovakia. Czechoslavakia is dismembered but war is averted.

October 1

German troops march into Czechoslovakia.

ister of Britain in 1937 and was vilified in later times for appeasing Hitler, drew criticism in his own day for boosting defense spending in response to German rearmament. He characterized his policy toward Germany as one of "hoping for the best, but preparing for the worst." Within his own Conservative Party, Chamberlain's policies of appeasement found little opposition. Hitler himself hoped for a deal with Britain that would allow Germany to expand on the continent unhindered by British troops or the formidable Royal Air Force. Not until he came up against the unyielding opposition of Winston Churchill, Chamberlain's successor, would he abandon that hope.

If Hitler failed to anticipate the full measure of British resistance to his plans, he appeared all but oblivious to the risk of arousing the fury of the world's two sleeping giants—the United States and the Soviet Union. But Hitler had reason to discount the military readiness of both nations. In Washington, President Franklin Roosevelt was preoccupied with efforts to ease the Depression and was keenly aware that most Americans were against involvement in another European war. Although the U.S. was an industrial behemoth, it favored worldwide disarmament, and its military posed little or no threat to Hitler. The reduced American armed forces consisted of a mere 170,000 men in uniform in 1939—only the 17th largest army in the world. In Moscow, Josef Stalin—a dictator every bit as ruthless as Hitler—was intent on purging his own regime of suspected dissidents in his effort to consolidate power. Stalin's Great Terror claimed the lives of thousands of Red Army officers, leaving Stalin ill-equipped to wage war against a major power and open to a pact of some kind with Germany that would allow both dictators to pursue their own agendas. Hitler, of course, had already targeted the vast expanses of the Soviet Union as the crown jewel of Germany's quest for *Lebensraum*. If he could prolong America's neutrality and befriend the Soviets until the time was right for attack, all of Hitler's goals were in reach.

Hitler embarked on his quest for supremacy with the immediate aim of avenging Germany's humiliating defeat in the last war by establishing a greater German Reich in central Europe. His long-term aims were nothing short of global domination. As of the mid-1930s, his potential foes showed little inclination to oppose him, and he stood a good chance of success. But if he expanded his territorial ambitions to absorb Europe too quickly, he risked becoming embroiled in a global conflict eerily similar to the one that brought Germany to its knees in 1918: a struggle against the combined resources of France, Britain, the Soviet Union, and the United States. In seeking to undo the past, he exposed his nation—and the world—to a haunting repetition of that earlier nightmare, rendered all the more terrible this time around by fearsome new engines of destruction.

1939

November 9 — ***Kristallnacht*: Anti-Semitic violence erupts in Germany.**

August 23 — **Germany and the Soviet Union sign a non-aggression pact.**

September 1 — **Germany invades Poland.**

September 3 — **Britain and France declare war on Germany.**

September 17 — **Soviet Union invades Poland.**

November 30 — **Soviets attack Finland.**

Benito Mussolini (below) helped to revive Italy's sagging self-esteem. The Duce's impending invasion of Ethiopia was designed to recapture the glory of the Roman Empire.

Rehearsal for War

Rows of Nazi police goose-step past Adolf Hitler at Nuremberg in 1939 (left), echoing the Third Reich's march to war. Members of the German Kondor Legion earned the Red Military Service Cross (below) for fighting in Spain's civil war.

"We were somewhere in North Africa when we heard a dull distant crash, which echoed to the farthest wastes of the desert." F. Scott Fitzgerald, scribe of the "Roaring '20s," had been living abroad in October 1929, and his words referred to the United States stock market meltdown, which was the beginning of the end for countless Americans' life savings. Wall Street's collapse plunged the country into a depression that had already crippled the rest of the world. In fact, the economic crisis in the U.S. intensified the problems elsewhere. Without American investors to foot a large part of the bill, international credit began to evaporate. Many nations passed high tariffs to stanch the flow of red ink in their economies, but no single government was capable of hauling the world out of the financial quagmire. By 1932 some 30 million people in industrialized nations were unemployed. A year later nearly half of all U.S. banks had failed, and world trade had plummeted to roughly one third of its 1929 total volume. Conditions were becoming more and more favorable for radical political solutions.

In the Far East, Japan, which missed out on the prosperity of the 1920s, was particularly ripe for change. With its banks already reeling from a recession and its agricultural system in disarray, the island nation, heavily dependent upon foreign trade, was ill-equipped to cope with the debilitating Great Depression. While its divided Parliament dithered over solutions, Japan's military leaders endorsed foreign conquest as the only means of establishing Japan as a preeminent global presence and restoring

the proud nation's dignity. Neighboring China—weakened by civil war—loomed as the most inviting target, and in September 1931, Japanese troops swiftly occupied the province of Manchuria. China pleaded to the international community, but the League of Nations failed to enforce its resolutions for Japanese withdrawal. Ignoring the outcry, Japan established the puppet state of Manchukuo and pulled out of the League of Nations in March 1933.

Its imperialist appetite whetted, Japan scanned the horizon for further conquest. Manchukuo was gradually expanded to include the provinces of Jehol and eastern Chahar and in 1937 undeclared war between China and

Japanese infantrymen (above) lay down an angled line of fire through holes in a Shanghai staircase in 1937. Injured Chinese villagers flee flaming buildings after the bombing of Chungking (center). Nationalist leader Chiang Kai-shek ultimately relocated his capital to this mountain city, which was impervious to ground assault but vulnerable to air attacks.

Japan erupted after a relatively minor skirmish on the Marco Polo Bridge, near Peking. Although Japan euphemistically called this conflict the "China Incident," many historians contend that the firefight on the Marco Polo Bridge marked the true beginning of World War II.

In Germany, Adolf Hitler's Nazi Party, which was attracting adherents with a vicious doctrine of racial hatred, took advantage of the dour social and economic conditions by blaming the nation's postwar misfortune on communists, Jews, and other non-Aryans. In dramatic public rallies, Hitler inspired awe for his oratorical prowess even among his rivals. "His words go like an arrow to their target; he touches each private wound... liberating the mass unconscious, expressing its innermost aspirations, telling it what it most wants to hear," wrote Otto Strasser, head of a competing party faction.

In September 1930 a restless and uneasy public elected 107 Nazis to the Reichstag—the party's largest gain up to that point. Sensing momentum Hitler began a furious 27-month campaign for the chancellery, employing all of the weapons at his disposal, including intense charisma, political finesse, and murderous coercion. Joseph Goebbels's Nazi propaganda apparatus—consisting of leaflets, speeches, newspaper articles, and even movies—hammered Germans with the message that they should unite under one Führer and attack their "real" enemies:

Hitler's blacklist of scapegoats and undesirables. Gangs of brown-shirted *Sturmabteilung*—the dreaded SA storm troopers—roamed the streets and terrorized any opposition. Hitler crisscrossed the country by airplane, speaking at wildly popular mass meetings. In 1932 as unemployment soared to 6,000,000—30 percent of the workforce—more and more Germans became susceptible to Hitler's intoxicating message and the Nazis won 230 of 608 Reichstag seats in the national elections. On January 30, 1933, a beleaguered President Paul von Hindenburg, a war hero and the head of the teetering German government, appointed Hitler chancellor of the German Reich. That night, as 25,000 celebrants streamed through the Brandenburg Gate, Nazi-controlled Radio Cologne broadcast the news across the land: "A million hearts are aflame! Rejoicing and gratitude pour forth!"

Hitler solidified his control by granting himself emergency powers after a largely manufactured communist-revolt "crisis." Individual freedoms were abolished and Nazi enemies were brutalized, locked up, or murdered. When Hindenburg passed away in August 1934, Hitler consolidated the offices of president and chancellor and assumed complete control. The Führer had become dictator, and even Goebbels was astonished at the

Hitler greets President Hindenburg (above), whose death in August 1934 conveniently paved the way for Hitler's ascendancy to absolute power. The Führer went to great lengths to legitimize his Nazi regime, approving the designs for minor military regalia—like this decorative Air Protection League dagger (inset).

all, Hitler would issue more than 400 decrees designed to systematically smash all political opposition, eradicate the Jewish people from German society, promote an Aryan "master race," and march Germany toward its destiny of world domination.

Hitler's decision in October 1933 to withdraw Germany from the League of Nations foreshadowed broader plans. Two years later, in utter defiance of Versailles, Germany began to fully rearm, greatly bolstering its economy in the process. Hitler's tactics succeeded in revitalizing German pride. When Hitler was appointed chancellor the Nazi party claimed 850,000 members; in 1940 that number exceeded four million. Bursting at the seams with nationalistic fervor, the Reich was poised to overflow its borders.

In Italy, *il Fascio di Combattimento*—led by a former teacher and journalist named Benito Mussolini—had ruled since 1922. The father of the fascist movement, Mussolini brutally suppressed all opposition and instituted capital punishment for any behavior that was even remotely seditious. Like Hitler, Mussolini was an anticommunist and antidemocratic demagogue who wanted to restore his country to a former state of glory. Ethiopia, in northern Africa, seemed the perfect target: It could be conquered easily, and it would boost Italy's morale by avenging an embarrassing Italian defeat in 1896. Defying the League of Nations, Mussolini mobilized his forces, and on October 3, 1935, Italian troops streamed into Ethiopia from the neighboring Italian colony of Eritrea. Adowa, the site of Italy's humiliation 39 years earlier, fell in three days. Seven months later, the capital city of Addis Ababa was in Italian hands as well. In Geneva, Ethiopian Emperor Haile Selassie's appeals to the League of Nations fell on deaf ears, while in Italy, Mussolini triumphantly bathed in floodlights on the balcony of the Palazzo Venezia and boasted to the crowd below that the Roman Empire had "reappeared."

Although they numbered some 100,000 men, Ethiopia's tribal troops (above) were often poorly trained and hopelessly under-equipped compared to the invading Italians.

fruits of the party's labors: "There is no more voting," he wrote with ebullience in his journal. "The Führer decides. Everything moves much faster than we dared hope."

Nazi ideology soon permeated every aspect of German life. Citizens were required to join a number of organizations, such as the Hitler Youth and the Reich Labor Service. In 1935 new laws made it illegal for Jews and non-Jews to marry one another or have sexual relations. In

The Spanish Civil War provided a convenient opportunity for both Germany and Italy to test their burgeoning militaries. With King Alfonso of Spain deposed, the resulting republic leaned more and more to the left—too much so for the tastes of the Spanish army and the Catholic Church. After the socialist Popular Front won elections in February 1936, tensions boiled over. Led by General Francisco Franco's army, Nationalists staged a revolt in July against the democratically-elected government.

Italy and Germany were quick to provide Franco, a dedicated fascist, with crucial military support. The Soviet Union, France, and Mexico were the only governments to aid the Republicans with anything more than words, sending tanks, planes, and supplies. But legions of students, radicals, workers, and intellectuals from across Europe and the United States—some 40,000 in all—volunteered to fight for the Republicans as part of international brigades.

Many volunteers viewed the conflict as a righteous struggle of freedom versus fascism. One African-American brigade member, Canute Frankson, wrote home: "On the battlefields of Spain, we fight for the preservation of democracy. Here, we're laying the foundation for world peace, and for the liberation of my people, and of the human race."

Of the estimated 3,000 American volunteers, nearly half would make the ultimate sacrifice for their ideals. Their efforts, though, were not enough to hold off the fascist onslaught. Soviet support gradually waned, and the Republicans lost control of Madrid in March 1939. Franco would rule Spain until his death in 1975.

Woodrow Wilson's vision of a sustainable peace had utterly dissolved, as the League of Nations proved powerless to contain aggression on three continents. Emperor Selassie's desperate plea for help after Italy's invasion of Ethiopia would serve as the League's epitaph: "It is us today. It will be you tomorrow."

Although they received military support from the Soviets, Republican forces (top and left) were poorly equipped compared to the Nationalists. A Republican poster (inset) urges Spaniards to resist Franco's army: "Defending Madrid is defending Catalonia." The capital, nevertheless, fell in March 1939.

Wählt Deutschvölkische Freiheitspartei
A 6517
Deutschvölkische Freiheitspartei
Was ihr wählen sollt
Wählt Deutschvölkische Freiheitspartei

SERVING IN STYLE
Adolf Hitler, Rudolph Hess (above, second from right) and the other imprisoned conspirators of the Beer Hall Putsch pose in a comfortable jail cell in 1924. The Putsch was a brazen coup attempt in which Hitler and a small force of *Sturmabteilung* (SA) troops stormed a meeting of Bavarian civil servants at a Munich beer hall. Armed with pistols, the aspiring militants claimed to have the building surrounded. The grab at power failed, however, and police arrested Hitler the next day. He served only nine months of his five-year sentence, using the time to strategize and start work on *Mein Kampf*.

GRASS ROOTS
A rickety truck bearing some of the Nazi faithful motors through Berlin's Brandenburg Gate (left) during an attempt to drum up campaign support in 1924. After discovering his considerable gifts for organization and oratory, Hitler quickly built the National Socialist German Workers' Party membership—a ragtag group of 54 when he joined in 1919—to more than 55,000 in 1923.

GROWING ANARCHY

After the Depression hit Germany and unemployment swelled, so did membership in both the Communist and the Nazi parties. Street clashes between the two groups and with the police (left) became increasingly common. In one five-week period of 1932, 133 Nazis, communists, and police were killed in the fighting.

MONEY TO BURN

German bank notes (left) in 1923 were more useful as kindling than as legal tender. When inflated prices reached their zenith in November, the German mark's value bottomed out at an incomprehensible four-trillionths of a single U.S. dollar. Germans needed to take wheelbarrows of marks to the market just to purchase daily household items. Many Germans blamed the crisis on the inefficiency of the Weimar government.

STRUGGLE FOR THE BASICS

German school children (right) crowd around a carriage distributing essentials in 1923. By the middle of that year, household staples could cost 1,000 percent more at dusk than they had in the morning. Inflation skyrocketed when Weimar treasuries began printing currency 24 hours a day in an effort to meet their World War I reparation obligations.

EXTERMINATION OF IDEAS

Flaming pages float up from a raging bonfire of books in Berlin (right) in May 1933—part of a nationwide cleansing of "radical" books and art. The Nazis had been stifling targeted artwork in an organized but limited fashion since 1927, when they created the Fighting League for German Culture. After Hitler's rise to power, free artistic expression was effectively quashed in a matter of months. Fortunately, many artists and writers escaped Germany and continued their work.

A SINGLE VOICE

A triumphant Chancellor Hitler (left, center) rejoices with Goebbels (far left) and Ernst Röhm, the head of the SA, after the 1933 election. By mid-July, Germans were banned from organizing rival political parties, making the Nazis the only official political organization for 40 million voters. Hitler himself was astounded at the swift demise of his adversaries, remarking, "One would never have thought so miserable a collapse possible."

SCAPEGOAT

Marinus Van der Lubbe (right), a retarded Dutch communist who set fire to the Reichstag in February 1933, cowers in his courtroom chair. The incident provided Hitler with an excuse to send an army of police and storm troopers into Berlin with a list of 4,000 communists and dissidents. By daybreak hundreds of people had been hustled off to jail, savagely beaten, or murdered. Citing the threat of communist revolutionaries like Van der Lubbe, Hitler proposed an emergency decree that severely curtailed Germans' individual rights. The next month, passage of the Enabling Act rendered the parliament impotent and delivered essentially all power to the Führer.

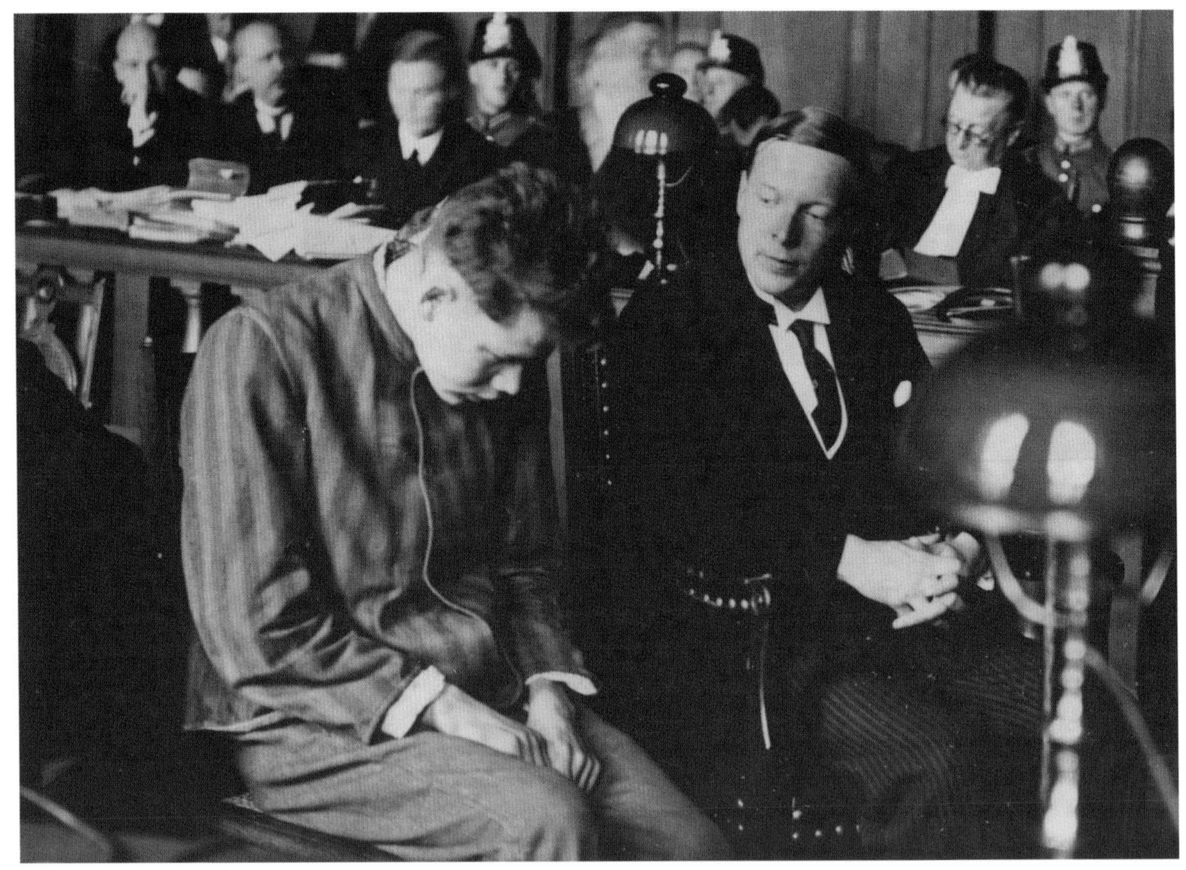

THE FUTURE OF THE REICH

The Hitler Youth (above) salutes the Führer in Nuremberg during the 1937 Nazi Party Congress. Over 50,000 children—almost 90 percent of them boys—attended the rally. Members were required to be, in Hitler's words, "slim and slender, swift as greyhounds, tough as leather, and hard as Krupp steel." Membership became mandatory as part of the complete Nazification of Germany. By 1938 the Hitler Youth—whose members began military training at age 11—was eight million strong.

PARAMILITARY MUSCLE

Hitler (left, center) strides down an arch of fervent SA members in October 1933, flanked by Goebbels (far left) and Hess. The SA had played a significant role in Hitler's rise to power. But the burgeoning ambitions of SA leaders, like Ernst Röhm, led Hitler to dissolve the group in June 1934 when he ordered the "Night of Long Knives." Hitler's new muscle—the *Schutzstaffel* or SS—began a bloody two-day purge that claimed the lives of some 200 "enemies of the state," including Röhm.

RAPE OF NANKING
After the fall of Shanghai, Japanese infantry and their supplies (right) lumber toward Nanking on a crowded roadway in December 1937. In a week's time the Japanese army would descend upon Chiang Kai-shek's provisional capital and drive the Nationalist army deeper into China. For several days thereafter, the invaders conducted a killing spree that claimed the lives of 40,000 Chinese civilians—an atrocity later referred to as the "rape of Nanking."

ABANDONED
Alone and bloodied, a baby (left) cries in the midst of the leveled South Railway station in Shanghai after a Japanese attack on August 18, 1937. The Japanese pummeled China with daily bombings during their campaign.

SUBTERFUGE
Japanese troops guard two captives (right) in the Chinese province of Manchuria after the Kwantung Army, acting independently of Tokyo, staged an explosion along the tracks of the Japanese-owned South Manchurian Railway as a pretext to stream across the border in September 1931. The Japanese installed a puppet government with Henry Pu Yi, last of the Manchu emperors, at its head. Rich in coal and iron, Manchuria had long been coveted by both Russia and Japan.

A PATCHWORK DEFENSE

A motley crew of Ethiopian soldiers (right) heads toward the southern front in 1935. Wary of militant Italian rhetoric, Emperor Haile Selassie rallied his countrymen before the outbreak of hostilities: "Warmen, gather around your chiefs, obey them with a single heart and thrust back the invader". With almost no air force and a disorganized army, however, Ethiopia was soundly defeated; Selassie was forced to flee to Palestine in May 1936.

TOUGH TERRAIN

Italian troops (left) scatter along a hillside near Makalle in late October 1935. The barren expanse of the Ethiopian highlands may have presented more resistance to the invaders than the native soldiers did. By December the Italian advance had ground to a halt, stymied by 400 miles of harsh, mountainous, and mostly roadless terrain separating them from Addis Ababa, the Ethiopian capital. But the Italians had a genius for road building, which literally paved the way for Mussolini's heavy artillery and mechanized units.

THE ROAD TO VICTORY

With flags fluttering from their bayonets, a company of Italian veterans (left) sings while marching to a train during the first leg of their trip to the East African front in late 1935. The actual fighting capability of the Italian army—which flooded across the Ethiopian border with trumpets blaring and banners waving—fell short of the bristling war machine presented by Italy's fascist propaganda. The conquest of Ethiopia was the only notable success Mussolini's military would enjoy.

OUTGUNNED
A cannon belches smoke as Republican forces (right) defend a Spanish hillside. What had started as an ideological rally to save democracy ended in disillusionment for many loyalist soldiers. The French novelist Albert Camus would later write, "It was in Spain that men learned that one can be right and yet be beaten, that force can vanquish spirit, that there are times when courage is not its own recompense."

DEATH OF A LOYALIST
In the arresting photograph above by famed war photographer Robert Capa, Frederico Borrell Garcia, a 24-year-old mill worker and Republican militiaman, is shot on the Cordoba Front on September 5, 1936. Republican forces were unable to quell the revolt in Cordoba and its neighboring Andalusian cities of Seville and Granada. In the months that followed, an estimated 100,000 Spaniards were murdered, executed, or assassinated as the opposing armies attempted to identify supporters and enemies within the areas they held.

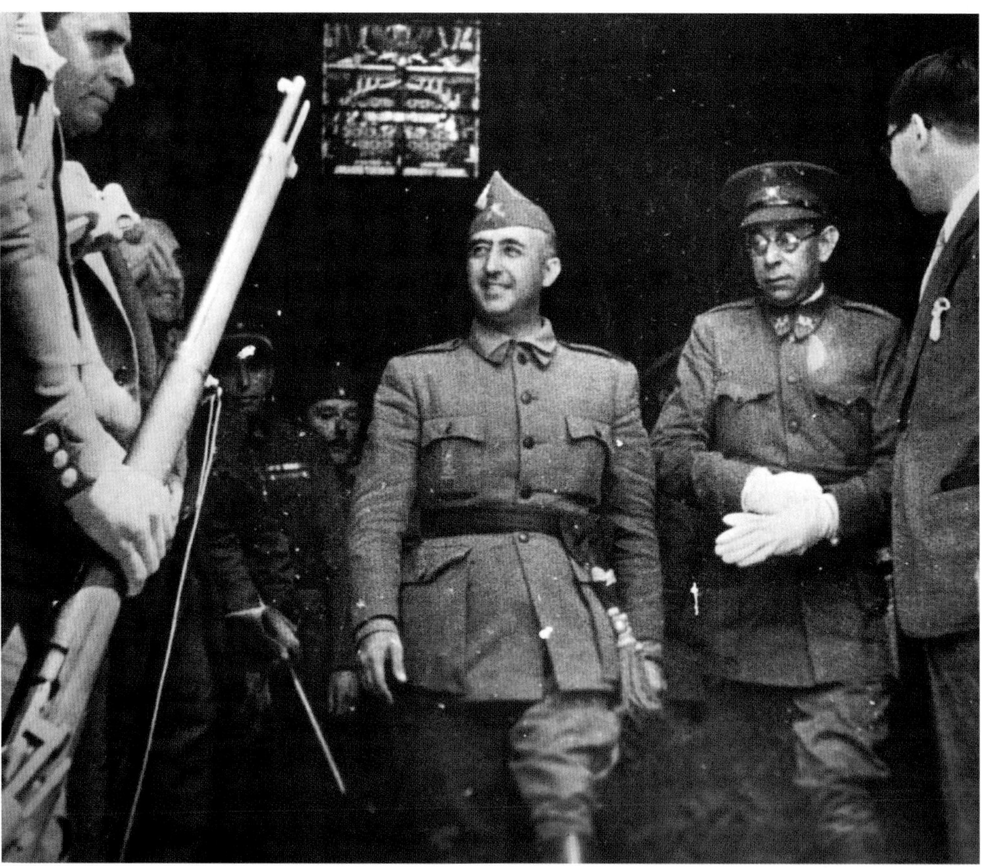

REBEL LEADER
A confident Francisco Franco (right, center) meets with his staff in North Africa in 1937. After winning the war, the wily Franco refused to join the Axis powers, despite benefiting from their considerable military support. His negotiation skills were so formidable that Hitler, after a long encounter, reportedly said he would rather have several teeth pulled than endure another conference with the generalissimo.

Adolf Hitler

The former Vienna vagrant employed charismatic leadership, diabolical genius, and a twisted vision of German glory to become the most dangerous man in Europe.

PLANS FOR EXPANSION
A smiling Führer (above) greets an adoring public in Nuremberg after ascending to the chancellorship in 1933. With supreme power only months away, Hitler would soon be in a position to actualize his dream of *Lebensraum*—living space—for a greater Germany.

A YOUNG WARRIOR
With a smartly waxed moustache, Corporal Adolf Hitler (near left) strikes a solemn pose with two fellow Bavarian soldiers and a dog (Hitler once remarked that dogs were his only friends) on New Year's Day, 1916. During World War I he earned the Iron Cross First Class—a distinction rarely achieved by enlisted men—and the praise of his superiors for bravely ferrying messages to and from the front.

WINGS OF IRON
The emblem of Hitler's Germany (inset), bespoke the Nazi obsession with power. Hitler adopted the swastika, an ancient good luck symbol, in 1920.

THE HITLER MYTH
An imposing Führer stands with an Aryan boy in a 1930s propaganda photo (above). This paternal imagery helped perpetuate public acceptance of Hitler as an infallible leader, the only one capable of delivering German salvation. By 1938 his rule was so absolute that not even his closest subordinates dared question him. Hermann Göring himself once admitted: "Every time I face Hitler, my heart falls into my trousers."

Der Deutsche grüßt: Heil Hitler!

Emailplakate 21. Ott, Weimar

Gesetzlich geschützt Behördl. genehmigt

A CULTURE OF OBEDIENCE
A poster (left) instructs the public to greet each other with the *Heil Hitler* (Long live Hitler) salute. In 1926 Goebbels made the greeting mandatory for Nazi party members.

Adolf Hitler

Mein Kampf

Eher-Verlag

MANUAL FOR RACISM
Hitler's autobiography/manifesto (inset) outlined his dreams for a new German empire. First titled an unwieldy "Four and a Half Years of Struggle against Lies, Stupidity and Cowardice," the book was re-named "My Struggle" and sold 10 million copies.

Der Stürmer
Deutsches Wochenblatt zum Kampfe um die Wahrheit
HERAUSGEBER: JULIUS STREICHER
Nummer 10
Nürnberg, im März 1939
17. Jahr 1939

Das Talmudweib

Die Jüdin Rosenberg in Wien treibt eine werdende Mutter in den Tod / Grauenhaftes Martyrium einer deutschen Familie

Haß ohne Maske

Aus dem Inhalt

Die Juden sind unser Unglück!

Anti-Semitism

Dour economic conditions combined with hateful intolerance to fuel the ignorant notion that Jews were parasites feeding off a struggling German nation.

CREATING AN ENEMY

A parade of actors dressed as caricatures of Jewish stereotypes (above) leads a float displaying a burning synagogue down a Mannheim street during an anti-Semitic carnival in 1939. Virulent rhetoric like that of the anti-Semitic weekly *Der Stürmer* (inset) was the genesis of the Nuremberg laws of 1935, which, among other restrictions, stripped Jews of German citizenship.

A MINORITY BESIEGED

A synagogue in Düsseldorf (above) is defaced with a slogan—"Death to Jews"—and a swastika in 1933. Despite the fact that Jews were well-integrated into German society, the growing tide of anti-Jewish sentiment thrived with little public dissent.

EARLY INDOCTRINATION

A children's book from 1936, *Trust No Fox in the Green Meadow and No Jew on His Oath* (below), illustrates the severe dehumanization of Jews that took place across German culture. The page at bottom contrasts the portrait of a slovenly, hunched Jewish merchant with that of the strapping, hard-working Aryan ideal of a citizen.

LEGALIZED PERSECUTION

A Nazi storm trooper hands out pamphlets (above) during a Hitler-backed boycott of Jewish-owned businesses on April 1, 1933. The boycott was not an overall success—many shoppers patronized the stores despite the SA's enforcement. A week later an undeterrred Hitler enacted a law that banned any non-Aryan employees from the 1.6-million-member civil service and began the systematic exclusion of Jews from German society.

NIGHT OF BROKEN GLASS

Germans stare at the shattered remnants of a Jewish-owned storefront (right) in the aftermath of *Kristallnacht*. Instigated by the death of a German diplomat who was shot by a Jewish refugee in Paris on November 7, 1938, mobs smashed and looted at least 7,500 Jewish-owned stores in Germany. Nearly 100 Jews were killed, and as many as 30,000 were carted off to concentration camps.

Outbreak

The images of conquest atop the gates of the government palace in Prague (left) fit the scene as Hitler's troops file into the Czechoslovakian capital on March 15, 1939. Troops who participated in the bloodless takeover won a bronze medal (below) with a special bar celebrating the annexation.

Londoners read about the invasion of Poland on September 1, 1939; Hitler had unleashed blitzkrieg before dawn. Two days later Chamberlain would announce that Britain was at war.

In the early morning hours of September 1, 1939, the disputed port city of Danzig was awakened by thunderous salvos fired from the 11-inch guns of an old German training ship, the *Schleswig-Holstein*. Firing from her berth on the Danzig waterfront, the battleship hammered the Westerplatte, a fortified Polish military post only a few hundred yards away. Overhead, the Luftwaffe's Stuka dive-bombers, with their piercing sirens, shrieked in support of German police and SS units on the ground as they assaulted the railway station and the customs house. The war that Adolf Hitler had so deliberately sought and that the rest of the world had hoped to avoid was at hand.

War wasn't merely advantageous for Hitler's expansive ambitions; it was necessary. He coupled his radical domestic policies with an aggressive and belligerent foreign policy bent on avenging the losses of World War I and extending *Lebensraum*—living space—for those of German heritage. To the south, Austria provided him with the first opportunity to test the limits of his growing clout and the resolve of the western allies. Following World War I the Paris Peace Settlements had severed the Austro-Hungarian Empire into several ethnically based smaller states, and under its terms Austria was specifically prohibited from joining in any political union with Germany. But by the early 1930s the crushing effects of the global economic depression, combined with Hitler's rise to power in Germany, generated increased support within Austria for an indigenous Nazi movement advocating *Anschluss*—annexation—by the Third Reich.

In 1933 Austrian chancellor Englebert Dollfuss outlawed the Nazi and Socialist parties. But his dictatorship—modeled after Benito Mussolini's regime—would be short-lived. In July 1934 a group of Austrian Nazis seized the chancellery, murdered Dollfuss, and announced a pro-Nazi government. Mussolini, the self-proclaimed protector of Austria and a close friend of the Dollfuss family, quickly amassed 50,000 troops along the Austrian border

Chamberlain (above, left) and Hitler (above, right) emerge after their second meeting to discuss the disputed Czech Sudetenland in September 1938. Hitler wanted the Sudetenland, where Sudeten-Germans (middle) saluted the arrival of Nazi militia in 1938, as part of his Reich. In a socialist appeal to the thousands of economically depressed Sudeten-Germans, a propaganda poster (inset) from 1935 promises "work, rights, and bread" to local voters who support the German effort to annex the region.

to discourage German intervention. Hitler was forced to turn his back on his Austrian followers—for the time being—and the coup quickly collapsed.

But Mussolini would not stand in Hitler's way for long. In 1936 Germany flexed its muscles by sending troops into the Rhineland region bordering France, a clear violation of the Treaty of Versailles. Hitler's bold maneuver impressed Mussolini, and France's failure to respond encouraged Italy to reconsider its alliances. When the Spanish Civil War erupted, both dictators supported the Nationalists, and after Italy and Germany signed an agreement creating the "Rome-Berlin axis" in October 1936, Mussolini—once Austria's proud defender—was aligned firmly with Germany.

Two years later Austrian authorities uncovered a second Nazi plot to overthrow the government, and thinking that a meeting with Hitler might avert another crisis, Dollfuss's successor, Kurt von Schuschnigg, arranged to meet the German dictator at the Führer's mountain retreat on February 12, 1938. Hitler bullied the Austrian leader with the threat of military intervention, strong-arming Schuschnigg into granting general amnesty to the Nazi conspirators and accepting several leading Austrian Nazis into his cabinet.

Desperate to avoid a Nazi takeover, Schuschnigg scheduled a plebiscite for March 13, 1938, to vote in favor of continued Austrian independence. But Hitler, certain that Italy would no longer oppose his aggression, sent in German troops on March 12. The following day the Führer installed a Nazi government, headed by Arthur Seyss-Inquart, and proclaimed Germany's union with Austria.

Polish foreign minister Joseph Beck (above, hatless) climbs the stairs of Hitler's mountain retreat to greet the Führer (back to camera) on January 5, 1939. Beck rejected Hitler's demands for the return of Danzig and a passage through the Polish Corridor to East Prussia.

Britain and France did little more than protest, and their reticence encouraged Hitler to shift his covetous attention to another neighbor—Czechoslovakia. A creation of the Paris Peace Settlements after World War I, Czechoslovakia had become an industrialized democracy by the 1930s, protected by a series of alliances, including a treaty with France. But the Czechoslovak republic contained a sizeable German minority in the Sudetenland, near its northwestern border. The economic strain of the Great Depression was particularly harsh in their industrialized region and—as was true in Germany and Austria—served to create a fertile breeding ground for the dissemination of Hitler's ideas and the formation of several militant German nationalist political parties.

In September 1938, Hitler's armies massed along the Czech border. Invasion seemed imminent. On September 29, Hitler, Mussolini, Britain's Neville Chamberlain, and France's Edouard Daladier met in Munich in a final effort to preserve the peace. Although Czechoslovakia was willing to go to war to defend itself, Britain and France—fearing German might—withheld their support in exchange for Hitler's pledge that he would seek no more territory. Czechoslovakia would cede to the Reich—by October 10—all portions of the Sudetenland that had a German population greater than fifty percent: essentially its entire frontier fortifications and nearly a third of its population. After Poland and Hungary followed Germany's lead and grabbed other regions of Czechoslovakia, the young nation had been almost erased from the map. But war, seemingly, had been averted and a triumphant Chamberlain returned home and proudly declared to an adoring London crowd that he had won "peace for our time."

France and Great Britain, however, had greatly misjudged Hitler and their policy of appeasement proved an outright failure. Changing tactics, Chamberlain and Daladier announced that they would guarantee the territorial integrity of Poland, Hitler's next target. But being completely unprepared for war, Britain and France hoped

The technological superiority of the Wehrmacht is embodied in this tableau as a Polish citizen and his horse-drawn cart pass a German mechanized unit on the first morning of the invasion (above). Although the Poles could count on 40 divisions to meet 62 invading German divisions, none were armored and their air force was hopelessly outdated.

to persuade the Soviet Union to keep Germany in check. The Soviet dictator, Josef Stalin, however, was miffed that he had not been included in the Munich Conference and believed that the western allies were incapable of standing up to Hitler. The suspicious dictator also feared that France and Great Britain might maneuver Hitler into turning against him, so in an about-face that shocked the world, he chose to make an alliance with Hitler.

On August 23, 1939, Stalin's representative, Vyacheslav Molotov, and Hitler's foreign minister, Joachim von Ribbentrop, signed a non-aggression pact. Under the terms of the agreement, Poland would be divided between them and Stalin would gain a free hand to take over the Baltic States. Finland would be fair game for Soviet conquest as well and, by the terms of a second, secret agreement, Germany would provide the Soviets with manufactured goods in return for raw materials and grain.

Freed from any Soviet threat, the Führer now turned his attention to Poland. The Paris Peace Settlements had granted the newly-created Polish state portions of German East Prussia, including a narrow strip of land that gave the otherwise landlocked Poles access to the Baltic Sea. This "Polish Corridor" separated East Prussia from Germany and converted the old German port of Danzig into a free port. Hitler issued a series of demands that included the annexation of Danzig and free passage through the corridor. Taking Chamberlain and Daladier's guarantee at face value, Polish foreign minister Joseph Beck rejected the Führer's ultimatums.

On September 1, 1939, the Germans struck, unleashing two units—62 divisions in all—across the Polish frontier. Vigorously employing its new tactics of mechanized war—dubbed blitzkrieg—the Wehrmacht's panzers, closely supported by Luftwaffe dive-bombers, plunged

into the Polish heartland, encircling and crushing Polish troop concentrations. German medium bombers struck at communications centers, paralyzing the Polish high command and preventing the coordination of field signals. The large but outdated Polish armed forces, led by Marshal Edward Smigly-Ridz, fought bravely but stood no chance against the German forces.

On September 3, Great Britain and France declared war on Germany. The French army massed on the German border but, mindful of its losses in World War I, did nothing to aid the beleaguered Poles. The Polish government left Warsaw on September 4, and by the 17th—the same day Stalin sent his Red Army into eastern Poland—the Wehrmacht pincers had closed on the Polish capital. Warsaw struggled valiantly under siege but finally surrendered on September 27. In Moscow the Polish ambassador received a curt note from Stalin explaining the situation. "A Polish state," its preamble read, "no longer exists."

In October, Stalin, wary of his new ally, moved to consolidate a buffer zone between the Soviet Union and Germany. The Soviet dictator bluntly demanded the cession of Finland's Karelian Peninsula as well as rights to construct a naval base on the Gulf of Finland. When the Finns refused, Stalin invaded. In the initial winter campaign, the Finnish army skillfully turned back the huge but poorly equipped Red Army. Ultimately, though, the sheer numbers of the Soviet juggernaut caved in the tiny Finnish army. With no aid forthcoming from the western Allies—the League of Nations merely voted to expel the Russians—the Finns reluctantly granted Stalin's demands.

On the western front, France and Great Britain prepared for war. Appeasement had failed. The war that they had worked so hard to prevent had erupted despite their best efforts and, to some extent, because of them.

An October 1939 cartoon (top) satirizes the unlikely alliance between Stalin and Hitler. The pact led to the Soviet invasion of Finland, whose soldiers (above, left), resisted fiercely, despite being heavily outnumbered. The Finns fitted their 20-mm antitank rifles (inset) with small skis for arctic use.

PRESIDENTIAL CAPTIVE
Escorted by Nazi military brass, Emil Hacha (left, clutching hat), the president of Czechoslovakia, inspects a regiment of Wehrmacht troops. On March 15, 1939, coerced by pressure and threats of military action from Hitler, Hacha signed over control of Czechoslovakia to Germany. Hacha, who had a heart condition, reportedly fainted during his early-morning meeting with the Führer, who had announced that an invasion would begin at 6:00 a.m. if the papers weren't signed.

BITTER PILL
Czech citizens (below) vent their rage at passing German troops as the Wehrmacht rolls into Prague on March 15,1939. The last surviving democracy in eastern Europe, Czechoslovakia was divided into three republics at the Munich talks of 1938, leading to its eventual dissolution.

THE FRUITS OF APPEASEMENT
A triumphant Hitler (left, standing in car) enters Prague in March 1939 to the cheers of adoring followers. Having had its fortified western frontier sacrificed at the Munich conference, Czechoslovakia was essentially defenseless. The blatant land grab sent a clear message about Hitler's aspirations and prompted both Britain and France to accelerate rearmament.

AN ULTIMATUM
Anxious residents of Warsaw (above) read Hitler's demand for surrender, issued on the eve of the German invasion. Two weeks later the Wehrmacht had fought its way to Warsaw and surrounded the city. Instead of surrendering, the Poles fortified the capital and lived under siege until September 27. Some 12,000 citizens were killed in the two-week stand, many entombed in buildings destroyed by Luftwaffe bombs.

SUPPLY ROUTE
As his sergeant (near right) stridently upbraids him for moving too slowly, a German soldier drives his horse-drawn supply wagon over a river in Poland. Although Germany would refine its blitzkrieg on the western front in 1940, the strike into Poland was primarily animal-driven: Nearly 500,000 horses were involved in the invasion. The Wehrmacht penetrated and dispersed the Polish front within the first three days of the invasion, and the Poles were never able to forge another. Approximately 910,000 Poles were taken prisoner, some 217,000 of them seized by the Soviet Union, which invaded from the East on September 17.

ERASING THE BORDER
Wehrmacht infantrymen (right) break a wooden barricade on the Polish border, punctuating their invasion of the country on September 1, 1939. In addition to igniting World War II, the massive attack unveiled a stunning new form of warfare: blitzkrieg. Waves of German infantry spread across the Polish countryside, quickly reaching Warsaw and, to the astonishment of Europe, subduing the entire country within a month.

NAZI COMMAND
Hitler (above, front and center) arrives in Poland with a group of his generals, including Erwin Rommel (to right of Hitler), who was the commander of the dictator's escort battallion at the time. Although the Wehrmacht's victory in Poland was convincing, some of Hitler's generals, including Walther von Brauchitsch (third from left), were skeptical of Germany's chances in a war against the west.

OBSOLETE WARRIORS
A poignant symbol of Poland's gallant but hopelessly outmoded military, the Polish cavalry (left) is put through a maneuver at Konskie in advance of the Nazi invasion. Not only were the Poles outgunned by Germany's superior technology, they were also greatly outnumbered. The Wehrmacht advanced with roughly 62 divisions in the north and south, six of them armored and 10 mechanized, and 1,300 state-of-the-art aircraft. Poland deployed 40 divisions—none of them armored—and possessed only a few outdated tanks. Further, most of Poland's air force was destroyed before it got off the ground on the first day of the invasion.

SCORCHED EARTH
On October 3, 1939, Wehrmacht infantrymen (above) advance through Poland, setting fires in the hedges and surrounding countryside to destroy every conceivable sniper position. Warsaw had fallen on September 27, and all Polish resistance would cease on October 6. Germany suffered only 13,891 fatalities in the monthlong campaign.

WARSAW BURNS

Wehrmacht infantrymen (left) monitor the shelling of Warsaw on September 17. The Germans had surrounded the city three days earlier, but rather than surrender, the Poles stubbornly resisted. In the first few days of the siege, Warsaw's residents tossed homemade firebombs, cast trolley cars across roads as barricades, and stationed snipers in buildings all over the city. Enraged by the surprising setbacks, the Germans ordered round-the-clock bombing.

TERROR IN THE STREETS

Warsaw residents run for safety seconds after Luftwaffe fire bombs blasted a working-class neighborhood (above). Describing the chaos that enveloped the city during the siege, one civilian said, "Everywhere corpses, wounded humans, killed horses." Food supplies were quickly exhausted, and the sight of starving Poles butchering fallen horses for food where they lay in the streets became commonplace.

GUNNER'S-EYE VIEW
Positioned in the nose turret as his pilot skims the aircraft over the target, a German machine gunner (left) takes aim at a Warsaw neighborhood. At the start of the invasion, the Luftwaffe bombed only strategic targets in the Polish capital, but during the siege they bombed indiscriminately, destroying one quarter of Warsaw in four days.

WARSAW FALLS

A young Polish boy (above) sits amid the rubble created by the Luftwaffe's nonstop bombing campaign in late September 1939. "There were fires every day," said one witness of the siege. "We slept fully dressed, with our suitcases containing the most indispensable objects next to our beds." Warsaw resisted stoutly, however, and only surrendered when it had run out of medical supplies, food, and water. The capitulation agreement was signed by Polish officials in a railway car in Rakow, just outside the city limits, in a ceremony overseen by German general Johannes Blaskowitz.

THE HORROR OF THE SS

A pair of Hitler's SS officers (left) search a Warsaw citizen following Germany's conquest of Poland. Poland's capital had fallen, but for many of its citizens the worst was yet to come. Possessing a weapon or anything resembling one was grounds for execution without trial at the hands of the brutal SS, which entered Warsaw, along with the Gestapo, to fulfill Hitler's orders to eliminate all of those people considered undesirable by the Third Reich.

DEATH TRAIN
A line of Polish Jews (left) waits to board a train from Warsaw to a Nazi concentration camp. Immediately after Poland's surrender, SS units rounded up Jews and other perceived enemies of the Third Reich. Some were executed, while others were shipped to ghettos in the first significant phase of the Nazis' "Extraordinary Pacification Action," their euphemism for genocide.

MARCHING ORDERS
A Soviet officer (right) reads orders to begin the invasion of Finland on November 30, 1939. Soviet troops were woefully undertrained and Red Army leadership was embarrassingly unprepared for fighting in the arctic environments. Only superior numbers enabled them to complete the conquest.

ARCTIC WARFARE
Towing their gear on reindeer-drawn wooden sleds, Finnish ski troopers (left) patrol a forest north of the Arctic Circle. In the first several weeks of the invasion, the Finns literally ran circles around the Soviet invaders, surrounding groups of them in the snowy forests of northern Finland and cutting them off from reinforcements. But by January 1940, the tide had turned in favor of the Soviet Union, which committed one million troops to the effort, compared to Finland's 175,000.

TAKING AIM
Two Soviet infantrymen fire their rifles while a third readies backup ammunition in a snowy trench on Finland's Karelian Peninsula. Uncomfortable with Finland's strategic proximity to Leningrad, the Soviets had demanded that the Finns turn over a swath of its territory. When the Finns refused, Stalin attacked. After weeks of bumbling maneuvers and embarrassing defeats, the Soviets finally broke through Finland's defenses with overwhelming force in February. On March 12, 1940, Finland, which lost 25,000 soldiers, signed a treaty conceding the Soviet Union's demand.

Ghetto Life

Surrender was only the beginning of the horror for Poland. Following the invasion, Germany isolated Polish Jews in ghettos to make room for Aryan "repopulation." It was the first step towards the Final Solution.

MARK OF DEATH
Two recently relocated Jewish men (left) contemplate their future in the Jewish ghetto in Kutno in October 1939. By November every Jew in Poland was required to wear the Star of David emblem (inset).

FENCED IN
Passage in and out of Jewish ghettos was strictly regulated and generally limited to daytime hours. Barriers of fencing and barbed wire—like the walls of the western Ukrainian ghetto of Munkacs (left)—contributed to the prisonlike atmosphere.

HUMILIATION
As a group of smiling civilians looks on (below), German soldiers force a Jewish man to cut the beard of a fellow Jew in Lodz shortly after Poland's capitulation. "It was forbidden to show even signs of sympathy or pity for the Jews," said one Pole. "The punishment was instant death."

ROUNDUP
A German soldier (below) barks at a crowd of Warsaw Jews after several "volunteers" have been loaded into a truck for work. The Nazis ruled through terror, and the Jewish community never knew what behavior could get them killed. "He who walked too quickly was shot," said one ghetto survivor. "He who fell on the way was shot. He who strayed out of line was shot. He who turned his head was shot."

SLAVE LABOR
Jewish children over the age of 12—like this young boy (left) from the Kovno ghetto in Lithuania—were required to work in the ghetto workshops.

The War Takes Shape: 1940-1941

The War Takes Shape: 1940-1941

As the diminutive 20th-century European conqueror surveyed the final resting place of his 19th-century counterpart, he couldn't contain his excitement. "This is the finest moment of my life," Adolf Hitler said as he viewed Napoleon's Tomb during a whirlwind victory tour of the French capital on June 23, 1940. The failed artist had finally made it to Paris. The bitter ex-corporal had finally exacted his revenge, and the rest of Europe trembled at his feet.

If Germany's rout of Poland provided only a clue that World War II was to be a very different war, the Wehrmacht's systematic dismantling of France's armed forces erased all doubt. German panzer divisions proved immobile French defenses utterly obsolete, and France's subsequent humiliation sent shockwaves around the world.

Hitler's blitzkrieg into Poland had been a blueprint for his 1940 invasion of France. Among those who studied the rapid German conquest of Poland at close quarters was General Paul Armengaud of the French air force. Sent to observe the fighting and advise Polish commanders, Armengaud summed up his conclusions in a memo to the French army's chief of staff, General Maurice Gamelin. "The German system consists . . . of making a breach in the front with armor and aircraft," he wrote, "then to throw mechanized and motorized columns into the breach." This was the essence of blitzkrieg, and Armengaud had no doubt that German armored divisions would soon try to punch through French lines in similar fashion. As he warned Gamelin: "It would be mad not to draw an exact lesson from this pattern and not to pay heed to this warning."

Gamelin recognized the growing mechanization of Europe's militaries, but he had neither the matérial nor the mentality needed to counter German intentions, which were signaled long before the war

Timeline: 1940-1941

1940

March 12

Finland signs a peace treaty with the Soviet Union.

April 9

Germany invades Denmark and Norway.

May 10

Germany invades Belgium, Luxembourg, and the Netherlands. Winston Churchill becomes prime minister of Britain.

May 12

Germany invades France.

May 26

Allied troops begin evacuation from Dunkirk.

June 10

Italy declares war on France and Britain.

began. In 1937, General Heinz Guderian had published a book entitled *Achtung—Panzer!* ("Attention—Armor!") advocating operations that combined armor with air power to puncture enemy defenses and overcome resistance. Allied chiefs who somehow missed Guderian's message had only to study neglected proposals from their own tacticians, including Captain Basil Liddell Hart, who in the 1920s had proposed British armored forces that could pierce enemy lines and deliver an "expanding torrent" of firepower. In France, an outspoken staff officer named Charles de Gaulle argued in vain for a mechanized army built for rapier-like offensives years before Germany assembled such a force.

Like the conflict itself, the contrasting military doctrines of the rival powers were rooted in the last world war. The Germans emerged from their defeat determined to avoid a repetition of the ruinous stalemate on the western front by creating a mobile fighting force that could achieve quick victories. Severe restrictions on the size of that force only helped the Germans in the long run by prompting them to retire commanders who were too old or too stubborn to change their ways. When Hitler took power and expanded the army, he inherited an innovative officer corps that was responsive to his demand for bold offensive operations.

Among the French and British, by contrast, the costly triumph in the last war induced a stubborn defensive-mindedness at high levels. French forces had suffered terrible losses early in World War I during fruitless offensives against entrenched German forces. Only by shifting to the defensive and fortifying their positions had the Allies managed to grind the Germans down. The 68-year-old Gamelin and his aides were shaped by that experience and planned to win the next war as they had the last: by building fortifications and defending a continuous and impregnable front.

June 15

The Soviet Union occupies Lithuania, Latvia, and Estonia.

June 22

France signs armistice with Germany.

July 10

German planes bomb southern ports in England. The Battle of Britain begins.

July 25

The United States imposes materials embargo on Japan.

September 13

Italy invades Egypt.

That attitude was reinforced by politicians who worried that an army designed to take the offensive would do so at the slightest provocation and plunge the nation into another bloodbath. Military spending slighted French armor and air power and favored strictly defensive measures like the Maginot Line, which shielded France's eastern frontier. A British officer who visited one of the forts on the line compared it to a "battleship built on land" and worried that it engendered "a sense of false security." Indeed, the Maginot Line defended France at its German border but failed to anticipate a possible invasion into northern France through the Low Countries. Gamelin's plans for realigning his forces north of the French border once that threat materialized left little in reserve to cope with German breakthroughs.

The British were in a better position to wage a defensive war. To be sure, British Expeditionary Forces that were sent to France risked being stranded should Gamelin's line of defense give way. But if the Germans then tried to carry the war across the Channel, they would have to overcome the British where they were strongest—at sea and in the air. Recent hikes in defense spending had yielded advances in radar and aircraft design that gave the Royal Air Force a fighting chance against Hitler's Luftwaffe. German submarines still posed the chief threat to British supply lines. Although Hitler and his naval chief, Admiral Erich Raeder, had diverted assets from submarine production—that corps would not be up to strength until 1942—to build a surface fleet, Germany was in no position to rule the waves. The scuttling of the *Graf Spee* in 1939 demonstrated that the *Kriegsmarine* remained subject to containment by the Royal Navy. German warships could not even be sure of breaking through the straits of Denmark and reaching the high seas.

To give his fleet access to the Atlantic and protect shipments of iron ore from Sweden, Hitler made plans in early 1940 to occupy Denmark and Norway. The operation was meant to enhance the navy's position, but it would expose the fleet to harm if the Royal Navy offered cogent resistance. Hitler was willing to take such chances to bring the war against France and Britain to a quick end. A

Timeline: 1940-1941

1940

September 27

Germany, Italy, and Japan sign Tripartite Pact.

October 28

Italy invades Greece.

1941

March 11

Roosevelt signs Lend-Lease bill into law, offering immediate aid to Britain and her allies.

April 6

Germany invades Yugoslavia and Greece.

June 22

Operation Barbarossa begins as Germany attacks the Soviet Union.

August 14

Roosevelt and Churchill meet off the coast of Newfoundland and sign the Atlantic Charter, outlining the goals and principles of the Allied war effort.

lengthy struggle would reveal flaws in his hasty rearmament program and strain German resources.

Other risks for Hitler lay in the uncertain intentions of his expansionist Axis partners, Italy and Japan. Since conquering Ethiopia at some cost, Mussolini had failed to improve the sagging morale of his forces or update their weaponry. Now he considered challenging the British in Africa and advancing from Albania into Greece. If the Italians became bogged down in the sands of Africa or the mountain passes of the Balkans, Hitler might have to divert German forces to rescue Axis fortunes in the Mediterranean and secure his southern flank.

Japan's bid for empire in Asia, meanwhile, was drawing fire in the United States. Washington threatened to cut shipments of oil and steel to the Japanese, who depended on American exports. Roosevelt's aim was to "slip a noose around Japan's neck and give it a jerk now and then." Yet Japan, with its unrivaled fleet of ten aircraft carriers, had the capacity to break out of that noose and wage a lightning war of its own against American and British assets in the Pacific. Like Germany, however, Japan would have to win that war quickly or risk losing its edge in weaponry to foes with vast industrial potential.

The Tripartite Pact, which Germany forged with Japan and Italy in September 1940, required Hitler to join his partners in war only if they were attacked by another nation not already at war (such as the U.S.). But success had gone to Hitler's head and he feared no rival—not the U.S. and certainly not the Soviet Union, whose recent difficulties contending with tiny Finland confirmed Hitler's impression that the Soviets would serve better as enemies than as allies. Even before the contest with France, he was looking ahead to a showdown with the Soviets. That would be the ultimate test for German forces: war against a nation with reserves so deep it could withstand repeated lightning strikes. Yet, Hitler faced that challenge with few qualms. "Germany is militarily far superior to Russia," he insisted. Like his hero, Napoleon, who made the same gamble in 1812, Hitler wagered the future of his empire on an invasion into the vast expanses of Russia against a massive, virtually unknown foe.

October 17

Hideki Tojo becomes prime minister of Japan.

December 6

The Soviet Union stops the German advance outside of Moscow and begins to counterattack.

December 7

Japan bombs Pearl Harbor, devastating the American Pacific Fleet. Japan also bombs Wake Island and Guam and invades Malaya and Hong Kong.

December 8

The United States and Britain declare war on Japan.

December 11

Germany and Italy declare war on the United States.

Blitzkrieg

Hitler's SS troops (left) patrol the streets near the Palais de Justice in Brussels, which fell to the Nazis in May 1940. After Luftwaffe planes attacked England in July, igniting the Battle of Britain, British combatants earned the medal below for fighting against Germany.

The world got its first glimpse of blitzkrieg in the fall of 1939, and it was a terrifying tableau indeed. Adolf Hitler had promised "an army such as the world has never seen," and though the statement was pure propaganda, few nations were prepared to doubt it after Germany's stunning success in Poland. While shocking Poland into submission in a matter of weeks, Germany unveiled a new style of mechanized, mobile warfare that relied on surprise, deception, versatility, and might. Coined later by an American journalist, the term blitzkrieg—or lightning war—was an apt description of the Wehrmacht's strategy of sudden, massive, penetrating offensives. With elements of surprise and audacity it not only allowed a nation to wage war with an inadequate army, but when combined with misinformation, it could also mask that inadequacy. Indeed, blitzkrieg functioned as a kind of bluff for Germany, like a cobra's hood, making its military appear larger and more formidable than it actually was. To a world fresh with memories of World War I—a more static, entrenched conflict—the flash invasion and toppling of Poland was an evolutionary leap forward in the practice of warfare.

Even though Great Britain and France declared war on Germany immediately after the invasion of Poland, neither nation moved offensively. Cowed by Germany's display of power and remembering their massive losses in the first world war, both countries maintained a defensive posture. Hitler, who had counted on such caution, took advantage of it to reorganize and rearm.

Churchill (below, left), criticized Chamberlain (right) and predicted war after the Munich Conference. On May 10, 1940—the same day that Germany invaded western Europe—Churchill became Britain's prime minister.

As Danish citizens peacefully line the Copenhagen docks, a German vessel loaded with invading troops steams into the harbor. The Danes had been instructed to surrender by King Christian X.

Thus began the Phony War—as one American politician labeled it—the dormant period from October 1939 to March 1940 when neither side took any action. Instead, French and German soldiers—often in view of one another—manned their respective borders in a tense waiting game. For the Germans manning their fortification at the French border, it was sitzkrieg.

The extended staredown was not unwelcome in France, where the military had spent a decade preparing for another prolonged stalemate. France had constructed the impregnable Maginot Line, a gigantic series of fortified bunkers, constructed along its 87-mile border with Germany. Named for André Maginot, the French defense minister when work began on the project in 1930, the barrier was a massive construction of underground passageways and chambers protected by 10-foot-thick walls. While it seemed the very essence of modernity, the Maginot Line was built to fight a style of warfare that no longer existed. The Wehrmacht would soon demonstrate its obsolescence.

The Phony War lasted until the spring of 1940, when Germany moved north. To secure control of the Baltic Sea and seize access to crucial mines in Sweden, German forces rolled into Denmark and Wehrmacht paratroopers dotted the skies over Norway on April 9, 1940. Denmark surrendered quietly under threat of bombardment, but Norway met the Wehrmacht with a small but courageous army. Supported by British and French troops, the Norwegians dealt the Germans serious setbacks at the port city of Narvik, but German offenses on the continent in May forced the western Allies to order their troops back home, allowing Germany to begin a contentious occupation of Norway.

German strikes began on May 10—the same day that Winston Churchill replaced Neville Chamberlain as Prime Minister of Britain—as hundreds of German gliders carrying paratroopers soared over Holland, Belgium, and Luxembourg. Behind the gliders came scores of bombers, which pummeled air fields and communications centers throughout the region. The Dutch surrendered after only five days. Belgium, which lost the linchpin of its defense, the fortress Eben Emael, to a relatively small detachment of German soldiers, followed suit at the end of the month.

Bypassing the Maginot Line to the north, the Germans turned their attention toward France. The Wehrmacht maneuvered its nimble panzers through the Ardennes forest in Belgium, a region previously thought to be impassable by armored vehicles. The Maginot Line thus became a poignant symbol of a

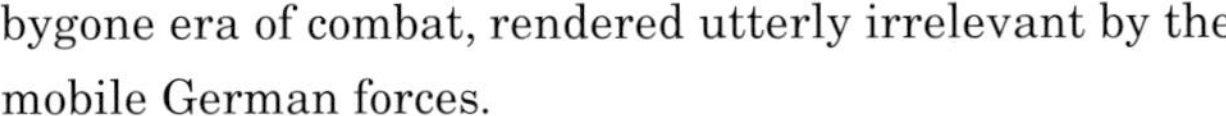

bygone era of combat, rendered utterly irrelevant by the mobile German forces.

Under General Erwin Rommel, Germany's Seventh Panzer Division ripped through northwest France and plunged all the way to the English Channel. South of Rommel, General Heinz Guderian led a panzer division eastward to the town of Abbeville, at the mouth of the Somme River, effectively splitting the Allied armies in two. France's defenses crumbled. In Paris, writer André Maurois recalled the unreality of the German onslaught: "We began to read in the papers and to hear on the radio quite unexpected names of places: Mantes, Pontoise. Was it possible the Germans were only half an hour from us by car, while we're living and working just as usual?"

France was clearly doomed, and the British Expeditionary Force—which amounted to only 13 ill-trained divisions in France by April 1940—was exhausted and cornered by the Germans near Dunkirk. "Nothing but a miracle can save the BEF now," admitted Lieutenant-General Alan Brooke, who commanded one of Britain's demoralized corps. The miracle came in the form of a stop order from Hitler himself. Fearing a British counterattack, Hitler halted his troops and tanks on May 24. His reluctance essentially saved the BEF and set in motion one of the most daring rescues ever attempted. Using all manner of watercraft, much of it conscripted from the citizenry, the British managed to evacuate 337,000 Allied soldiers, including the majority of the BEF, safely across the channel to Britain.

Although 100,000 French troops were among those who escaped from the beaches of Dunkirk, France's fate was sealed. The French army was completely overwhelmed by the German blitzkrieg. "The war has become practically a lightning Tour de France," Rommel wrote to his wife. "Within a few days, it will be over for good." Paris was all but evacuated, and on June 14, German troops entered the capital without facing a single shot. Alone

After retreating to London, Charles de Gaulle (top left) inspects his Free French troops (its flag inset) in the British capital on Bastille Day in 1940. De Gaulle's counterpart in the Vichy government, Philippe Pétain, was lampooned in a political cartoon (top right) by Ted Geisel, better known as Dr. Seuss.

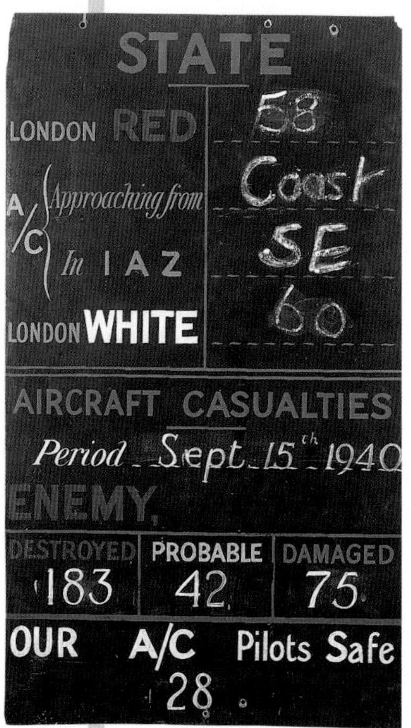

At British Fighter Command in Bentley Priory (right), members of the Women's Auxiliary Air Force (WAAF) keep track of incoming German squadrons and the positions of RAF fighters during the Battle of Britain. A blackboard (above) helps British headquarters keep score by listing the number of destroyed German aircraft.

among the French leadership, General Charles de Gaulle favored continued resistance. Relocated to London, he energetically attempted to revive the French military and morale, with the hope of retaking France. Britain recognized de Gaulle as the Free French leader, but on June 17 Marshal Philippe Pétain, the new head of the tottering French government, announced, "It is with a heavy heart that I tell you today that we must stop fighting."

Five days later in the Compiègne Forest, site of Germany's surrender to France after World War I, the French signed an armistice. Indeed, the same railway car in which Germany had capitulated in November 1918 was wheeled out for France's final disgrace. Pétain's new government, centered in Vichy, remained in power, but the Germans occupied the northern portion of the country, including the entire strategic Atlantic Coast. The humiliating terms of the Treaty of Versailles were finally avenged. "The great battle of France is over," wrote a young German officer. "It lasted 26 years."

Despite the miraculous evacuation at Dunkirk, Hitler hoped that Britain could be forced to capitulate, if not by diplomatic means then certainly after a short bombing campaign. He believed that the British were already beaten and just needed a small push to recognize that fact. But there would be no appeasement or negotiation from Churchill, who told his Parliament in early June, "We shall fight on the beaches, we shall fight on the landing grounds, we shall fight in the fields

King George VI (left, in military uniform) and Queen Elizabeth stop to chat with a workman who is conducting repairs to a London building damaged by Luftwaffe raids during the Battle of Britain.

Ration books (insets) became a fact of life in England during the Battle of Britain and would remain so throughout the war.

and in the streets, we shall fight in the hills; we shall never surrender."

On July 10 the Battle of Britain—the first all-aerial conflict in history—began. Hitler's "small push" to help the British recognize their defeat evolved into a furious air duel that leveled Britain's cities but failed to crush her spirit. For three months in 1940, German bombers and British Spitfire fighters sparred high above Britain's cities. On the ground, the British populace absorbed the brunt of the fighting. The heaviest German bombing came in August, and on September 7, frustrated by their lack of progress on the coast, the Germans began bombing central London. Roughly one week later, after two waves of German bombers were decimated by British fighters east of London, Hitler postponed Operation Sea Lion—his plan for invasion—until further notice. The battle was over. Sophisticated radar technology, superior aircraft production, and the bravery of hundreds of pilots—including Poles, Czechs, Canadians, and Australians—enabled Britain to turn back the Luftwaffe. "Never was so much owed by so many to so few," declared Churchill in a tribute to the young men—some still teenagers—who won the battle above Britain. German air raids would continue throughout the war, but Hitler would never again seriously consider an invasion of the Isles.

NARVIK BURNS
The Wehrmacht was stymied in the northern Norwegian village of Narvik (above), where the Allies sank 10 German destroyers in April 1940. Germany had hoped to seize the port town and its valuable railroad link to the iron-rich mountains of Sweden. The outnumbered German soldiers—led by General Eduard Dietl—made a daring escape to Sweden. The setback would prove temporary, as the Germans returned to Narvik when the Allied troops were called home in June to defend western Europe.

CROSSING THE FJORDS
German mountain troops paddle the icy waters near Narvik (left). Hitler had insisted that Germany invade Norway to prevent the British Royal Navy from using Norweigan ports and intercepting German ships. The Norweigans, however, would prove as difficult for the Germans to subdue as the Finns had for the Soviets during their Winter War.

BLITZKRIEG IN HOLLAND

At the foot of one of the country's iconic windmills (above), a German tank commander asks a group of fellow soldiers in the Netherlands for directions to the front in May 1940. Employing blitzkrieg tactics, the Nazis overran Holland, a neutral country that had not waged war since 1830, in five days.

SHOCK TROOPS

German paratroopers (right) relax after their stunning triumph at the Belgian fortress of Eben Emael in May 1940. A series of concrete and steel emplacements, the fort housed 700 soldiers and was thought to be impenetrable. In an operation which cost them only 21 casualties, the Germans landed on the structure in gliders, destroyed some of the emplacements with hollow charges, then kept the Belgian forces at bay until reinforcements arrived.

SUDDEN HOMELESSNESS
A Belgian woman and her children (left) wander through their town after a Luftwaffe air raid. To establish bases for its eventual invasion of France and Britain, the Wehrmacht invaded Holland, Luxembourg, and Belgium on May 10 and gained control of all three by the following month. Though the British and the French criticized Belgium for not joining their preinvasion alliance, the Germans would come to respect the Belgians' fierce, but futile, resistance to the invasion.

GERMAN CONQUERORS
Wehrmacht troops (right) smile and wave for the camera as they march across the border from Belgium into France in 1940. With French reinforcements crumbling around it, the Belgian army had surrendered on May 28. Paris fell roughly two weeks later. The Germans streamed into the French capital on June 14 and completed their conquest of France on June 25. The French counted 90,000 dead in the Battle of France, compared to only 27,000 German fatalities.

PANZER COMMANDER
German general Heinz Guderian (left), one of the architects of the tactics that came to be called blitzkrieg, consults battle maps in France in June 1940. Guderian had long been a proponent of developing the Panzer arm of the Wehrmacht, and he was occasionally frustrated by the German high command's reluctance to deploy the tanks with untrammeled aggression.

MOBILE ARMOR
Panzer units (right) negotiate narrow, winding streets in France in June 1940. The nimble tanks were an integral part of blitzkrieg tactics, which called for massive and highly mobile offensives. To gain access to the French interior, the Panzers cut through the thick Ardennes Forest in Belgium. The action allowed the Germans to bypass the heavily fortified Maginot Line and invade France from the north. Indeed, no weapon in the Wehrmacht arsenal contributed more to France's downfall than the panzers.

GUERIN BARBIER
CHOCOLATS BISCUITS
HÔTEL DE FRANCE
WH
HALTE

VICTORY TOUR

Eager German soldiers (left) greet Hitler at Le Bourget airport in France on June 23, 1940, after the Führer had toured Paris following the French surrender. In a whirlwind three-hour visit, the dictator stopped at most of the well-known destinations in the City of Lights, including the Louvre, the Place de l'Opera and the Arc de Triomphe.

OCCUPATION

With the Eiffel Tower visible in the gloomy distance, a Nazi flag (right) flies atop the Arc de Triomphe on June 14, 1940, the day Wehrmacht troops seized Paris. Most of the capital's citizens had fled in advance of the Nazi forces, and there were not even pockets of resistance. Indeed, the Parisians who remained behind welcomed the German conquerors as tourists, staying open for business as usual and watching peacefully as Wehrmacht troops enjoyed the sights of one of Europe's most beautiful cities.

COURAGE UNDER FIRE
A line of British soldiers (left) waits to be evacuated. The troops executed the removal operation with almost unerring precision, and many of them sustained a mood of surprisingly good humor along the way: With enemy fire bursting all around them, one group of British infantrymen sang a jovial song with the lyrics, "Oh, I *do* like to be by the seaside."

SHORE TO SHIP

Columns of British and French soldiers (above) await rescue from the beaches of Dunkirk. Surrounded by advancing German forces, the British Expeditionary Force and the French divisions in the region had no choice but to retreat across the English Channel. The Allies had hoped that Operation Dynamo could save 45,000 men, but more than 330,000 French and British soldiers escaped aboard a patchwork of boats and ships.

MEN OVERBOARD

With their life raft sinking beneath them, a group of sailors (right) from the French destroyer *Bourrasque*, which was sunk by a mine off the coast of Dunkirk, haul themselves aboard a British rescue boat. The remarkable evacuation at Dunkirk from May 26 to June 4 caused the British *Daily Mirror* to keen "BLOODY MARVELLOUS!" in its next day's headline, but Churchill soberingly reminded Great Britain that "Wars are not won by evacuations."

DOUSING THE FLAMES

Members of the London Auxiliary Fire Service attempt to control a blaze ignited by German firebombs near the Whitehall section of the British capital. As pivotal as it proved to be, the Allied victory in the Battle of Britain came by the narrowest of margins. During the height of the conflict, in August and September 1940, Britain lost 832 fighter planes compared to the Luftwaffe's 668. Germany also lost 600 bombers in that span, a figure that gave the formerly overconfident Hitler pause and prevented him from committing a potentially overwhelming force to Operation Sea Lion.

SPARED

The hightest point in the landscape, St. Paul's Cathedral (left), is miraculously untouched, but the remainder of its central London neighborhood shows heavy damage from Luftwaffe bombs during the Battle of Britain, which began on July 10, 1940, and raged through the fall. The Germans started shelling London on a daily basis on September 7, and even after the battle's official end in October, the Luftwaffe made sporadic bombing raids on the British capital.

SHELTER FROM THE BLITZ

In lieu of bomb shelters, citizens crowd into the Elephant and Castle tube station (right) to take cover from another German raid. Following the official end of the Battle of Britain in October, Germany continued to bomb London in a series of nighttime raids that terrorized British citizens but did little to advance Germany's military cause. Borrowing from the term that described Germany's overall tactics in the war, Londoners dubbed this period the Blitz.

AIR RAID

As sirens blare their warning of an impending Luftwaffe attack, Royal Air Force pilots sprint to their planes to take to the air in defense. History's first conflict to be decided entirely by airpower, the Battle of Britain dealt Nazi Germany its first loss of World War II. The majority of the courageous airborne defenders, who numbered only 2,500, were British citizens, but a prominent minority were Canadians, Australians, New Zealanders, South Africans, Irishmen, and Americans. Czech and Polish refugees also played a heroic role in the pivotal campaign.

OFF TO THE COUNTRY

In anticipation of the impending Battle of Britain, a group of British schoolchildren (right) is evacuated from London to a safer location in the British countryside. In two years, the relocation program rescued two million children and countless pregnant mothers and old people from the cities.

ELEPHANT & CASTLE
PHILIPS
LAMPS

INSPECTING THE DAMAGE
To the obvious delight of the citizenry, Churchill (left, with cigar) takes a walking tour of London to inspect damage wrought by Luftwaffe bombs during the Blitz. "We can take it," he often said during these morale-boosting rounds, and London, despite losing some 40,000 of its inhabitants to the bombing raids, proved it could withstand the pummeling.

Winston Churchill

Churchill's courageous and imaginative leadership embodied Britain's spirit of resistance during World War II. Uniting his country against Nazi aggression, he led his people in their "finest hour."

FEARLESS LEADER
Taking over as Prime Minister from Neville Chamberlain on May 10, 1940, the same day that Germany invaded western Europe, Churchill immediately established a tone of stout and determined leadership. Fueled by optimism, as the British World War II poster (inset) attests, Churchill believed that his entire life had been but a prelude to his "walk with destiny" as British prime minister. When he took the office, he promised the British people his "blood, toil, tears, and sweat."

FORMIDABLE DUO
Churchill's easy rapport with American president Franklin Roosevelt helped win Britain political and military support from the United States. Although the U.S. remained officially neutral until Pearl Harbor, Roosevelt's Lend-Lease policies helped the British weather Germany's biggest blows in 1940 and 1941.

HOMECOMING
Churchill (right) greets Londoners with his trademark V-for-victory sign upon his return to 10 Downing Street from the Trident Conference in Washington, D.C., in May 1943. A skilled negotiator, Churchill was also imbued with a nearly prescient grasp of international affairs. Before he became Prime Minister, he correctly called the Munich Conference of 1939 "a total and unmitigated defeat" for the Allies.

YOUNG JOURNALIST
Having served the British military in Egypt and Turkey in 1897 and 1898, young Churchill (left) turned to journalism in 1899, acting as a correspondent in the Boer War for the London Morning Post. He was captured in an ambush during the conflict but escaped and, upon his return to England, launched his political career. His first position, which he took in 1900, was as Conservative member of Parliament for the town of Oldham.

BUDDING STATESMAN
Churchill (above, right) walks with David Lloyd George, Chancellor of the Exchequer, on Budget Day in 1910. When Lloyd George became Prime Minister in 1916, Churchill served as his minister of munitions, commissioning the production of thousands of tanks for the British Army. From 1919 to 1921 Churchill was Lloyd George's secretary of state for war.

American Isolationism

With a tradition of isolationism stretching back to the Founding Fathers, many Americans opposed the war, even as Germany and Japan menaced their neighbors and threatened America's interests.

MOTHERS AGAINST LEND-LEASE
Leaders of the American Mothers' Crusade Against Lend-Lease (top) meet with Michigan congressmen Clare Hoffman (left, with flag) and Roy O. Woodruff (second from right), both of whom supported the Mothers' cause, in Washington, D.C., on February 26, 1941. Lend-Lease favored giving war materials to Britain and her allies in exchange for a promise of repayment after the war was won. Isolationists like the American Mothers' Crusade believed the policy was a prelude to American intervention.

AMERICAN NAZIS
German-Americans perform the Nazi salute (above) at the second annual German Day celebration at Camp Siegfried, in Yaphank, Long Island, on August 29, 1937. Only a small fraction of German-Americans condoned Hitler's actions and even a smaller percentage were actually Nazis. But like many other Americans, some hoped that the United States would remain neutral.

ISOLATIONIST AVIATOR
Charles Lindbergh (above, right) and Senator Burton K. Wheeler of Montana salute at an America First (button inset) rally in New York City on May 23, 1941. Lindbergh drew criticism from Roosevelt for making pro-German speeches on behalf of the isolationist group. The famous pilot doubted America's ability to defeat Hitler's war machine after his celebrated visit to Germany in 1936.

ANTIWAR MASTERPIECE
The film version (left) of Erich Maria Remarque's classic World War I novel, *All Quiet on the Western Front*—copies of which Hitler had publicly burned in 1933, for the novel's "treachery toward the soldiers of the World War"—won the 1930 Academy Awards for Best Picture and Best Director and contributed to the strong antiwar sentiment of the day in the U.S.

THE RADIO PRIEST
Father Charles Coughlin (left), a staunch proponent of isolationism, showcases his fiery speechmaking at a 1938 rally. A Catholic priest from Detroit, Coughlin preached anticommunist, anti-Semitic propaganda to an audience of 40 million on his Sunday afternoon radio broadcasts.

War Around the Mediterranean

Erwin Rommel (below), nicknamed the Desert Fox, was perhaps the greatest general of the war. In North Africa he led his troops to brilliant effect until they ran into superior Allied forces.

British desert commandos, like these members of the Special Air Services (left), caused "more damage than any other British unit of equal strength," according to Rommel. Other Commonwealth troops also distinguished themselves in the desert. The Seventh Armored Division—the Desert Rats (badge below)—earned its nickname for its lethal "scurrying and biting" activities.

On October 28, 1940, Adolf Hitler stepped from his personal coach onto the flag-decked platform of the rail station in Florence, Italy. Awaiting him was fellow dictator Benito Mussolini. The Duce was ecstatic, "Führer, we are marching!" he proclaimed. "This morning a victorious Italian army has crossed the Greek frontier!" Poker-faced, Hitler congratulated his ally. In reality he was furious. Mussolini had not informed Hitler of the planned offensive, and all of the Führer's carefully crafted diplomacy in the Balkans promised to unravel.

For over a year Hitler had maneuvered to maintain a tenuous balance among the fractious Balkan states in order to secure a southern flank for his planned invasion of the Soviet Union. Despite the 1939 non-aggression pact between Germany and the Soviet Union, Hitler viewed the Bolshevik giant as the greatest threat to his Reich and considered conflict with the Red Army inevitable. Without the assistance—or at least neutrality—of his Balkan neighbors, Hitler's planned crusade to the East might be doomed from the outset.

Satisfying all the Balkan states while countering the Soviets' influence was difficult enough for Germany without Mussolini's interference. In August, Bulgaria and Hungary had made territorial claims on Romania. At a summit in Vienna, Germany awarded portions of Romania to its neighbors but dispatched military missions to guarantee Romania's remaining territory and oversee the protection of the vital Ploesti oilfields. Unable to extinguish the civil unrest that followed the

dismemberment of his country, however, Romania's King Carol II abdicated in favor of his 19-year-old son, Michael, and granted dictatorial powers to fascist general Ion Antonescu. Antonescu immediately requested German military support, and Hitler obliged him with Panzer divisions and several fighter squadrons. In

In late 1940 the strategic Balkan peninsula was fraught with conflict. Mussolini's army invaded Greece and encountered unexpected resistance, a blunder lampooned in the cartoon above. The poorly conceived invasion disrupted Hitler's plans and encouraged him to send German troops into Romania, the domain of his new ally, General Ion Antonescu (above, near right).

November, Hitler pressured Hungary, Romania, and Slovakia to join the Tripartite Pact with Germany, Italy, and Japan. As part of the alliance, both Hungary and Romania promised to allow free transit of German forces across their borders for a possible invasion of Greece.

Hitler's plan to interfere in the Balkans came just in time. Italian fortunes around the Mediterranean had approached a crisis. By November the Italian invasion of Greece had bogged down, and a series of fierce counterattacks had not only driven the Italians out but also permitted Greek forces to overrun nearly a third of Italian-occupied Albania. Britain had begun to land troops on the island of Crete and dispatched RAF units to Greek airfields near Athens. In North Africa a smaller British force under Major General Richard O'Connor smashed an Italian army of 300,000 men led by Marshal Rudolfo Graziani in northeast Libya and drove it back to the fortress city of Bardia.

On January 3 a second British operation forced the Bardia garrison to surrender—80,000 Italians were taken prisoner—before driving on to capture the port city of Tobruk. In the first week of February, O'Connor completed his conquest of Cyrenaica by sending his Seventh Armored Division on a 170-mile trek across the desert to cut the Italian line of retreat between Bengazi and El Agheila. With Italian forces surrendering in droves, the Führer felt obligated to rescue his Italian ally—in North Africa as well as in the Balkans—from humiliation.

After Hitler finally succeeded in pressuring Bulgaria into joining the Axis, lead elements of the German army entered Bulgaria and moved toward the Greek border on March 2. Six days later a 58,000-man British expeditionary force arrived from Egypt to help defend Greece. On March 27, only two days after a reluctant Prince Paul, the regent of Yugoslavia, had directed his diplomats to sign the Axis pact, General Dusan Simovic led a

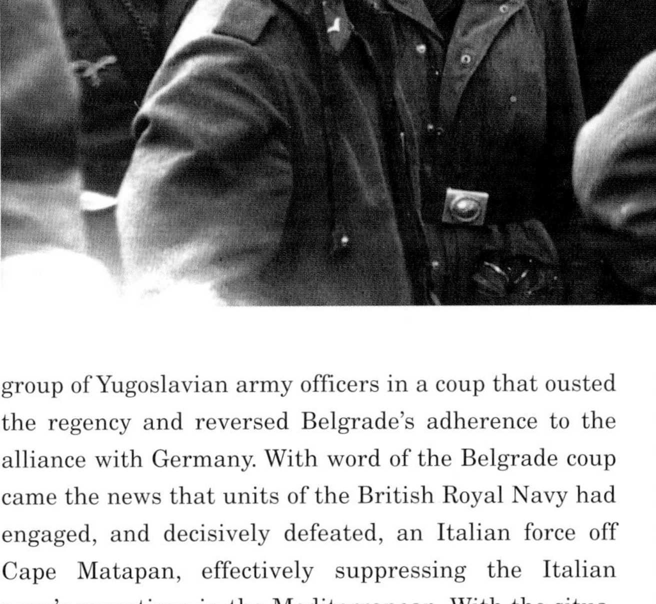

General Kurt Student (above, right), architect of the German airborne invasion of Crete, instructs a unit of paratroopers. Some airborne officers carried M-38s (above inset), but most paratroopers—who earned diving-eagle badges (top inset) when they graduated from jump school—carried only pistols and relied on weapons drops to augment their firepower.

group of Yugoslavian army officers in a coup that ousted the regency and reversed Belgrade's adherence to the alliance with Germany. With word of the Belgrade coup came the news that units of the British Royal Navy had engaged, and decisively defeated, an Italian force off Cape Matapan, effectively suppressing the Italian navy's operations in the Mediterranean. With the situation on his southern front deteriorating, Hitler determined to crush Yugoslavia along with Greece.

On April 6 the Germans attacked Yugoslavia. Field Marshal Wilhelm List's 12th Army crossed the Bulgarian frontier and advanced into southern Yugoslavia while Maxmilian von Weichs's Second Army smashed toward Zagreb from the north. By April 12 the Germans had captured Belgrade, and the remnants of the Yugoslav army surrendered five days later. On the same day that the Wehrmacht invaded Yugoslavia, elements of List's 12th Army, the XL Panzer Corps, hooked through Yugoslavia and passed through the Monastir Gap into Greece. While mountain troops of the German XVIII Corps smashed through the massive fortifications of the Metaxas Line along the Bulgarian border, the Second Panzer Division pushed south toward Salonika. The XLI Panzer Corps' armored spearheads turned west to cut off and isolate the Greek First Army along the Albanian frontier, and by April 22 most of the Greek forces had capitulated.

With northern Greece secure, German armored columns advanced south through Greece to converge on the pass at Thermopylae. Brushing aside a British rear guard, the Germans occupied Athens on April 27. By the second week of May the survivors of Britain's expeditionary force abandoned all of their armor and heavy equipment and were evacuated from Greece to the

Panzers roll across the Western Desert in May 1941 (above). The Afrika cuff title (inset) designated those German soldiers who had fought in the African theater for six months. Masks and goggles (inset, far right) allowed soldiers to breathe and see despite the hurricane-force winds in the desert.

island of Crete. The disastrous campaign cost the British over a quarter of their forces—11,000 prisoners and 2,100 killed or wounded. In addition, more than 200,000 Greeks surrendered. German losses in the Balkans amounted to a mere 5,000 casualties.

With the fall of Greece, one last major obstacle to the stabilization of Germany's Balkan flank remained—the island of Crete. Strategically located in the eastern Mediterranean and within bomber range of Romanian oil fields, Crete was now occupied by a large British force, recently increased in size by the troops withdrawn from the Greek mainland. With the island guarded by the Royal Navy, any marine operation would be fraught with risk. Taking full advantage of their air superiority in the eastern Mediterranean, the German high command determined upon Operation Mercury—an ambitious plan to capture Crete using paratroopers and gliders of Germany's elite *Fallschirmjäger* battalions.

In the early morning hours of May 20, German assault troops in gliders descended on the northern coastal town of Maleme to seize a vital airfield. At the same time, massive parachute drops of several battalions leapt from their Junkers-52 transports to support the glider troops. Farther east along the coast, other airborne units landed around Canea and, after a three-hour delay, a second wave of paratroopers landed around Retimo and Herak-lion. Unfortunately for the Germans, Ultra codebreakers had deciphered German intentions and informed British intelligence of the planned invasion. With the failure to seize Crete in a lightning coup, the fighting raged for more than a week, with the Germans airlifting battal-ions of elite mountain troops to reinforce their belea-guered, widely dispersed paratroopers. In the waters around Crete, the Royal Navy lost three light cruisers and six destroyers in a desperate battle against the Luft-waffe. By the last week of May, the Commonwealth com-

mander on Crete, New Zealander general Bernard Freyberg, was authorized to withdraw his troops to Egypt.

At the same time that Hitler ordered the German high command to make preparations for the conquest of Greece, he took steps to repair Axis fortunes in North Africa. On February 6, 1941, the Führer ordered General Erwin Rommel to take command of two mechanized divisions that were to be dispatched to Tripoli to assist the Italians. An advocate of tank warfare, Rommel brilliantly adapted his strategies to the desert landscape. Within days of his arrival Rommel decided to take the offensive with his new Afrikakorps. With British North African forces drained by operations in Greece and Crete, Rommel's attacks drove the British out of Agheila and Mersa Brega by March 31.

Ignoring orders to hold his position, Rommel and two Italian divisions captured Agedabia on April 2 and encircled the bulk of the British armor near Benghazi and Mechili. By April 7, Axis forces had reconquered all of Cyrenaica except for Tobruk. The port was defended by the Ninth Australian Division, which stubbornly resisted Rommel's attempts to storm the town. Throughout May and June, Rommel was able to reject two British attempts to relieve Tobruk, but his failure to capture the port meant that his own supply lines were dangerously overextended. Rommel was forced to halt his advance at the Egyptian border, and the situation in North Africa reached a stalemate.

Following the lightning campaign in Yugoslavia and Greece, the Axis powers set about the disposition of their conquests. Yugoslavia was erased from the map. Croatia and Montenegro were recognized as independent states. The Yugoslav province of Macedonia was divided between Bulgaria and Albania. Greece was occupied by Germany, Italy, and Bulgaria. It had taken four months for Germany to rescue Italian fortunes, but the vulnerable Balkan flank of Europe had been secured, and the path was open for Adolf Hitler's crusade against the Soviet Union.

The Australian infantry (above) helped capture Bardia, where a number of Italian generals and their staffs were taken prisoner. British and Commonwealth troops relied on sun compasses (inset) to guide them in the featureless desert.

IN THE TRENCHES
In a scene repeated all over Yugoslavia in April 1941, a frightened infantryman surrenders to German forces. Resistance to the Nazi invasion was weak and disorganized. The Yugoslavian army was beset by internal conflicts, and many Croats and pro-German Yugoslavs welcomed the invaders as liberators.

OPERATION PUNISHMENT
After a coup deposed the regime of Prince Paul in Yugoslavia, an enraged Hitler ordered an invasion of the Balkan nation. The "Ghost Division," as the 11th Panzer Division of General Ewald von Kleist's First Armored Group was called, charges through the city of Nis (left). The unit covered the 140 miles to Belgrade in just four days, and the conquest of the upstart nation was completed just eight days after the invasion had begun. Perhaps the most difficult part of the process for the Germans was finding someone to sign an instrument of surrender, since the political leadership had already fled the country.

ANOTHER RETREAT

An overloaded truck (right) hurries British soldiers to the southern ports of Greece for evacuation to Crete. Only a handful of Commonwealth troops had been sent to help defend Greece from the German invasion, but the citizens of Greece appreciated every ounce of effort and sacrifice. "They threw flowers to us," remembered one British soldier, "and ran beside us crying, 'Come back. You must come back again . . . Good luck.' "

RESISTING THE AXIS

Greek troops enthusiastically rush to the front (right) to meet Mussolini's challenge. The Greeks' spirited resistance repelled the poorly planned and poorly executed Italian advance. Despite significant numerical superiority, Mussolini's soldiers were unable to break through the Greek mountain strongholds.

FINISHING TOUCHES

German bombers buzz the ancient monuments of the Acropolis in Athens (below). After Italy's debacle in Greece, Hitler dispatched the Wehrmacht from positions in Yugoslavia to save his ally from humiliation. Greece's capital city fell to the Germans after less than three weeks of combat in April 1941.

ΣΕΚ
Z.5M

BLITZKRIEG FROM ABOVE

German paratroopers descend through a plume of smoke (above) emitted by a crippled troop carrier. Luftwaffe airborne forces were used over the Aegean island of Crete in the first airborne invasion in history. Though small and isolated, Crete was of great strategic importance; an Allied presence on the island would have left Hitler's southeastern flank vulnerable. After 10 days of battle, the gritty paratroopers delivered the island into German hands.

FINAL ASSAULT

Two German paratroopers (above) rush an Allied position on Crete. The final parachute drop of the invasion was launched against the airfield and harbor at Heraklion, an ancient Minoan port three miles north of Knossos. Many paratroopers never made it out of their transport planes, 15 of which crashed in the hail of antiaircraft fire. The victory in Crete was costly—4,000 German soldiers were killed, and 220 out of 600 transport aircraft were destroyed—and their subsequent occupation of the island would not be easy.

FLYING DEUTSCHE-MEN

German paratroopers (left) disarm British soldiers. The battle for Crete was costly for both sides, and the lessons for future airborne assaults were inconclusive. Although the British were defeated, heavy German losses led General Student to conclude that "the days of the paratrooper are over." This conclusion would be disproved in Sicily and Normandy, where Allied airborne troops were used effectively.

DOWNCAST AND DISENCHANTED

Italian soldiers (right), captured during the British victory at Bardia, march glumly toward a British base. Mussolini's troops were quickly losing faith in their cause, and some in North Africa surrendered without a fight. The British steamrolled the coasts of Egypt and Libya with astounding speed and efficiency in late 1941 before Hitler could dispatch his own forces.

PAPER TIGER

In a move calculated to showcase Italy's military strength and triple the size of its holdings in Africa, Mussolini launched an invasion of Egypt in September 1940. Italian troops rolling into Egypt presented a formidable picture (left), but the reality was quite different; Italian tanks were so flimsy that they often broke down in the harsh terrain.

CLEAN-UP CREW

British Commonwealth troops (right) storm through the ruined town of Bardia, searching for remaining enemy troops. Protected by a garrison of 45,000 Italian troops and surrounded by an 18-mile ring of defenses, Bardia was believed to be impenetrable. However, in January 1940 the RAF launched a bombardment from the air while three Royal Navy battleships assaulted the shorefront. Within two days, the Italian flag in Bardia was lowered, and the British swept toward Tobruk.

DESERT FOX

General Erwin Rommel (left) directs troop movements in 1942. He arrived in North Africa in February 1941, just as British troop concentrations were shifted to Greece. Barely a month after his arrival Rommel and his troops went on the offensive and quickly reversed Axis fortunes in the desert.

LONG-RANGE PLAN

Rommel compared waging war in the desert to fighting on the sea. In such terrain, "whoever has the weapons with the greatest range has the longest arm," he told his officers. He believed the 88-mm gun (left) gave the Germans an advantage over the more mobile British, who had recently been reinforced with tanks. The long-range 88-mm was traditionally an antiaircraft weapon but served quite well against tanks in the desert.

A SEA OF SAND

German soldiers (right) trudge over dunes near El Alamein. The troops fighting in the sands of North Africa faced extraordinarily harsh conditions. Sand itself, which plugged nostrils and got into wounds, made life miserable. One frustrated soldier wrote home, "We have more sand than hair on our heads."

A FORTRESS HOLDS ITS OWN

Commonwealth troops (left) patrol the beleaguered town of Tobruk in 1941. They had captured the strategic port and its extensive fortifications in January, and its defenses—built by the Italian army—became a maddening obstacle to Rommel. The Germans attempted several unsuccessful assaults on the stronghold, and the embattled town became a cause célèbre. Churchill told the commander of the garrison, "The whole Empire is watching your steadfast and spirited defense of this important outpost . . . with gratitude and admiration."

LAST STAND

British gunners in Tobruk (right) man a captured Breda gun and prepare to fire at any German aircraft that might appear. In May 1941 Rommel was attempting to capture the city with fewer than half the men in the defending force. He eventually scaled back to patrols and artillery duels and focused his energies elsewhere. In June 1942 the Afrikakorps returned in greater strength, reclaimed the vital port, and took nearly 35,000 prisoners.

THE KEY TO THE DESERT

Taking Tobruk proved much easier for the British than holding it. After the fall of Bardia in early 1941, British troops passing through barbed wire (above) were virtually unopposed on their way to Tobruk. After Rommel and his Afrikakorps steamrolled most of the British army in 1942, however, Tobruk gained added significance. British general Archibald Wavell ordered his men to hold the city at all costs: "There is nothing between you and Cairo," he said.

Erwin Rommel

Assigned to reverse Axis fortunes in North Africa, the celebrated Desert Fox brilliantly outmaneuvered the British as his Afrikakorps swept across the continent.

SUPERMAN

Rommel (above) inspired awe even in his adversaries. British leadership believed the key to beating the Germans in North Africa was eliminating Rommel's aura of invincibility. "Rommel is becoming a kind of magician . . . to our troops," said Sir Claude Auchinleck, the British commander in North Africa in 1942. "Rommel represents something more than an ordinary German general." Rommel used his compass (inset) and what he called *Fingerspitzengefühl*—an "intuition of the fingers" or a sixth sense—to guide him.

BORN TO LEAD

Lieutenant Rommel (below) appears at home in the trenches of France's Argonne Forest in 1915. Rommel's only ambition in life was to be a professional soldier; by age 25 he was regarded as an authority on battlefield tactics.

EARLY SUCCESS

Rommel (above) supervises the surrender of Fortune's 51st Highland Division in St. Valéry, France, on June 12, 1940. His role in the defeat of France made him a hero, earning him a promotion to Major General and an assignment to command the Afrikakorps in North Africa.

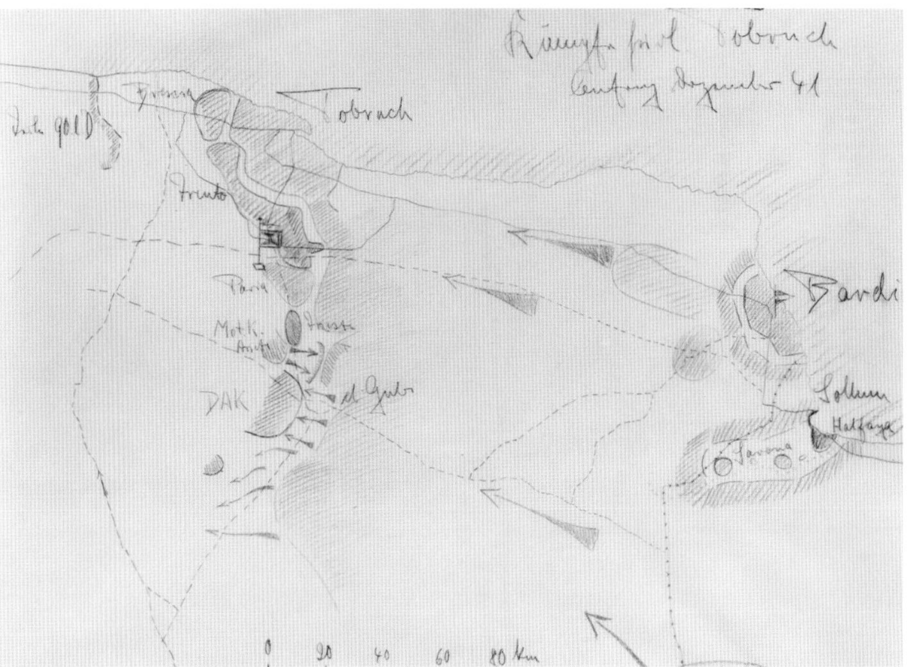

MAPPING VICTORY

Rommel sketched troop locations between Bardia and Tobruk (above) in December 1941. Tobruk eluded the Afrikakorps for eight long months, and its symbolic value grew to equal its strategic importance. On June 18, 1942, Rommel tightened the noose around the tiring Commonwealth defenders. "To each one of us," Rommel said, "Tobruk was a symbol of British resistance and we are now going to finish it for good."

CELEBRITY

Rommel was already a media darling by the time he made the cover of *Signal* magazine (right) in May 1941. The charismatic officer possessed a flair for the dramatic that added to his larger-than-life image and won him the admiration of his troops and superiors.

Benito Mussolini

The father of Fascism and an aspiring Caesar, Mussolini led Italy to ruin in his quest for a new Roman Empire. Bungled operations in Egypt and Greece reduced Italy to a mere appendage of German power.

THE DUCE
Like Hitler, Mussolini won a following with charismatic public addresses, like this rally in Rome in 1920 (above), and maintained support with brutal repression of the opposition. Pins (inset) celebrated the two dictators'1936 Pact of Steel, which allied the two fascist nations. As a politician, Mussolini's willingness to please others helped him to power but ultimately limited his effectiveness as a leader. "He wants everybody's blessing," said one early observer of the Duce, "and changes his coat 10 times a day to get it."

POLITICAL MUSCLE

Although the 1920 elections failed to produce even one Fascist Party victory, Mussolini and his legions of Black Shirts (above) continued to fight for power in vicious street battles against Italian socialists and communists. Two years later King Victor Emmanuel III invited Mussolini to form his own Italian government.

EVOLVING RELATIONSHIP

Mussolini and Hitler (below) ride through the streets of Florence during Hitler's state visit in 1938. Although Mussolini came to power several years before Hitler and initially dismissed the Führer as a "mad, little clown," Hitler assumed the dominant role in the relationship once the war began.

FIRST TASTE OF WAR

Corporal Mussolini (below, in 1917) abandoned the Socialist Party during World War I. Backed by the French government, Mussolini reversed his antiwar rhetoric and urged Italy to join the Allied cause.

THE PRINCE OF VANITY

Mussolini took great care with his appearance, exercised fanatically, and scorned overindulgence in food and drink. As he rose to power, however, he shocked conventional Italians by appearing at official functions unshaven. When he did choose to shave, he did so in typical Duce fashion, using an ornate gold shaving set (right).

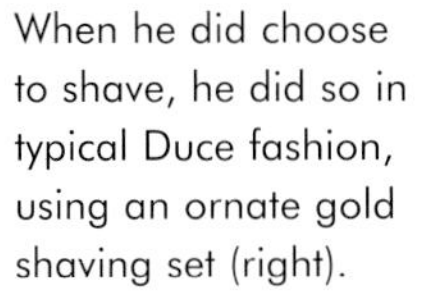

Barbarossa

Wehrmacht troops (left) traverse a wind-whipped plain outside Moscow in December 1941; German soldiers with at least two weeks of experience on the eastern front received the medal below, sarcastically called the "Frozen Meat Medal."

"We have only to kick in [the Soviet Union's] doors," Adolf Hitler told his generals in the summer of 1940, "and the whole rotten structure will come crashing down!" Despite the 1939 non-aggression pact, Hitler never doubted that Germany would eventually go to war with the Soviet Union. Hitler had had the Soviet Union in his sights since he had come to power in the early 1930s. He considered the Bolshevik nation not only his ideological enemy but the only barrier preventing the realization of his dream of German *Lebensraum*. He regarded the Soviet people as sub-human and believed that Germans, as the superior people, were entitled to the living space then occupied by the Soviet population. Indeed, in terms of Nazi ideology, the war in the east was a crusade to fulfill the destiny of the Aryan race to rule the world. The Nazis viewed Bolshevism as a noxious Jewish conspiracy and the continued existence of the Soviet Union as a threat of apocalyptic proportions. In 1937 Hitler called the Soviet Union "the greatest danger for the culture and civilization of mankind."

The Führer never intended to honor the German-Soviet non-aggression pact. For him it was merely a political expediency to clear the way for the Nazi invasion of Poland. Ambitious in his own right, Soviet dictator Josef Stalin had agreed to the treaty mainly because it secretly divided eastern Europe between the two nations, and he believed it would encourage Hitler to focus his energies on western Europe and thus delay a German invasion of the Soviet Union.

Hitler (below, right) studies a map of the eastern front with field marshals Walter Warlimont (left) and Walther von Brauchitsch (center) on June 30, 1941—one week after the launch of Barbarossa.

Developments in 1941 convinced Hitler that the colossal Soviet empire—a nation of more than 170 million people covering one-sixth the earth's land—was ripe for dissolution. On the western front, German military victories fueled Hitler's growing sense of invincibility. France had fallen in a matter of weeks. Britain was barely holding on after almost a year of heavy bombardment, and the United States remained neutral. In the east, the Soviets' poor showing in their war against Finland only encouraged Hitler's thinking: Attack the Soviet Union now while the western allies licked their wounds.

General Fedor von Bock (below), awarding the Iron Cross to German soldiers in 1941, ably led Army Group Center despite warning Hitler that the Soviet Union was "an enormous country whose military strength was unknown"; a pair of Wehrmacht troops (right) keeps watch from a position outside Moscow. By December 1941, however, the Germans would be on the defensive as the Soviets launched a major counterattack.

Operation Barbarossa—named for Emperor Frederick I, a crusader of the Holy Roman Empire—was designed to crush the Soviet Union in a fast, brutal attack modeled after the German blitzkrieg victories in Poland and France. The invading force of 150 divisions, including 19 panzer tank units and 14 motorized infantry units, was split into three groups: North, Center and South. Army Group North targeted Leningrad; Army Group Center plunged toward Smolensk and Moscow; while Army Group South drove toward Kiev and the Ukraine. Hitler believed that Germany would need only 10 weeks to destroy the Soviet army.

On Sunday morning, June 22, 1941, three million German soldiers roared into the Soviet Union as Barbarossa began. Although the Red Army received reports of German military activity on their front, it was stunned by the overwhelming size and speed of the attack. Stalin had foolishly maintained a non-aggressive stance until the day before the invasion. Hoping the reports of German military activity represented merely an exercise, he took careful steps not to maneuver his army in any way that might provoke the Germans. The Red Army, therefore, was totally unprepared—and unqualified. Since he had purged his military in the late 1930s, two-thirds of Stalin's officers had been in their jobs for less than a year. Their incompetence contributed to the incomplete redeployment of Red Army forces that had been enforcing the annexations of Latvia, Lithuania, and Estonia in 1940. Not surprisingly, the Soviets' initial response to the German invasion lacked organization, lending credence to Hitler's belief that the Soviet Union would soon collapse completely and surrender.

General Heinz Guderian, commander of the German panzer forces, had anticipated supply problems and tried to dissuade Hitler from employing blitzkrieg tactics in Barbarossa. But the panzer units performed well in the initial attack, some of them covering 100 miles in the first three days. Within two months Germany's Army Group Center seized Smolensk and captured 138,000 prisoners.

Since Stalin (top left) had purged the ranks of the Red Army (propaganda poster, inset) in the late 1930s, many of his officers, including Marshal Zhukov (top right), led inexperienced and disorganized troops.

In the north the Wehrmacht advanced to within 100 miles of Leningrad. While the invasion forces encountered some poorly organized resistance, German soldiers invading the Ukraine found themselves welcomed as liberators. Stalin had annexed the western Ukraine from Poland in 1939 and severely repressed its population. The beleaguered Ukrainians believed German propaganda that Hitler would free them from the yoke of Soviet rule and reestablish an independent Ukrainian state.

Days after the invasion, however, Hitler's troops revealed their true intentions. They dissolved the Ukraine's newly-formed separatist government and arrested its supporters. The Ukraine was the Soviet Union's most productive agricultural region as well as a major industrial center, and Hitler planned to resettle the area with Aryans and use it to supply the German fatherland. In the Ukrainian city of Kharkov an estimated 100,000 people died of starvation while German troops requisitioned the local food supply for themselves. The execution of Ukrainian Jews quickly became commonplace as the Wehrmacht carried out Hitler's plan to depopulate the area.

The Wehrmacht's behavior in the Ukraine was not unique. Hitler viewed the assault on the Soviet Union as a "war of extermination." The murder of civilians was therefore an acceptable tool of terror. German infantry as well as SS units known as *Einsatzgruppen*—task forces—enacted orders to liquidate so-called ideological enemies, including "Communist party officials and Jews in the service of the party or state." The Germans regarded partisans with particular hatred and targeted them for especially gruesome, often public, deaths.

While Army Group South terrorized the Ukraine, Group North and a Finnish-German force encircled Leningrad. Their orders were to level the city and eliminate its population. By the end of August, Wehrmacht troops had started cutting Leningrad's supply lines and destroying the city's existing food stores. By early winter, food supplies were almost totally depleted.

The siege of Leningrad had been intentionally planned for winter to maximize the number of deaths by starvation. But the brutal cold actually provided

German soldiers (top left) made straw snow boots (inset) to contend with the bitter cold. The Wehrmacht attacked the Soviet Union with the largest force in European history but underestimated the ability of the Soviet troops (top right) and the bitter conditions of the Russian winter.

Leningrad's starving citizens with their best hope for survival. To the east of the city lay Lake Ladoga, and on its eastern bank were rail links to Moscow and the rest of the Soviet Union. Beginning in January 1942 a network of roads across the frozen lake allowed supplies to flow back into the city. By March, lack of food was no longer a major problem in Leningrad, and though the siege continued until 1944—and claimed more than one million Russian lives—life in the city gradually returned to relative normalcy.

Hitler's insistence on taking Leningrad—over the objection of his commanders—delayed a German attack on Moscow until October 1941. By that time, the weather was so severe that the offensive thrust lacked the speed and firepower needed for success. Nevertheless, German commanders believed they could secure a quick victory after General Hermann Hoth's Third Panzer Division cut the Leningrad-Moscow railway and moved into position 70 miles northwest of the city on October 14. The fall of Moscow seemed imminent.

But weeks of heavy rain produced swamp-like conditions around the Soviet capital. While Wehrmacht troops slogged toward Moscow, some of them coming within sight of the city, their tanks bogged down behind them in the muck, and supplies fell far short of the front lines. The Soviets also introduced the T-34 tank, which was far more capable in the sloppy terrain than the Wehrmacht's panzers and so well-armored that German antitank ammunition proved useless against it. Oblivious to the difficulties facing his troops, Hitler ordered them to push on to Moscow.

Unbearable winter conditions and increasingly stubborn Soviet resistance began to affect German morale. Studying his maps near Moscow on December 4, Walter Schaefer-Kehnert realized that if his German panzer unit had a long-range cannon, it could shoot at the Kremlin. A 10.5-cm gun was duly dispatched, and

Stalin dubbed the war with Germany the Great Patriotic War and urged all of his people to join the "relentless struggle" against the Nazis. Siberian soldiers (left) of the Red Army were instrumental in tipping the balance of the battle for Moscow in favor of the Soviets. Heroes of the fighting—in which some 25 million Soviets perished—were awarded the Order of the Red Banner (above).

the Germans opened fire on the seat of Soviet power. Though the weapon was too small to do any significant damage, Schaefer-Kehnert said, "We thought only of the morale consequences on the citizens of Moscow—shooting at the town and the Kremlin!"

But the largely symbolic act of firing upon the Soviet capital could not hide the fact that Schaefer-Kehnert and the Germans were in trouble. The very next day, they were unable to defend themselves against a Soviet attack—subzero temperatures froze the firing mechanisms in their weapons. They also had no winter clothing. "We had huge losses from frozen fingers and toes during the night," Schaefer-Kehnert said. "There was an order that a guard had to go around every two hours and look because you would freeze to death and you would not realize it was happening." Crippled by the cold and reeling from the Red Army's first significant counterattacks, the German invasion stalled 10 miles from the Soviet capital. As December wore on, the Red Army effectively exploited its newfound advantages and forced the Germans to retreat from their positions around Moscow.

In the early months of 1942 the conflict hardened into stalemate as the German army fortified and held previously secured positions away from the Moscow front. The chink in the German armor had been revealed, however, and the Wehrmacht could advance no farther on the capital city. Although German soldiers remained on Soviet soil until 1944, their failure to capture Moscow proved to be a turning point. The United States entered the war in December 1941, and British and American aid began to flow into the Soviet Union in 1942. Germany was soon fighting an Allied force that included the U.S. in the west, and a fully mobilized and equipped Red Army in the east. Hitler's arrogant assumption that he could defeat the Soviets before the end of 1941 proved to be his greatest miscalculation, and the war between Germany and the Soviet Union turned out to be the bloodiest conflict in history.

SMILING CONQUERORS

A truck full of Wehrmacht troops (right) traces a muddy route through the Ukraine in June 1941. By September the Germans had surrounded the Red Army near Kiev, capital of the Ukraine and charter city of Russian civilization. The encirclement trapped 665,000 Soviet soldiers, the largest number of combatants ever taken in a single military operation. Thousands of them were then marched west to German prison camps—a vast column of Soviet soldiers dogged by disease, battle wounds, and exhaustion. Said one observer, "All the misery of the world seemed to be concentrated there."

PULVERIZING POWER

A German 240-mm howitzer (left) bombards Soviet strongholds in the summer of 1941, while its operators shield their ears against the booming report. After capturing Minsk on July 9, the Wehrmacht surrounded approximately 25 Soviet divisions near Vitebsk, Mogilev, and Smolensk, the largest group of Soviet soldiers the Germans had yet neutralized. But the trapped Soviets held out until August 5, when a detachment of Bock's motorized infantry and panzer divisions temporarily abandoned their drive on Moscow to join the Wehrmacht outside Smolensk.

TAKING STOCK

General Heinz Guderian (right, center), panzer commander in Army Group Center, confers with one of his location officers on the eastern front in 1941. Along with Field Marshal Erich von Manstein, Guderian would spearhead some of the Wehrmacht's most significant victories on the eastern front, plunging ahead with his tanks and helping to clear a path toward Moscow. But along with the entire Wehrmacht offensive, Guderian was stymied by the onset of the fearsome Russian winter. Temperatures plunged well below zero and caused some 100,000 cases of frostbite among German troops.

SNIPER FIRE
Two German soldiers (left) of the 71st Infantry Division take aim from a house they've captured in Kiev during the bitter fighting for the Ukrainian capital on September 19, 1941. Seven days later the Wehrmacht killed Red Army general Mikhail Kirponos, commander of the Kiev military district, in an ambush and completely surrounded the city.

TO THE VICTORS
Standing in the upper reaches of the citadel in the center of town, two German soldiers (left) look out over the spires of Kiev and the Dnieper River on September 23, 1941. The Germans secured the city three days later and took 665,000 Soviet soldiers prisoner.

BOGGED DOWN
The bitter Russian winter wasn't the only natural obstacle facing the Wehrmacht. As the motorized German infantry (right) slogging toward Kiev attests, the rainy Russian autumn was equally paralyzing for an invasion force that relied heavily on mobility.

WINTER WARRIORS
Soviet troops (above) march in a traditional military parade in Moscow's Red Square in November 1941. After the pomp and pageantry came a harsh reality: The soldiers marched straight into battle against the Germans, who were advancing upon the capital. Far better equipped for the cold than the Germans (U.S. manufacturers provided the Red Army with 13 million pairs of boots before the war's end), the Soviets mounted several successful counterattacks. The Soviets forced German retreats at Rostov-on-Don and Tikhvin before settling in for a stalemate that lasted until May.

HELPING HANDS
Citizens of Moscow dig an antitank trench (left) at the perimeter of the Soviet capital in the fall of 1941, before the first frosts of the season harden the ground and make such a task impossible. On November 16 the Wehrmacht launched the final stage of its assault on Moscow. The Germans hoped to take the city in time to use it as shelter from the imminent heavy snows but never advanced closer than 10 miles from the capital.

UNDERSUPPLIED

A group of German troops (above) awaits orders outside a command post in the Moscow suburbs in November 1941. Their chilly discomfort, caused by a lack of winter clothing, grew worse as the infamous Russian weather descended upon them. German general Alfred Jodl had denied winter gear to his troops on the eastern front, lest the soldiers get the impression that their mission to conquer the Soviet Union might not be accomplished on schedule.

COLD COMFORT

Two Wehrmacht infantrymen (left) share a cigarette and huddle together for warmth in a shallow foxhole along the eastern front. The extreme conditions of the Russian winter of 1942 devastated the Wehrmacht. More than 2,000 soldiers underwent frostbite-related amputations, and many men froze to death in their sleep.

BITTER WIND

A pair of German soldiers (left) follow a horse-drawn sleigh of supplies along a Ukrainian railway in early 1942. To the north, Germany's Army Group Center pushed on to Moscow in the face of increasingly harsh weather conditions.

MOSCOW MIRACLE

The bloodied corpse of a German soldier lies on a frigid, snow-covered plain as a Soviet T-34 tank rolls forward. The Wehrmacht advance, which had swallowed up hundreds of miles of Soviet territory in the summer of 1941, began to falter in the autumn. By the winter of 1942 the Germans were retreating from positions they had gained on the outskirts of Moscow and were accumulating casualties from the weather as well as the combat.

IVAN THE TERRIBLE

Boosted by increased production in its domestic factories, thousands of new conscripts, and most importantly, the addition of 10 divisions from its Siberian forces, the Red Army (left) counterattacked Germany on December 6, 1941. The Siberian troops, which Stalin had been reluctant to deploy for fear of an attack by Japan from Manchuria (he received reliable intelligence that Japan would strike east, not west), proved pivotal to the Soviets' success. By Christmas the Soviet Union had retaken most of the territory the Wehrmacht had claimed in the latter phases of its drive toward Moscow.

Josef Stalin

A dictator whose legacy of ruthlessness rivaled Hitler's, "Uncle Joe" used cunning diplomatic skills to unite his nation and befriend the western democracies.

UNHOLY ALLIANCE

Flanked by his foreign minister, Vyacheslav Molotov (above, far right) and the German foreign minister, Joachim von Ribbentrop (far left), Stalin (in white coat—without ceremonial shoulder strap, inset) beams over the signing of the Soviet-German non-aggression pact in Moscow on August 23, 1939. The treaty, which stunned the international community, temporarily shelved hostilities between the two nations and cleared the way for Germany's invasion of Poland—which it secretly promised to split with the Soviet Union.

HAPPIER DAYS

Stalin shares a jovial moment with his daughter, Svetlana (above), in 1937 at the dictator's country house in the suburbs of Moscow. Svetlana later renounced her father and emigrated to the U.S.

FATHERS OF THE REVOLUTION

At the eighth meeting of the delegates of the Bolshevik Communist Party (left) in Moscow in 1919, Stalin (second row, second from left) sits next to Lenin (middle), the man he would succeed as Soviet leader.

RISE TO POWER

Stalin (right, in 1930) was educated at the Tiflis Orthodox Seminary until he was expelled for espousing Marxism. Having secretly consolidated power within the Party for years, Stalin ascended to the Soviet leadership after Lenin's death in 1924, even though his mentor had warned that Stalin was "too crude" for the nation's highest office.

SHOEMAKER'S SON

Born Josef Djugashvili, the son of a Georgian cobbler, Stalin entered the Bolshevik underground at the turn of the century and was soon arrested and sent to Siberia. After escaping in 1904, he joined the illegal Bolshevik Central Committee in 1912, when the St. Petersburg imperial police created a file (above) on the future Soviet leader.

Soldbuch
zugleich
Personalausweis

Einsatzgruppen

Special commands of German SS and militia, innocuously called "task groups," carried out the systematic extermination of Europe's "undesirables."

PUBLIC HANGING

Wehrmacht troops (above) witness and photograph the public execution of several Russian partisans in January 1942. Every SS agent carried a "Soldbuch" (left) in which to record his daily observations and murderous activities. Many were expressed in euphemisms such as "resettlement measures" or "cleansing actions."

IN BARBAROSSA'S WAKE

Behind the advancing Wehrmacht troops of Operation Barbarossa came the dreaded SS troops, who corralled Soviet Jews (above) in work camps, forced them to wear the Star of David, and summarily executed them. Between June and November 1941, Heinrich Himmler, chief of the SS, oversaw the massacre of one million Jews in Soviet territory.

SYSTEMATIC ATROCITIES

Himmler (above, right) greets a group of Soviet peasants outside their ruined village during Barbarossa. At a meeting in January 1942 in the Berlin suburb of Wannsee, Himmler received governmental permission to carry out the slaughter of the Jews.

WAR CRIMES

An SS officer prepares to execute a Ukrainian civilian (above) in the fall of 1942, outside the city of Winniza. Such executions and mass graves were common, but Himmler regarded them as inefficient and established concentration camps in their place. By the summer of 1944 there were 20 concentration camps and 165 work camps, all of which carried out the genocide of Jews, Gypsies, homosexuals, and indigents.

NO ONE SPARED

A group of women and one child (left) huddle together in front of a mound of slaughtered prisoners at a Latvian concentration camp in December 1941. Prisoners of camps connected to industrial centers were usually worked to exhaustion before being executed.

Japan Moves South

Though he was opposed to the Tripartite Pact and discouraged a war with America, Admiral Isoroku Yamamoto (below) planned the attack on Pearl Harbor.

A Japanese carrier crew (left) cheers as one of its planes takes off to attack Pearl Harbor. Japan attacked several Allied bases in the Pacific that day, including the Philippines, where American general Jonathan Wainwright earned the Medal of Honor (below).

In the early hours of December 7, 1941, a fearsome Japanese armada of 31 warships carrying 353 attack planes steamed stealthily into position 230 miles north of the Hawaiian island of Oahu. Elite pilots, equipped with postcard aerial maps of Pearl Harbor provided by a Japanese operative in Honolulu, lifted off from their carriers after a final communiqué from Admiral Isoroku Yamamoto, architect of the impending attack: "The rise or fall of the empire now hinges on this battle."

Japan's decision to go to war with the United States was fraught with risks. Just 15 months earlier Yamamoto himself had told his prime minister, "If I am told to fight regardless of the consequences, I shall run wild for the first six months or a year, but I have utterly no confidence for the second or third year." Other powerful voices in the Japanese leadership echoed Yamamoto's concerns, but the need for expansion was nevertheless overwhelming. Japan, with an island population of nearly 80 million, could never be self-sufficient in food and raw materials. Japan had already looked toward China to augment its resources. Suffering from civil strife and dependent on Western aid, China appeared ripe for conquest. The Imperial Army had been gobbling up Chinese territory on the continent since 1931, but the deeper it chased the elusive Chinese Nationalist leader, Generalissimo Chiang Kai-shek, into China, the more it foundered on poor, unpaved interior roads. Moreover, the U.S., which considered itself China's protector, had in turn punished Japan for her aggression with crippling trade restrictions.

As the China campaign encountered military and political resistance, the Imperial Navy shifted its attention south. By exploiting the riches of European colonies—oil in the Dutch East Indies, raw metals in British-controlled Burma and Malaya, and rubber plantations in French Indochina—Japan hoped to establish a new Greater East Asia Co-Prosperity Sphere, a perimeter of power in the central and south Pacific. The Allied

Japanese ambassador Kichisaburo Nomura and envoy Saburo Kurusu (above) exit the State Department on December 7, 1941, shortly after their country's planes had attacked the U.S. Fleet in the Pacific. Sporting a black armband, President Franklin Roosevelt (above, right) signs the declaration of war against Japan on December 8. Pearl Harbor would not soon be forgotten by FDR nor the myriad of Americans who used it as a rallying cry (button, inset).

powers in Europe were fighting a losing battle against Germany and were helpless to protect their colonial jewels. Only the U.S. stood in Japan's way.

To ward off the Americans, Japan forged the Tripartite Pact with Germany and Italy in late 1940, committing the Axis powers to aid each other if attacked by a nation not involved in the European war. Buoyed with confidence, Japan grabbed Indochina from Vichy France in July 1941. Abandoning rhetoric for action, President Franklin Roosevelt froze Japan's assets in the U.S. and ordered a debilitating oil embargo. American and Japanese diplomats worked furiously to reconcile their remote positions, but neither side wavered. Secretary of State Cordell Hull's hard line was reinforced by his knowledge of Japan's true aims and intentions—the U.S. had cracked Japan's code nearly a year earlier. For his part, Japanese prime minister Hideki Tojo simply wouldn't countenance the U.S.'s three-pronged ultimatum: Renounce the Tripartite Pact, pull all troops out of Southeast Asia and China, and give up all territory gained since 1931. The U.S.'s rigid demands left Japan no "wiggle room" to save face. "I am afraid we would become a third-class nation in two or three years" if Japan capitulated, Tojo told his emperor in November. The only course was war.

On the morning of December 7, radar trainee Private George Elliott, working all night at an Oahu tracking station, had noticed two waves of blips registering some 137 miles north of the island. By the time his instructor got Lieutenant Kermit Tyler on the phone, the radar scope was flooded with contacts within 92 miles of the islands. Aware that a flight of B-17s was due from California that morning, Tyler said, "Well, don't worry about it," and hung up.

The Japanese achieved utter surprise. When their bombers screamed over the harbor, American servicemen thought Navy fliers were buzzing them as a prank, until the torpedoes hit the water. Explosions rocked several ships at once. The battleship *Oklahoma* was hit first with a one-two torpedo punch. Within 20 minutes, she rolled to port and caught on the muddy harbor bottom. Some of her crewmen scrambled onto the slick upturned hull and watched in a daze as the bombs fell around them. The battleship *California* was also hit twice but sank straight into the mud, leaving her guns operational during the battle. The battleship *West Virginia*, aft of the *Oklahoma*,

EXTRA!

WAR!

San Francisco Chronicle

The City's Only Home-Owned Newspaper

FOUNDED 1865—VOL. CLIII, NO. 146 SAN FRANCISCO, MONDAY, DECEMBER 8, 1941 DAILY 5 CENTS, SUNDAY 10 CENTS

JAPAN ATTACKS U.S.!

Hawaii and Manila Bombed; Chute Troops Off Honolulu!

25 YEARS AGO TODAY IN S. F. HEADLINES

LLOYD GEORGE ACCEPTS BRITISH PREMIERSHIP . . . CONVICT WALKS OUT AT SAN QUENTIN . . . SEA-TO-SEA STEAMER LINE FINANCED TO CURB RATES . . . STREET CARS HERE CARRY MORE PASSENGERS THAN IN L. A.

Robt. Burns Panatela de Luxe 10¢

The Sophisticrat of Cigars

Bulletins

HONOLULU, Dec. 7 (AP)—A naval engagement is in progress off of Honolulu, with at least one black enemy aircraft carrier in the action against Pearl Harbor defenses.

WASHINGTON, Dec. 7 (AP)—The White House announced at 3:35 p. m. (EST) today that the army had just received word that an American vessel, believed to be a cargo ship, had been sending out signals of distress approximately west of San Francisco. Whether it had been torpedoed was not immediately learned.

The Time

Eyewitness Reports Sound Of Terrific Cannonading In Pearl Harbor Area

HONOLULU, Dec 7 (UP)—Parachute troops were sighted off Harbor Point today.

By EUGENE BURNS

HONOLULU, Dec. 7 (AP)—At least two Japanese bombers, their wings bearing the insignia of the Rising Sun, appeared over Honolulu at about 7:35 a. m. (Honolulu time) today and dropped bombs.

The sound of cannons firing comes to me here in Honolulu as I telephone this story to the San Francisco Associated Press office.

Reports say the Japanese bombers scored two hits, one at Hickam Field, air corps post on Oahu island, and another at Pearl Harbor, setting an oil tank afire.

Shortly before I started talking on the transpacific telephone, I saw a formation of five Japanese planes flying over Honolulu.

The sound of cannonading coming from the direction of Pearl Harbor has been continuing for an hour and a half. So far, there are no reports of casualties. No bombs have fallen in Honolulu itself, so far as I coud determine before making this call.

There is much commotion going on, with planes in the air and anti-aircraft firing.

The citizens of Honolulu have been cleared from the streets by military and naval units, assisted by

Continued on Page 11, Col. 2

THIS IS WHERE IT STARTED: The Japanese yesterday attacked Hawaii and all naval bases in the Philippines. Japanese troops were also reported on route to Thailand.

Bolivia Gets Lease-Lend

35 Cars of Nazi Wounded Daily

FDR Calls Cabinet; Army and Navy Ordered To Battle Stations

WASHINGTON, Dec. 7 (AP)—The President decided today after Japan's attack on Pearl Harbor and Manila to call an extraordinary meeting of the Cabinet for 8:30 o'clock tonight and to have congressional leaders of both parties join the conferenc at 9 p. m.

By the Associated Press

WASHINGTON, Dec. 7-Japanese airplanes today attacked American defenses bases at Hawaii and Manila, and President Roosevelt ordered the army and navy to carry out undisclosed orders prepared for the defense of the United States.

The White House said Japan had attacked America's vital outposts in the Pacific--Hawaii and Manila--at 3:20 p. m. (EST) and that so far as was known the attacks were still in progress.

Announcing the President's action for the protection of American territory, Presidential Secretary Sephen Early declared that so far as is known now, the attacks were "made wholly without warning--when both nations were at peace--and were delivered within an hour or so of the time that the Japanese Am-

Continued on Page 11, Col. 8

also sank into the mud with its guns blazing and its deck in flames. Suddenly, the exploding din of war—a cacophony of strafing Zero fighters, heavy, armor-piercing bombs, hastily manned antiaircraft guns, and the popping of small arms—was interrupted by a detonation of colossal proportions: A Japanese bomb scored a direct hit on the forward ammunition magazine of the battleship *Arizona*. The shock wave was so strong that Japanese air commander Mitsuo Fuchida's bomber, circling more than half a mile away, was buffeted like a feather in the wind. After three more hits the *Arizona* was swallowed by the harbor, taking more than 1,000 sailors with her.

After a second wave of attacks the raid abruptly halted. The swarm of Japanese warplanes rose above the wreckage and slipped away through the rising smoke. In less than two hours the invaders had sunk or crippled 18 warships, destroyed 188 planes, and damaged 159. More than 2,400 Americans were killed and nearly 1,200 were wounded, while Japan lost only 29 planes.

But Pearl Harbor was just one of several coordinated attacks across the Pacific. Even as Fuchida's flock of warplanes neared Oahu, Japanese shells hammered the Malayan coast and assault troops overran the Thai beaches of Singora and Pattani. Singapore was bombed as well, where the British were so unprepared that they sent

A small rescue craft speeds toward the *West Virginia* (above, left) after the battleship was hit in the surprise attack on Pearl Harbor. A life preserver (inset) from the *Arizona* provides a sad reminder of the sunken ship, which took over 1,000 men to their watery graves. News of the Japanese bombing was boldly plastered on tabloids across the country (above).

As a Japanese officer looks on, General Wainwright (top) makes a radio address ordering his remaining troops in the Philippines to surrender. Japanese troops (top right) celebrate after taking Bataan. The fall of the Philippines was nearly as catastrophic as the losses at Pearl Harbor and contributed to Japanese propaganda (poster, inset) that the Allies were weak.

no fighters to intercept, fearing that inexperienced antiaircraft gunners would inadvertantly down their own fliers.

Japanese forces also targeted American airfields on Luzon, the largest island of the Philippine archipelago, and caught General Douglas MacArthur's B-17 bombers still on the ground. On December 10 the Japanese crushed the small American garrison on the tiny island of Guam and dealt the Royal Navy a catastrophic blow in the South China Sea. Eighty-eight Japanese bombers caught up with a six-ship British task force led by the *Repulse* and the brand-new battleship *Prince of Wales*. Both ships had been recently deployed to the region to symbolize British naval superiority, but the Japanese sent both to the bottom at the cost of only four planes.

As their war machine raged down the Malayan peninsula, the Japanese needed only 70 days—a month ahead of schedule—to conquer Singapore. When the Union Jack was lowered on February 15, Japanese forces accepted the surrender of 130,000 Commonwealth troops. The Dutch East Indies toppled in short order as well. After Japan routed Allied naval forces in the decisive Battle of the Java Sea, the Dutch formally surrendered on March 9, ending 300 years of colonial rule.

In the Philippines a massive invasion force of 43,000 Japanese troops hit the beaches of Luzon on December 22. MacArthur ordered his relatively disorganized American and Filipino army to withdraw and establish a line on the Bataan peninsula. After taking fortified refuge on the nearby island of Corregidor, MacArthur finally abandoned the fight on direct orders from Roosevelt. On March 11 MacArthur departed for the relative safety of Australia, where he famously promised, "I shall return."

The troops left behind at Bataan, now led by General Jonathan Wainwright, bravely battled the Japanese onslaught and the crippling effects of attrition. Malaria, starvation, and exhaustion proved as lethal as the Japanese. In early April the Japanese mounted a final offensive and broke through. For the Americans who survived, surrender replaced the hell of combat with an

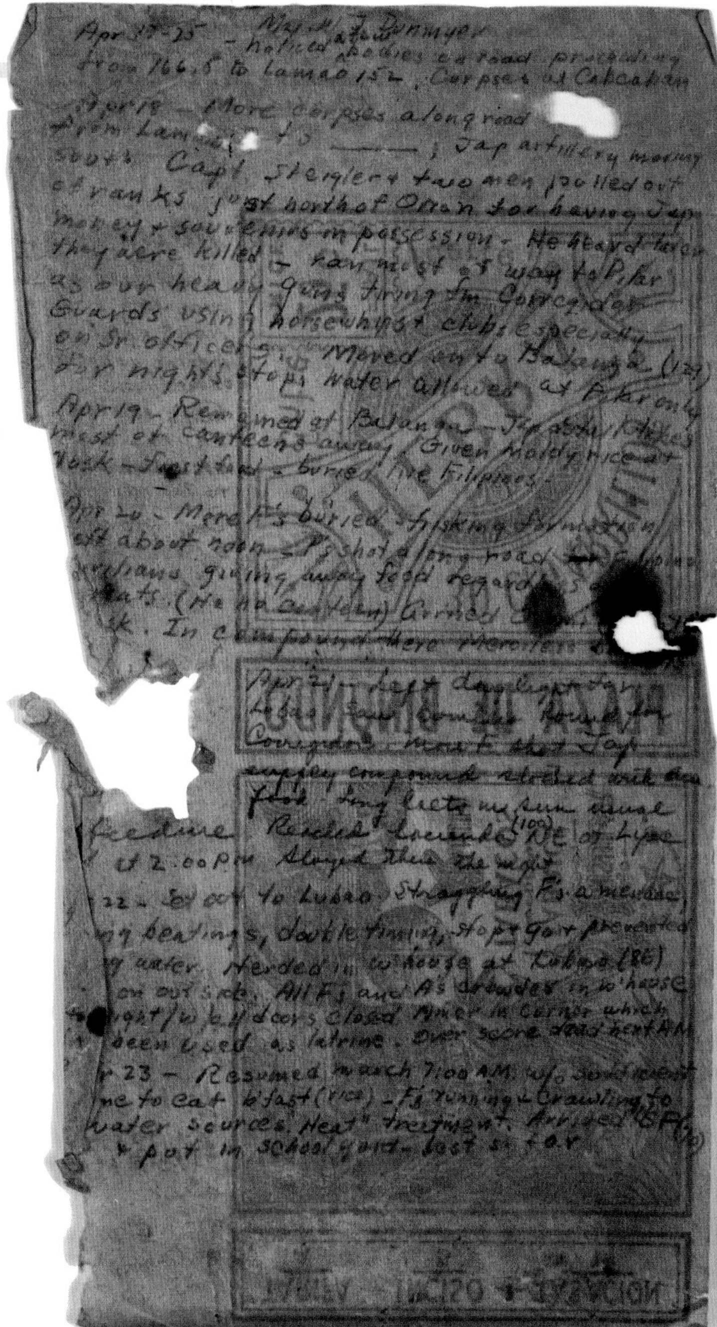

entirely new, though equally vivid, horror. The Japanese military code frowned upon the shame of surrender; thus the Japanese did not deem the large, sickly group of prisoners worthy of mercy. They herded the prisoners into line and marched them off to the north. During a 65-mile trek that became known as the Bataan Death March, the Japanese beat and executed prisoners who were not able to keep pace. Of the 70,000 men who began the trek, one in 10 died from exhaustion or ill-treatment.

The Japanese had waged ferocious and lightning-quick campaigns across the Pacific, but the Allies were not defeated. Although devastating, the surprise attack on Pearl Harbor had not dealt a mortal blow. U.S. aircraft carriers, at sea on the day of infamy, were spared altogether. And despite all the wreckage at Pearl Harbor, only the *Arizona*, the *Oklahoma*, and the *Utah* could not be salvaged. The other 15 warships damaged that morning survived. Despite their horrible losses, the Allies emerged eager to exact revenge. The Japanese diplomatic deceit and the horrible tales emerging from Bataan only hardened the Allies' resolve. No one understood that more than Yamamoto, who had spent time in Washington before the war as a naval attaché. After the stunning success of his meticulously-planned Pearl Harbor attack, he said, "We have awakened a sleeping giant and have instilled in him a terrible resolve." The Pacific war had only begun.

U.S. Army colonel Albert Svihra kept an account of the horrors of the Bataan Death March on cigarette paper (left). Over 70,000 American and Filipino soldiers who were captured at Bataan were forced to take part in the brutal 65-mile march (above) to internment camps. Thousands died from exhaustion, from disease, and often at the hands of their captors.

INFAMY

In the early morning hours of December 7, Japanese torpedo planes attack the ships and airfields around Ford Island at Pearl Harbor (above). Many U.S. servicemen, unprepared for the onslaught, thought they were witnessing a routine air-raid drill. Of the 780 antiaircraft guns mounted on the American ships, only a quarter were manned. After the intitial torpedo attacks, Japanese bombers dropped armor-piercing bombs on ships moored on both sides of the island.

DAZED AND DEVASTATED

Sailors at the Ford Island airfield look on in disbelief as the U.S.S. *Shaw* explodes in the background (right). Naval Aviation Ordnanceman Joe Morgan recounted, "We saw two bombs drop and, when the pilot pulled out, the emblem of the rising sun underneath his wing. I realized we were at war." Many of the American aircraft were destroyed and damaged before they could even get off the ground. To guard against sabotage, they had been parked close together, inadvertently creating easy targets.

LAST GASP

Still belching smoke and fire, the last remains of the *Arizona* (right) provide a grisly marker for the many lives lost on the battleship. The *Arizona* had already been hit by torpedoes when a bomb cut through the deck and exploded in her forward magazine. Almost simultaneously, the bomb and the *Arizona*'s ammunition exploded, shooting flames 500 feet high. The crippled ship was hit with three more bombs before finally succumbing.

ORIGIN OF ATTACK

On the Japanese aircraft carrier *Shokaku*, an officer (above) looks on as planes take off for Pearl Harbor. The words inscribed behind him encourage the pilots to proudly carry out their missions. At take-off, crewmen would rally their brothers-in-arms with the war cry of "Banzai!"

THE ELUSIVE ZERO

The single-seat Japanese Zero fighter (right) proved to be a troubling foe to Allied fighters in the early years of the war. The speedy and highly maneuverable plane was made of a light aluminum alloy, which enabled its relatively small 950-horsepower engines to fly the Zero farther and higher than most other planes at that time.

8941
8941

SURRENDER

On April 9, 1942, 76,000 American and Filipino troops (above) surrender to the Japanese after defending Bataan for 14 weeks. One month later, the last pocket of resistance was snuffed out when 13,000 soldiers on the island of Corregidor gave up under intense shelling. For American and Filipino POWs, the nightmare was only beginning.

ON THE ROAD TO MANILA

Armed with light tanks, Japanese troops (left) advance south toward the Philippine capital of Manila. The United States, a presence in the Philippines since the Spanish-American War in 1898, had taken the Filipino army into its service in July 1941. General Douglas MacArthur had concentrated his troops close to the capital, but the strength of the Japanse offensive forced him to move his men to the Bataan peninsula.

HUMILIATING DEFEAT
After calling for a ceasefire, British officers begin the process of surrendering to the Japanese in Malaya (above). Though they outnumbered the Japanese troops by a two-to-one margin, the British were overwhelmed by Japanese tanks and air support. Over 130,000 soldiers were taken prisoner in what Winston Churchill referred to as "the worst disaster . . . in British military history."

PATH OF DESTRUCTION
Japanese soldiers approach a smoking building in Kuala Lumpur, a southwest Malayan city, during Japan's march south. Only 70 days after the Japanese invaded from the north on December 8, 1941, Malaya's southern port of Singapore surrendered.

ABANDON SHIP! Sailors from the British battleship *Prince of Wales* (left) abandon ship as it sinks off the southern coast of Malaya. On December 10 the *Prince of Wales*, and the battle cruiser *Repulse*, were destroyed in a Japanese bombing raid. A total of 2,081 men were rescued but 820 lives were lost. The *Prince of Wales* was one of the newest additions to the Royal Navy—Churchill himself had sailed to the Atlantic Charter conference aboard the ship in August. Its loss shattered the confidence of the Royal Navy in the Pacific.

WINNING PINS
There was never any shortage of visible support (pins, inset) for Roosevelt from backers who were won over by FDR's enthusiasm and his reputation as a do-er. In his first day as president, FDR created an emergency banking bill, which Congress passed in 38 minutes. *The New York Times* proclaimed, "The President is the boss, the dynamo, the works."

Franklin Roosevelt

An unapologetic interventionist, Franklin Roosevelt knew that the United States could not ignore aggression and avoid war forever. Pearl Harbor gave him the war; it just wasn't the one he wanted.

PRESSING THE FLESH
FDR (above) came from a wealthy New York family but never lost touch with the common man. Americans responded to his tough yet upbeat manner, and millions tuned in to hear his "fireside chats" on the radio. With the country still suffering through the Depression, Roosevelt reassured it in his inaugural address saying, "We have nothing to fear but fear itself."

DRAFT No. 1 December 7, 1941.

PROPOSED MESSAGE TO THE CONGRESS

Yesterday, December 7, 1941, a date which will live in ~~world history~~ infamy, the United States of America was ~~simultaneously~~ suddenly and deliberately attacked by naval and air forces of the Empire of Japan.

The United States was at the moment at peace with that nation and was ~~continuing the~~ still in conversations with its Government and its Emperor looking toward the maintenance of peace in the Pacific. Indeed, one hour after Japanese air squadrons had commenced bombing in ~~Hawaii and the Philippines~~ Oahu, the Japanese Ambassador to the United States and his colleague delivered to the Secretary of State a formal reply to a ~~former~~ recent American message ~~from the Secretary~~. While this reply ~~contained a statement~~ stated that diplomatic negotiations ~~must be considered at an end, but~~ it contained no threat ~~and no~~ or hint of ~~an~~ armed attack.

It will be recorded that the distance ~~of Manila, and especially~~ of Hawaii, from Japan makes it obvious that the attack ~~s were~~ was deliberately planned many days or even weeks ago. During the intervening time the Japanese Government has deliberately sought to deceive the United States by false statements and expressions of hope for continued peace.

INFAMOUS WORDS
Roosevelt's first draft of his declaration of war address to Congress (above) reveals that its famous first line originally read "a date which will live in world history." Roosevelt himself edited the text to the more powerful, "a date which will live in infamy."

HOLIDAY CHEER
In fine holiday spirit President Roosevelt returns from Easter services with First Lady Eleanor in 1938 (above). Mrs. Roosevelt was an active, high-profile first lady. After her husband's death in 1945, she served as the United States' delegate to the United Nations.

JUST SWIMMINGLY
Though the crippling effects of polio eventually relegated him to a wheelchair, Roosevelt (above) swam frequently to remain active and never lost his optimism: "If you've spent two years in bed trying to wiggle your big toe, everything else seems easy."

SIGNATURE SPECS
A big part of Roosevelt's persona was his pince-nez glasses (left), which lacked temples and attached to the nose by a spring.

Japanese-American Internment

The disgraceful relocation of more than 110,000 people of Japanese descent, motivated by racial paranoia after Pearl Harbor, was a black eye on the face of American liberty and democracy.

MASS UPHEAVAL

The Mochida family (above) stands proudly with their bags during "evacuation" to an internment camp. The incarcerations were authorized by President Roosevelt in Executive Order 9066 on February 19, 1942. Entire families were often given a scant few days to settle all their affairs and cull only their most basic possessions before being herded inland by the military. A tersely worded poster (inset) issued directives and a sobering timetable to the detainees.

IRONY OF SERVICE

A mother sits with her son (below) at a camp in Arizona and displays a photo of her other son, a U.S. soldier. About 1,000 volunteers from the camps entered military service, where Japanese-American units served with honor and distinction.

CAMP LIFE

In an American propaganda photo (above), a family unit is shown sharing a meal at Manzanar, Calif., in April 1942. In reality, fathers were often separated from their loved ones at "relocation centers." The general loss of privacy inherent in large camps additionally tore at the fabric of family life.

DESOLATE PRISON

A dust storm (above) enshrouds two children and a line of barracks at the Manzanar camp. Many camps were located in the desert. "Sand filled our mouths and nostrils and stung our faces . . . like a thousand darting needles," one internee recalled.

SILENT PROTEST

Despite adorning his shop in Oakland, Calif., with a public statement of loyalty (left), the owner, a University of California graduate, was forced to sell his business at a crippling loss. The internment of Japanese Americans was finally halted by the courts in 1944. Decades later the U.S. government admitted its error, and reparation payments were made to many whose lives and dreams were summarily disrupted without due process.

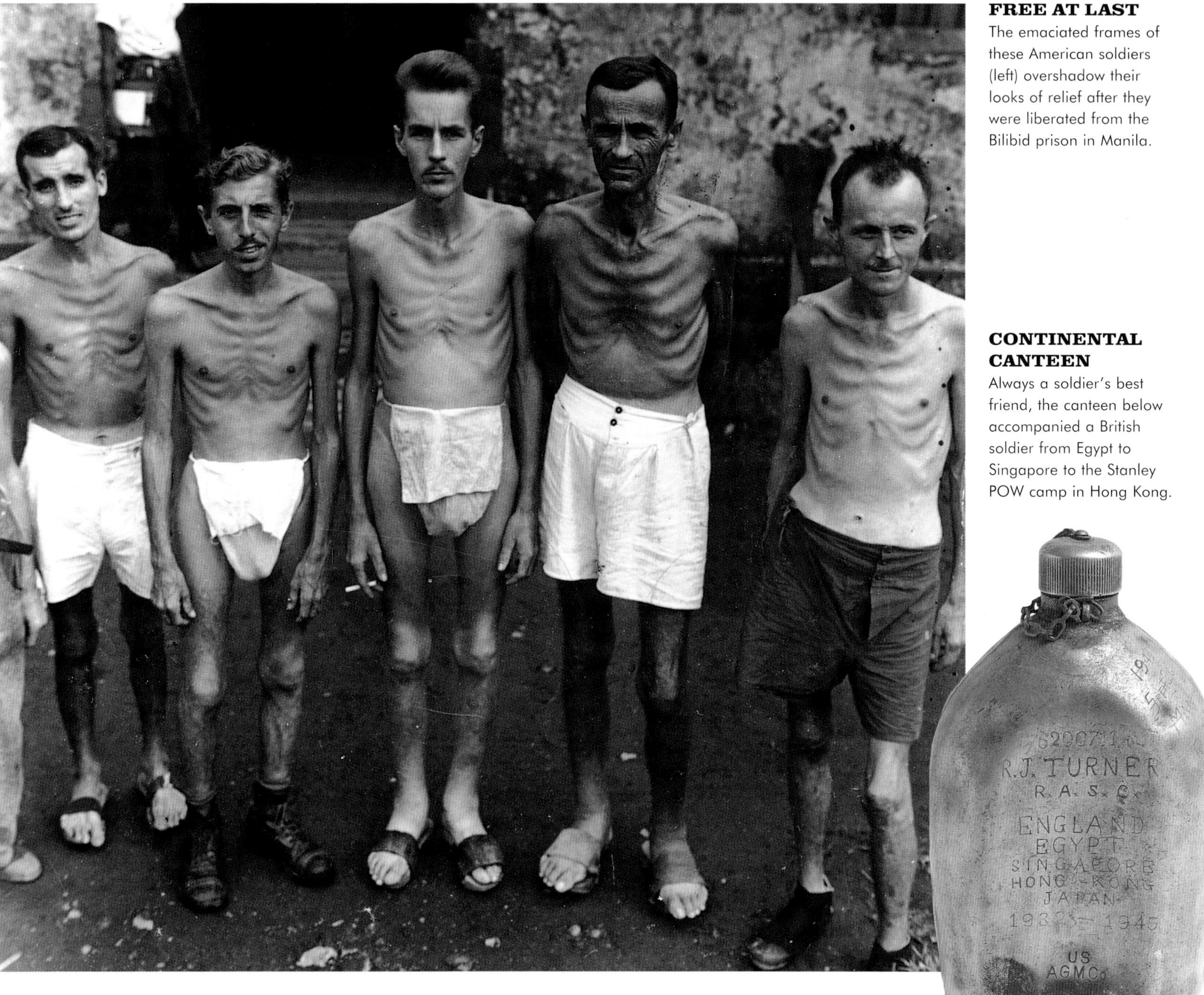

FREE AT LAST
The emaciated frames of these American soldiers (left) overshadow their looks of relief after they were liberated from the Bilibid prison in Manila.

CONTINENTAL CANTEEN
Always a soldier's best friend, the canteen below accompanied a British soldier from Egypt to Singapore to the Stanley POW camp in Hong Kong.

Prisoners of Japan

The treatment of wartime prisoners is notoriously poor. But Japanese culture—which frowned upon the disgrace of surrender—produced soldiers who offered little mercy to defeated Allied troops.

FROM DEATH MARCH TO DEATH CAMP

The brave and lucky men who survived the Bataan Death March were sentenced to spend their days at the equally hellish Camp O'Donnell in North Bataan (left). Japanese military photographers often selected healthier-looking POWs to photograph, but the actual condition of the inmates was abysmal. Most of the men who did make it to Camp O'Donnell did so "on the marrow of their bones," said an American doctor imprisoned there.

CAPTORS BECOME CAPTIVES

Dejected Japanese soldiers turn away as gaunt yet relieved Australian and British troops (above) take their leave of a prison camp on Formosa after liberation by American Marines. Some of these men had been held in the camp for three-and-one-half years.

PRISONER PARAPHERNALIA

Among the items worn by POWs in Japanese prison camps were this pair of heavily patched tropical shorts (inset, below) and a wooden POW sick tag (inset, right). Prisoners did their best with what little they had: POW doctors fashioned artificial limbs out of bits of scrap metal and rubber for inmates who had lost limbs in combat or from illness.

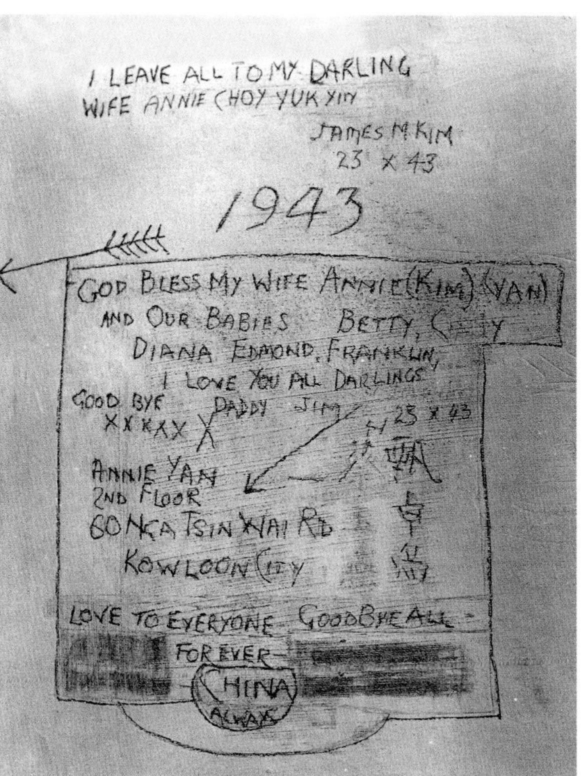

FAREWELL

James Kim, a condemned Chinese member of the Hong Kong Defense Force, recorded his final thoughts (left) on the wall of his cell in Stanley Prison prior to his execution in 1943.

Global War: 1942-1943

Global War: 1942-1943

When Adolf Hitler learned of Japan's convincing victory at Pearl Harbor, he gushed to his generals, "Now it is impossible for us to lose the war; we now have an ally who has never been vanquished in 3,000 years." When Winston Churchill heard the same news, he replied, "So we have won the war after all."

Although rival belligerents may have drawn ironically identical, if diametrically opposed, conclusions of the same event, there is no doubt that the United States' entry into the war changed the conflict's course and complexion. Pearl Harbor solidified what had been, up to that point, three separate wars fought on three different continents. America's entrance into the war enabled the formation of a unique coalition composed of the world's greatest colonial, industrial, and communist powers. Only a threat as dangerous as Hitler's Germany could have made such an alliance work.

President Franklin Roosevelt was personally and politically prepared to go to war, but his nation's military was not. The U.S. was years behind the Axis powers in military mobilization and much of America's Pacific Fleet lay at the muddy bottom of Pearl Harbor. The pressure on Roosevelt had never been greater, for the U.S. was suddenly at war with both Japan and Germany. A war leader like Hitler—who second-guessed his generals and immersed himself in operational details—might have been overwhelmed by that challenge. But Roosevelt had his own way of handling the military. When he found commanders who possessed both strategic and executive skills—the ability to make the most of the assets at their disposal—he left them to their own devices. So when he appointed Admiral Chester Nimitz as the new commander of the battered Pacific Fleet, he gave him one order: "Get the hell out to Pearl and stay there till the war is won."

Timeline: 1942–1943

1942

February 15

Singapore falls to the Japanese.

February 19

President Roosevelt orders Japanese Americans on the West Coast to internment camps.

April 9

U.S. troops at Bataan surrender to the Japanese.

April 18

Doolittle Raid: B-25s from the U.S.S. *Hornet* stage a surpise attack on Tokyo.

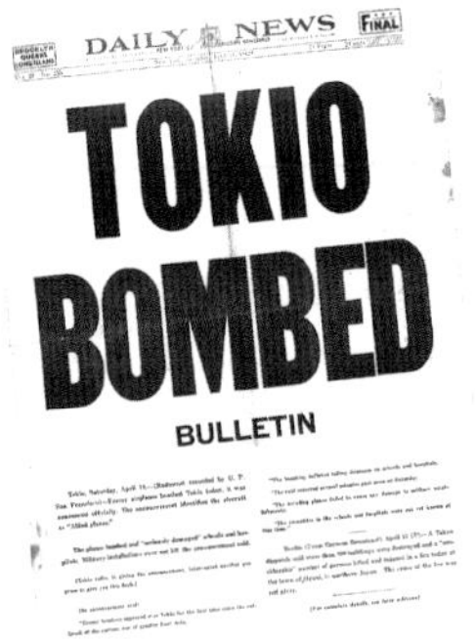

DAILY NEWS FINAL

TOKIO BOMBED

BULLETIN

May 7/8

The U.S. Navy halts a Japanese southern advance in the Battle of the Coral Sea.

May 30

Allies launch the first 1,000-bomber air raid, against the German city of Cologne.

Free to handle matters as he saw fit, Nimitz reached out to the demoralized naval officers at Pearl Harbor. Rather than assign blame, he asked for their help in putting the fleet back in order. Much like Roosevelt, he exuded a sense of calm amid the crisis and a conviction that defeat could be overcome through renewed effort rather than recriminations. But nothing he did to raise morale would have mattered if the Japanese had succeeded in all of their Pearl Harbor objectives. Among the targets they failed to destroy were a submarine base and the fleet's aircraft carriers, which luckily had been out to sea on December 7. The Japanese also failed to destroy a tank farm holding 4.5 million barrels of oil. If those oil reserves had gone up in smoke, the fuel-starved American fleet would have had to return to California.

Fierce competition for oil and other supplies had transformed the war into a truly global struggle. The Japanese had attacked Pearl Harbor and the Philippines in response to American trade restrictions, and they widened their offensive in early 1942 by seizing Dutch and British oilfields in Java and Burma. In the process, they closed off the Burma Road—a major supply route for Chinese troops fighting Japanese occupation forces. Although China became increasingly isolated and the Chinese army was consistently outclassed, Japan failed to land the knockout punch that would eliminate China from the war.

China was only one area of concern for Japan, whose forces were dispersed across a vast theater. Australia had become a staging ground for Allied forces under General Douglas MacArthur. His first task was to defend Australia and its barrier islands, but he was anxious to take the offensive and return to the Philippines. The American ships that survived Pearl Harbor presented another threat to the Japanese. Admiral Isokoru Yamamoto hoped to lure Nimitz's carriers into a deci-

June 4/6

U.S. Navy deals the Japanese a crippling naval defeat at Midway.

June 21

Erwin Rommel and the Afrikakorps capture Tobruk.

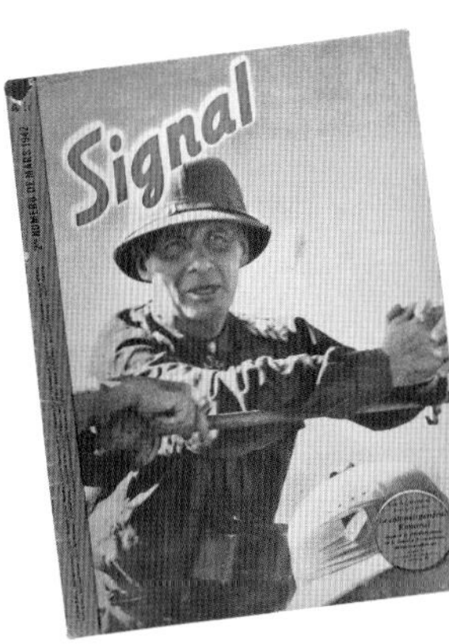

August 7

The U.S. launches its first offensive in the Pacific at Guadalcanal.

August 19

Allied landings at Dieppe, France, are repelled by German forces.

August 23

The Battle of Stalingrad begins.

sive battle and shatter the Pacific Fleet before it could be reinforced with new vessels from American shipyards. In 1942 the odds favored the larger Japanese fleet, but Yamamoto failed to recognize a hidden American asset—Commander Joseph Rochefort and his team of naval codebreakers. Yamamoto's strict radio silence had prevented Rochefort from anticipating the Pearl Harbor attack, but Rochefort was determind to prevent another naval debacle. As he told his codebreakers: "Forget Pearl Harbor and get on with the job!"

Codebreaking also figured prominently in the Battle for the Atlantic, the all-important struggle for control of the sea lanes linking the U.S. to Britain. The Allies had little hope of defeating Hitler if they failed to defend those sea lanes against predations by German U-boats, prowling in so-called wolf packs. American shipments provided the British with much of their food, among other essentials, and were crucial to Allied plans to reconquer Europe. "The only thing that ever really frightened me during the war," wrote Winston Churchill after the war, "was the U-boat peril."

In other arenas as well, the quick gains of the Axis powers's lightning war had given way to the Allies' slow, brutal efforts to rob enemy forces of the will and means to fight. The strategic bombing of German cities and industries that began in earnest in 1942 was one such campaign—a protracted attempt by the Allies to pound Hitler into submission. Risks were great for the air crews involved, and no one knew whether the raids would crush opposition or stiffen resistance. But British air marshal Arthur "Bomber" Harris had witnessed the German incendiary bomb attacks on London during the Blitz and was convinced that air power could win the war. "Victory, speedy and complete," he wrote Winston Churchill in 1942, "awaits the side which first employs air power as it should be employed."

Ground offensives were also dictated by strategic concerns for economic resources. General Erwin Rommel's advance toward Cairo in 1942 gave Hitler hope of seizing Middle East oil fields, but Rommel's own oil and ammunition reserves dwindled as his supply lines grew longer and more vulnerable to Allied interdiction. Nowhere did oil

Timeline: 1942–1943

1943

October 23/November 4

Battle of El Alamein: Rommel is defeated and retreats to Tunisia.

November 8

Operation Torch, the American invasion of North Africa, begins.

January 14/24

Casablanca Conference: Roosevelt announces that the Allies will accept only the Axis powers's "unconditional surrender."

February 2

German forces surrender at Stalingrad.

April 19

Warsaw Ghetto Uprising: The SS attacks Jewish resistance in the Polish capital.

May 13

German and Italian troops surrender in North Africa.

play a bigger role in the fighting than in the Soviet Union, where Hitler ordered his forces southward into the oil-rich Crimea in 1942. As with Rommel's advance, this offensive overextended German supply lines and invited enemy counterattacks. The fate of two nations would culminate in a momentous battle at Stalingrad.

Much depended on the ability of rival leaders to adapt to this grueling war of attrition, a contest in which victory would go not necessarily to the swift but to the well-supplied. Hitler, convinced that sheer will power could triumph over adversity, seldom allowed his generals to cut their losses and protect supply lines by yielding ground. And he paid little attention to the vital task of maximizing German war production, which was hampered by inefficiencies. Stalin, by contrast, was forced by his near defeat in 1941 to address his weaknesses. He insisted that his generals tell him the truth about Soviet setbacks. Some feared for their lives if they did so, but their disclosures helped improve tactics and weaponry. Meanwhile, Soviet workers were moving entire factories to safe sites east of Moscow and turning out armaments at a furious pace. Such productivity was due partly to Stalin's dictatorial power to regiment the workforce. But Hitler's invasion of the Soviet Union had given the Soviets the greatest incentive to work hard for victory.

Soviet economic feats were rivaled only by the capacity of American industry. The lethargy of the Great Depression vanished as America's economy mobilized with a speed that Hitler had never imagined when he declared war on the U.S. four days after Pearl Harbor. Hitler's hasty declaration was a gift for Roosevelt, making it politically easier for him to give the war against Germany priority over the struggle against Japan. That policy of "Europe first" was encouraged by Churchill, who used his influence to hold Roosevelt to the commitment. Churchill believed that America's seemingly unlimited resources would ultimately overwhelm the Axis powers, but he knew that the war could be won only through desperate struggles on the battlefield. As General Dwight Eisenhower wrote in his diary in 1942, after hearing politicians talk glibly of economic victory: "Not one man in twenty in the government realizes what a grisly, dirty, tough business we are in."

May 24

Germany withdraws U-boats from the Atlantic, ending the Battle for the Atlantic.

July 10

Allies land in Sicily.

July 25

Italian authorities arrest Benito Mussolini, and Marshal Pietro Badoglio is named prime minister.

September 8

Italy surrenders to the Allies.

November 28/December 1

Tehran Conference: Stalin, Roosevelt, and Churchill meet together for the first time.

Battle for the Atlantic

With a Nazi flag billowing in the sea breeze, a Type VII German U-boat (left) pulls into its home port of Lorient, in occupied France, in 1940. The Submarine War Badge (below) was given to all German submariners after their first combat patrol.

On the night of January 14, 1942, the 9,500-ton Norwegian tanker *Norness* steamed northward in the crowded shipping lanes 60 miles off Long Island's Montauk Point lighthouse. Although Norway and much of the world was at war, the *Norness'* captain steamed straight ahead with his lights on, at a steady speed of 10 knots. At a little after midnight *Kapitänleutnant* Reinhard Hardegen, commander of the German submarine *U-123*, launched two torpedoes at a range of 800 yards toward the unsuspecting tanker. One torpedo struck the *Norness,* and a boiling column of flame surged high above her mast. While her crew abandoned ship, two more torpedoes sent the burning wreck to the bottom. The first shot in the battle for the American coast had been fired, but the *Norness*' distress call went unheard and United States naval authorities remained unaware that German U-boats were gathering off their shores.

The *Norness* was the first victim of Operation *Paukenschlag*—Operation Drumroll—Admiral Karl Dönitz's submarine onslaught against the poorly-guarded American coast. Shortly after Germany's declaration of war on the United States, Dönitz radioed orders to assemble a pack of U-boats to initiate operations against Allied ships in American waters. Hardegen's *U-123* converged on the American coast with four other German submarines, and within two weeks of the sinking of the *Norness*, they had sunk 35 vessels between Newfoundland and Bermuda. Over three-quarters of these losses were tankers carrying vital supplies to Great Britain. All along the coast, American cities continued peacetime habits and refused to consider nighttime blackouts. German U-boat skippers were able to pick out targets silhouetted against the glow of city lights. To make matters worse, Admiral Ernest King, commander in chief of the U.S. Navy, lacked ships to protect Atlantic coastal shipping and defend vital American ports, concluding that vessels were safer sailing on their own. Events were to prove him terribly wrong. Soon, residents of U.S. coastal cities could see the smoke and flames of burning ships offshore, as oil and debris darkened the beaches from New Jersey to Florida. Attacks on poorly escorted con-

Admiral Karl Dönitz, commander of U-boat operations, (below, right) awards a submarine captain the Order of the Iron Cross in April 1940. Dönitz would later lead the German navy in January 1943.

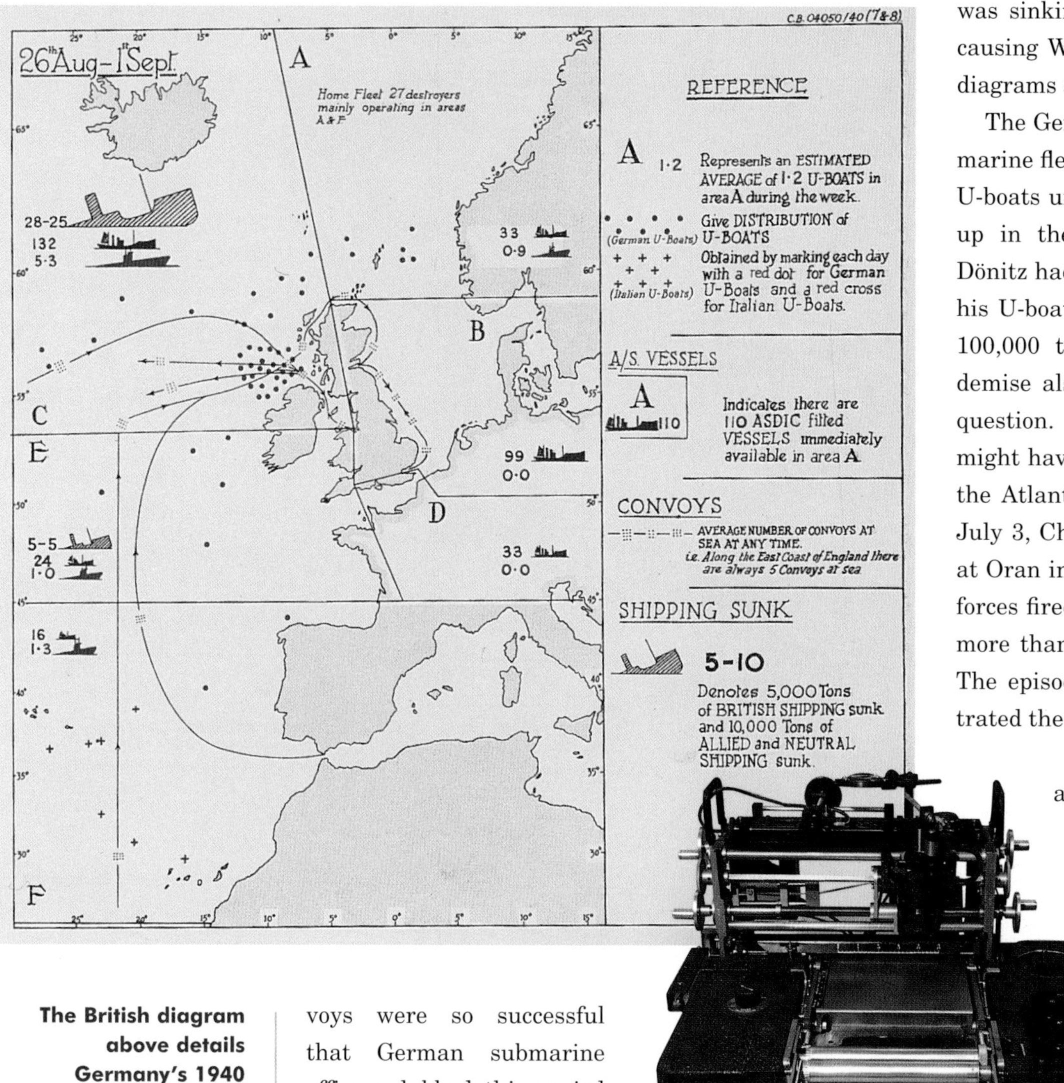

The British diagram above details Germany's 1940 attempt to blockade the industrial cities of Liverpool and Bristol with U-boat deployment in the Irish Sea. A British ASDIC range-finding machine (inset), when operated by an experienced technician, could pinpoint submerged U-boats via sound waves.

voys were so successful that German submarine officers dubbed this period "Happy Time."

The naval war that shifted to America's shore in 1942 had, in fact, been waged with increasing savagery since the beginning of hostilities. The Battle for the Atlantic, especially for the British Isles, was a fight for survival. Britain relied on the world's largest naval fleet to prevent the isles' strangulation. Dönitz's pre-war "Z-plan," which called for the creation of a German U-boat fleet of 300 by 1942, threatened to produce just that outcome. In 1941, Germany was sinking more shipping than Britain could replace, causing Winston Churchill to face industrial "statistics, diagrams and curves . . . incomprehensible to the public."

The German navy was restricted from building a submarine fleet until 1935. By 1939, however, Dönitz had 57 U-boats under his command. His fleet was often bottled up in the North Sea, but after France's surrender, Dönitz had a 2,500-mile coastline from which to unleash his U-boats. By the summer of 1940 they were sinking 100,000 tons of Allied shipping per month. France's demise also placed the status of the French navy into question. If Hitler had seized control of the fleet, he might have dangerously altered the balance of power in the Atlantic. Britain could not allow that to occur. On July 3, Churchill ordered an attack on the French fleet at Oran in Algeria. For the first time since 1805, British forces fired on French ships, and six French vessels and more than a thousand Frenchmen went to the bottom. The episode strained Anglo-Franco relations and illustrated the severity of Britain's desperation.

Isolated by Nazi Europe, Britain looked across the Atlantic for assistance. In May 1940, Churchill asked the United States Navy for its obsolete "four-stack" destroyers. Four months later, President Franklin Roosevelt responded by authorizing the loan of fifty World War I destroyers to Britain in exchange for 99-year leases for the establishment of U.S. military bases on British possessions in the Western Hemisphere. American isolationists criticized Roosevelt for pushing America towards war, but his administration only increased its support of the Allies. In March 1941, Roosevelt pressured Congress to authorize the Lend-Lease policy, which provided Britain with more crucial war materials. In addition, American destroyers joined in protecting Allied convoys across the Atlantic. In October, after a German U-boat sank the American destroyer the *Reuben James*, Roosevelt called for "armed neutrality" and warned that any Axis submarine operating in American-controlled waters would be subject to attack. If the U.S. was not yet at war with Germany, Roosevelt was taking his nation to the brink.

***Kriegsmarine* troops (left) stand at attention as a U-boat embarks on a mission to sink British shipping. The German submarine fleet almost choked the British Isles into submission, but the costs were atrocious: the death rate of Germany's 35,000 submariners would reach a staggering 82 percent over the course of the war.**

Between Pearl Harbor and the summer of 1942, the crisis in American coastal waters and the mid-Atlantic intensified. German operations extended to the Caribbean, and by the middle of the year it seemed as if Dönitz's fleet might sever Britain's ocean lifelines. Wolf pack tactics drastically increased German U-boat efficiency. When an Allied convoy was located, its position was immediately radioed to German headquarters. Orders to converge on the target were then transmitted to other submarines within range. A wolf pack could harry a convoy for days, confusing the escorts and sinking cargo vessels. In the month of June alone, the Allies lost 173 ships to U-boat attack. By the end of the year, German subs had sunk more than 6,000,000 tons of Allied shipping.

New technology also favored the German U-boat fleet. The Type IX U-boat, an effective long-range sub, could operate farther into the Atlantic, out of range of shore-based aircraft. By 1942 the *Kriegsmarine* also introduced the Type XIV submarine tanker—nicknamed *Milchkuhe*, or "Milk Cows," by U-boat crews—which rendezvoused with U-boats to refuel and replenish weapons and supplies. This greatly extended the operational range and endurance of the Type IX boats.

The Allies responded by improving the safety of convoys and by creating "hunter-killer groups"—unattached units composed of destroyers and corvettes—which could respond to a wolf pack attack by greatly augmenting the antisubmarine assets of a convoy. The Royal Navy also intensified efforts to analyze German radio traffic in order to pinpoint German wolf packs and predict attacks. One of the bright spots of this period was the successful passage of the American convoys bound for the invasion of North Africa. Tight security and strong escort forces limited Allied losses to only 23 ships out of a total of more than 1,000. The U.S. Navy had been hesitant to adopt British convoy techniques, but the tragic losses during the first months of American involvement con-

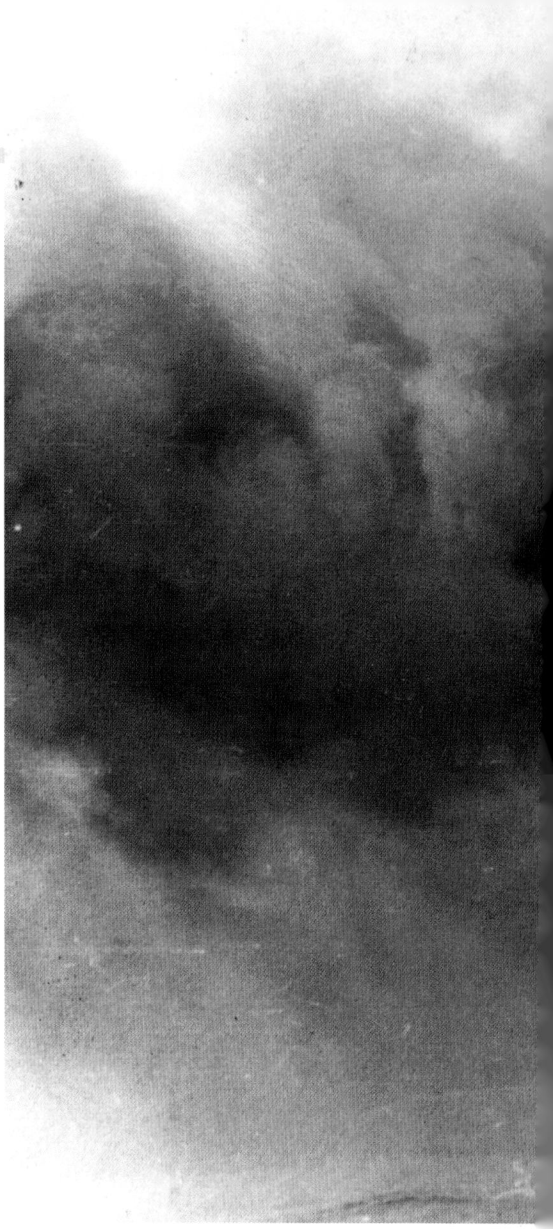

Sailors from the German battleship *Bismarck* (above) are pulled from the seas in a chaotic rescue scene shot from the H.M.S. *Dorsetshire*. The sinking of the *Bismarck*—and the death of more than 2,000 ot its crewmen—effectively ended Germany's use of heavy surface ships in the Atlantic.

vinced its leadership to change strategy. Nevertheless, Allied losses were reaching unacceptable levels by March 1943, and only the immense production capacity of American shipyards maintained any sort of balance.

By spring, however, the tide began to turn. In January at Casablanca, the Allied leaders resolved that the war against the U-boats should become a priority. Allied air forces diverted strategic bombing units for attacks on German shipyards and U-boat bases. The Allies also introduced improved radar capable of detecting a U-boat when it surfaced to recharge its batteries, even in darkness and bad weather.

Another threat to the U-boats was the deployment of American B-24 Liberator bombers modified for long-range anti-submarine patrol. The Liberators and other long-range aircraft flew from bases in Newfoundland, Iceland, and Scotland to cover the North Atlantic. A final Allied breakthrough was the increased ability of the cryptanalysts at Britain's Bletchley Park to decipher German naval codes—an effort greatly aided by the capture of an Enigma cipher machine and codebooks from German U-boats.

During the interwar years, Germany had focused primarily on producing submarines and "pocket" battle-

The *Graf Spee*, a German "pocket" battleship (center), lists to starboard, her decks choked with smoke. Scuttled in December 1939, she burned for four days. The battleship *Tirpitz* (above) survived nearly 20 attacks from British bombers during the war before finally succumbing in 1944.

ships that were designed to circumvent the Treaty of Versailles's naval restrictions. As a result, Germany's surface fleet was not very effective at challenging Britain's mastery of the high seas. The *Graf Spee*, a fast, commerce-raiding gunboat, was cornered by the British in Montevideo, Uruguay, and scuttled by its captain in December 1939. In May 1941, the *Bismarck*, a powerful new battleship and the pride of the German navy, was destroyed near occupied France after an epic showdown with British battleships. Even in northern waters, where the German navy experienced some success interrupting Allied convoys destined for the Soviet Union, their surface ships were soon outclassed. The loss of the *Bismarck* haunted Hitler, and he ordered his remaining major ships to avoid "any unnecessary risks." The German battleship *Tirpitz*, the sister ship to the *Bismarck*, was relegated to raiding Allied convoys. Nevertheless, she came under attack by RAF bombers and midget submarines of the Royal Navy. After suffering damage, she remained stranded in Norway, where she was bombed and capsized at her moorings in November 1944.

By mid-1943 the "Happy Time" for Hitler's U-boats had ended. Despite the introduction of improved submarines and snorkels, devices that enabled U-boats to recharge their batteries while submerged, U-boats had become the hunted rather than the hunter. The *Kriegsmarine* lost 696 of 830 U-boats and an astonishing 25,870 of 40,900 crewmen. "We had lost the Battle of the Atlantic," admitted Dönitz after the war, referring to the tragic demise of his fleet in 1943. In May 1943, he withdrew his submarine fleet from the ocean.

WARY LOOKOUT

A crewman (above) watches aircraft return to the escort carrier H.M.S. *Tracker* after an antisub patrol. In the early months of the war, merchant shipping convoys heading west were escorted only part of the way across the Atlantic. Their protectors then met up with eastbound convoys and ushered them back to Allied shores. By May 1941, however, Iceland became an Allied base, and fleets of ships were afforded protection from marauding wolf packs for the entire journey.

NUMBERS GAME

A single tail-gun points at the ready (right) while a convoy of vessels steams forward in the escort ship's wake. With U-boats on the prowl, defense planners calculated that convoys needed at least three escorts plus ten percent of the number of ships in the convoy for adequate defense.

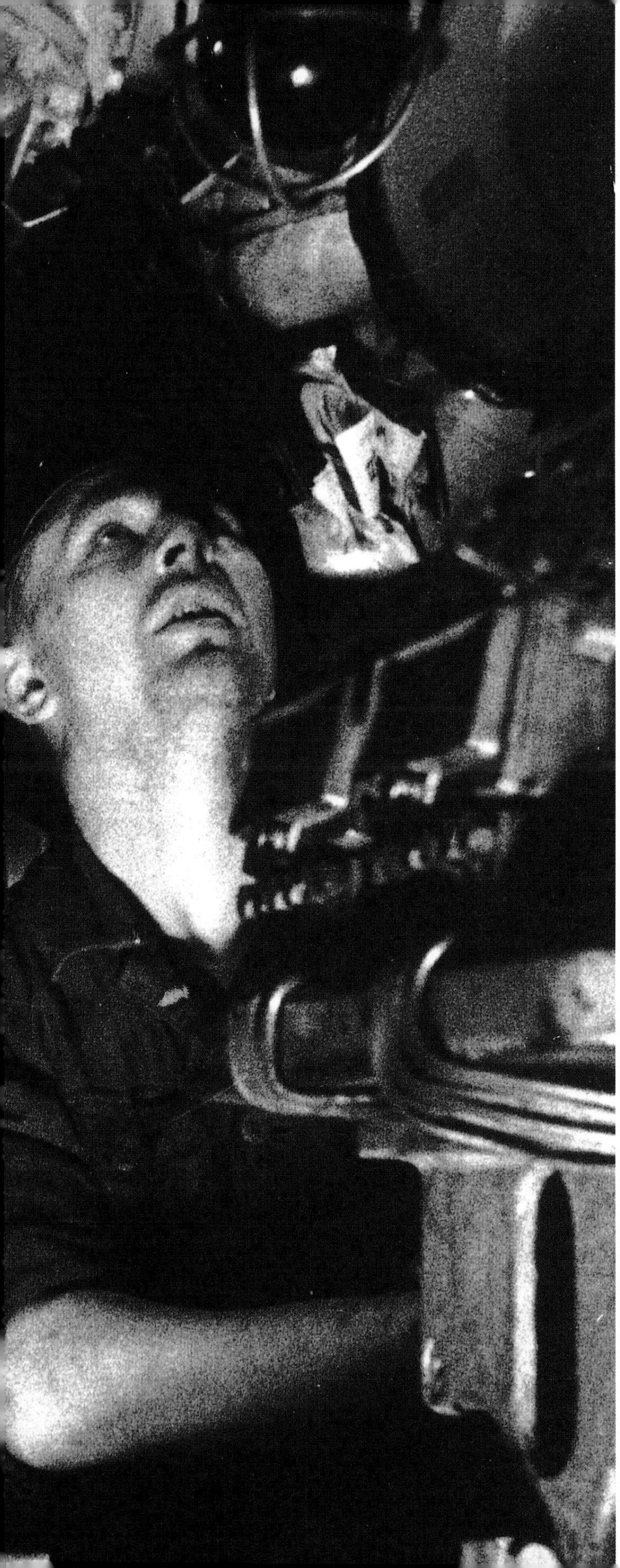

A WOLF PACK'S FANGS
Crewmen gingerly secure torpedoes in the cramped hull of *U-124* (above). In early 1943, the most intense period in the Atlantic, Dönitz averaged more than 100 U-boats patrolling the waters each month. German wolf packs hounded virtually every North American convoy in March and sent a half-million tons of Allied shipping to the bottom.

THE STRATEGY OF THE HUNT
Determined men from *U-96* (left) monitor their stations while engaging a British escort. The art of Dönitz's wolf pack warfare, highly effective in the war's early years, was to deploy a wide arc of submarines that intersected likely shipping lanes. When any one U-boat detected a convoy, it summoned its fellow hunters via radio. The pack converged and attacked its prey from the rear and flank.

UNDER THE SEA
Men on *U-96*'s tower (above) signal a sister boat while patrolling the North Atlantic in 1941. Life aboard a submarine required a special breed of man—one who could cope with both high stress and tight quarters. Erich Tropp, one of Germany's finest U-boat aces, said, "When a U-boat man leaves port and closes the hatch in the tower, he says good-bye to the world of color, the sun, the moon, the stars, and the diverse beauty of the earth."

A QUICK PEEK
A U-boat captain and his lookout crew (left) train their binoculars on the horizon in the summer of 1942. In normal operations, submarines spent as much time on the surface as possible—their surface speed was often double that attainable while submerged, where their air was fouled with carbon dioxide after only a day. It became increasingly risky, however, for U-boats to surface at all by mid-1942, as the Allies reaped the benefits of their centimetric airborne radar, a powerful U-boat tracking system with a range of nearly 100 miles.

A WATERY GRAVE
A wounded British tanker (right) yaws up out of the seas on its way to the bottom while an anonymous victor observes. The losses on both sides of the Battle for the Atlantic were nothing short of catastrophic. In 68 months, some 2,000 Allied vessels, representing around 14.5 million tons of matériel, were sunk; about 80 percent of the U-boats that inflicted the damage—not counting German midget submarines—were lost in the grim struggle for control of the shipping lanes of the Atlantic Ocean.

A HARDENED ADVERSARY

A bedraggled German survivor (left, center) of a shelled U-boat is helped along the deck of a U.S. cutter by two young Coast Guardsmen in September 1943. A technologically revitalized wolf pack fleet had re-entered the fray that month, after having been pulled from the Atlantic by Admiral Dönitz in May. The Allies were able to counter the new advances, and by the end of the year, more U-boats had been lost than Allied vessels.

THE DEATH OF U-175

A mushrooming depth-charge explodes as the U.S. Coast Guard cutter *Spencer* (right) zeroes in on *U-175* while protecting a convoy in April 1943. A punishing barrage of 22 depth charges forced the crippled submarine to the surface, where it suffered a withering salvo of machine gun and artillery fire. More than 40 German sailors were rescued as *U-175* sank.

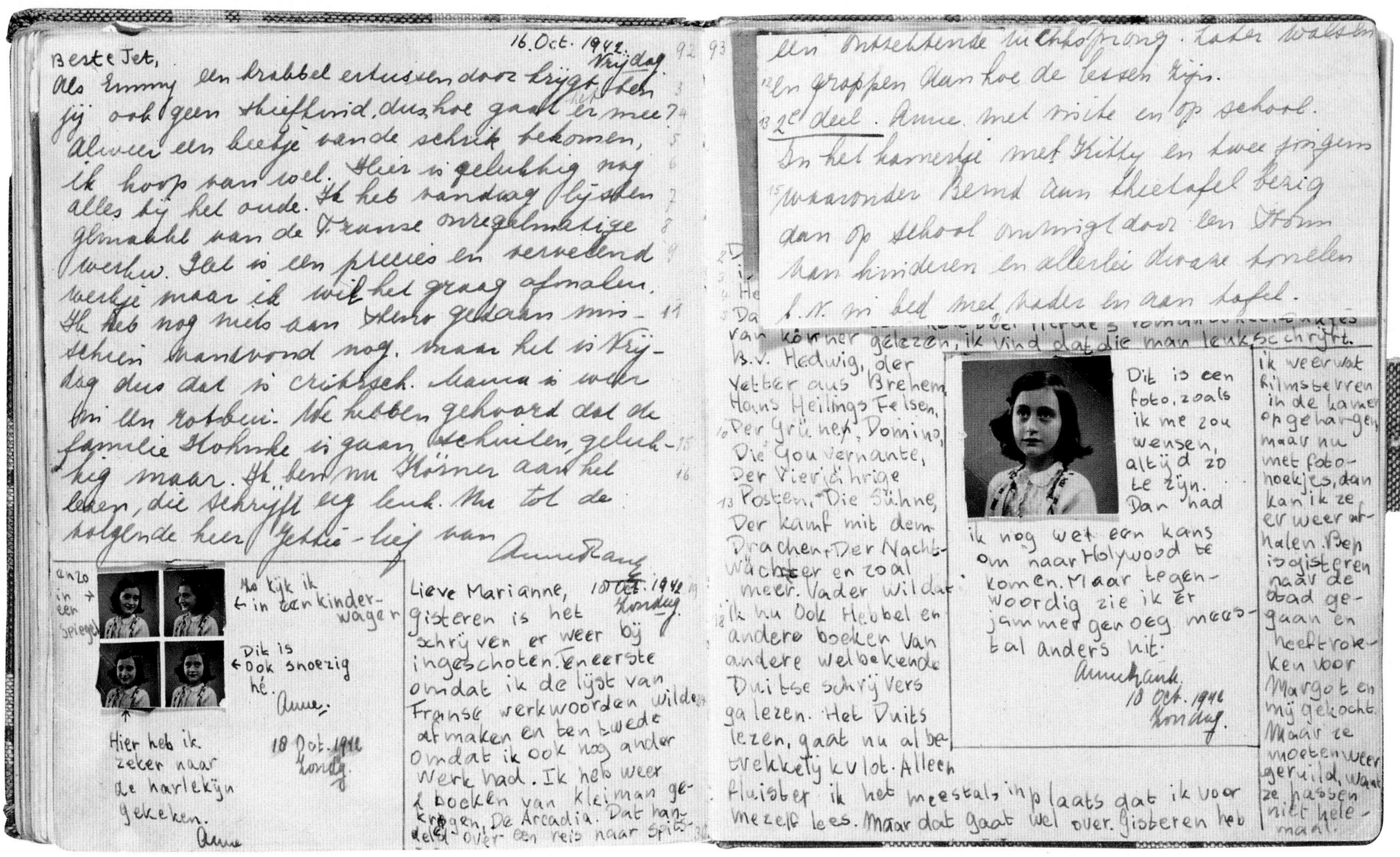

Anne Frank

The fears, hopes, and dreams of Anne Frank come alive in the diary she kept while her Jewish family hid from the Nazis in Holland. Discovered and deported in 1944, she died in a German concentration camp, but her story endures as a tragic reminder of Nazi oppression.

DEAR DIARY

Anne received her first diary on her 13th birthday, on June 12, 1942, one month before her family went into hiding. She made her first entry on her birthday, and by the end of 1942 the red-and-white-checkered book was nearly full. "I hope I will be able to confide everything to you," she wrote in her diary. "I have never been able to confide in anyone, and I hope you will be a great source of comfort and support."

LINK TO THE OUTSIDE WORLD

Miep Gies—with her husband on their wedding day in 1941 (below)—was Anne's father's secretary. She secretly supplied the Franks with goods. Anne especially appreciated the books that Gies brought: "We long for Saturday because that means books. We're like a bunch of little kids with a present."

MARGOT AND ANNE

Anne and her older sister, Margot (below, left), were both born in Germany. Once Hitler came to power, however, Otto Frank moved his family to Holland. "Because we're Jewish, my father emigrated to Holland in 1933, when he became the managing director of the Dutch Opekta Company, which manufactures products used in making jam," Anne wrote.

SECRET ANNEX

After Anne's sister, Margot, was called up to report to the SS on July 5, 1942, the Franks decided to go into hiding. Their father had been preparing an empty storage area in the back of his office building (left) since the spring of 1941. For the next two years, the Franks, the van Pels family, and Fritz Pfeffer—eight people in all—would live in the annex virtually isolated from the outside world. Anne wrote extensively about each person in her diary, especially Peter van Pels (below), with whom she shared her first kiss.

THE FACE OF INNOCENCE

Anne (left, at school in 1941) dreamed of becoming a writer or journalist when the war was over. Her diary helped her escape from the claustrophobia of the annex and the nightmare that unfolded outside its confines. "The nice part is being able to write down all my thoughts and feelings; otherwise, I'd absolutely suffocate," she wrote.

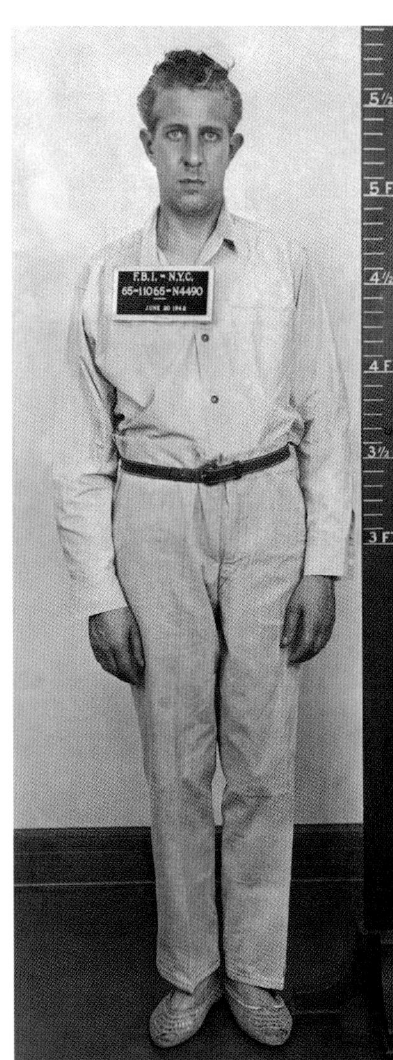

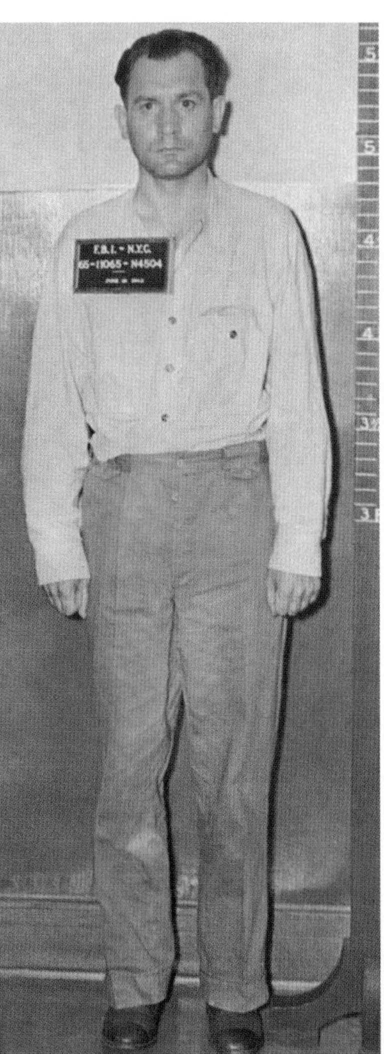

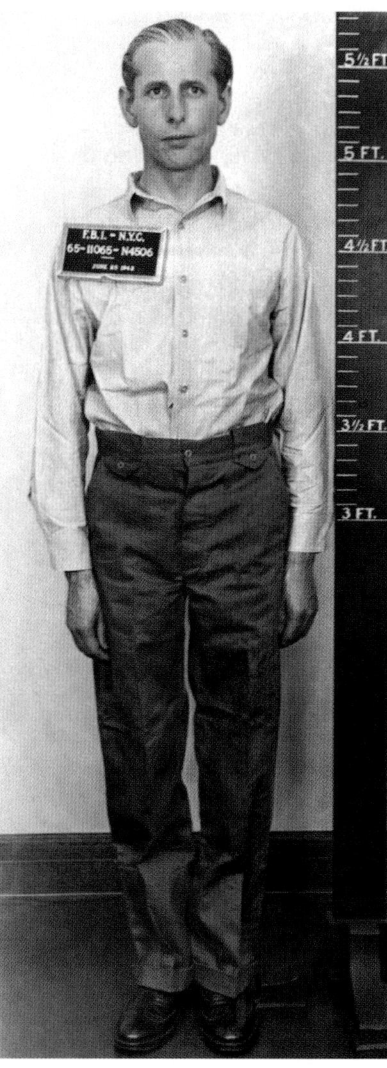

Secret War

Spies, subterfuge, and sabotage all played major roles in the war of intelligence, a war in which no one was who he seemed and where seemingly innocuous objects often contained deadly surprises.

THE EYES OF SPIES

Americans were advised that enemy agents were lurking everywhere (inset), and in some cases, it was true. Eight Nazi operatives (four pictured above) arrived in the United States in June 1942 to sabotage factories. All eight men were captured after one of them, claiming to be an anti-Nazi leftist, turned himself in to American authorities. Six of the other conspirators were eventually put to death. Although the British were the undeniable masters of espionage, the U.S. also had its share of successes. German-born American William Sebold worked as a double-agent and was responsible for the arrest of 33 enemy agents.

SPY GUY

William "Wild Bill" Donovan (right), a successful Wall Street lawyer and close friend of President Roosevelt's, modeled the Office of Strategic Services (OSS) after Britain's successful espionage and information-gathering agencies.

PERSONENBESCHREIBUNG

Staatsangehörigkeit: Frankreich
Beruf: Bootsmann
Geburtsort: Paris
Geburtstag: 27.7.08
Wohnsitz oder Aufenthaltsort: Hamburg
Gestalt: mittel groß
Gesicht: oval
Farbe der Augen: braun
Farbe des Haares: braun
Besondere Kennzeichen: /

16

Unterschrift des Inhabers

PASSPORT TO DANGER

Spies and saboteurs masked their identities and conducted business in enemy territories with the help of fraudulent passports. This forged German passport (above) belonged to an agent with the British SOE who was part of Operation Vivacious, a plan to sabotage engineering works in Berlin.

SLY BOOTS

Phony footprints (above) were issued to the Special Operations Executive (SOE) operatives to disguise beach landings. Agents would strap the feet to the bottoms of their boots, thereby leading the enemy to think their tracks were left by locals.

CAMERA SPY

Spying implements came in all sorts of shapes and packages, as evidenced by this camera hidden in a matchbox (above), which was developed by Kodak. The label on the cover of the box could be changed to correspond to the country in which the camera was being used.

TOOLS OF THE TRADE

To destroy important enemy equipment, saboteurs often carried pocket-sized destructive devices. These British time-delay "pencil" fuses (left) look harmless enough but contain a corrosive liquid in their casing, which under certain conditions proved an effective alternative to explosives. A special deck of playing cards (above) could sometimes mean the difference between imprisonment and freedom. Hidden portions of escape maps lay beneath each card and could be pieced together to plot a safe route out of enemy territory.

Carrier Warfare

An American torpedo plane circles the U.S.S. *Yorktown* (left) near the Coral Sea in April 1942. The ship's antenna was photographically retouched by censors to cloak American radar technology. U.S. soldiers with 30 days of active service in the Pacific earned the Asiatic Pacific Campaign medal (below).

Lieutenant Richard Best scanned the empty ocean from an altitude of 10,000 feet. He and his fellow dive-bomber pilots from the U.S.S. *Enterprise* were desperately searching for the Japanese carrier force that had just attacked Midway Island on the morning of June 4, 1942. The pilots' squinting, suntanned faces reflected their concern; with fuel running low, the planes would soon have to turn back empty-handed.

Suddenly, a lone Japanese destroyer appeared on the horizon, steaming north at full speed. The Americans tailed the escort vessel and were soon rewarded with a sight every dive-bomber pilot dreams of: Three wide, white wakes roiled the blue surface of the Pacific, and at the head of each wake lay the unmistakable outline of a Japanese carrier. The pilots peeled out of formation and started their bombing runs. Best picked his target and nosed his sturdy SBD Dauntless over into a screaming, near-vertical dive. "As I started my bombing run on the. . . *Akagi*, I saw its great big tan-colored deck with a tremendous orange Rising Sun painted on the deck just forward of the bridge." Best put the Japanese emblem in his crosshairs and released his bomb. Little did he and the intrepid handful of American pilots realize that the next five minutes would determine the outcome of the battle and irrevocably change the course of World War II.

In the dark days following Pearl Harbor, Japan's military—on both land and sea—appeared invincible. In the air Japanese pilots clearly enjoyed a technological advantage over their American opponents. The Zero fighter could outfly and outmaneuver its counterpart, the F4F Wildcat, an infinitely less nimble "little beer bottle of a plane," as one pilot described it. Said Best of dogfighting with Zeroes: "It was like taking the stairs while they took the elevator." In torpedo bombers the Japanese Kate—equipped with the deadly Type-95 "Long-Lance" torpedo that had proved so successful at Pearl Harbor—far outclassed the clumsy Devastator and its equally unreliable Mark-13 torpedo, which often failed to explode. Only the SBD Dauntless dive bomber matched its opposite number, the Japanese Val, in performance and accuracy.

An F4F Wildcat (below), its .50-caliber machine gun bays open for inspection, sits on the deck of the *Enterprise* before entering the fray in the Coral Sea in May 1942.

But despite these shortcomings, and even as Japanese

A B-25 rises off the deck of the *Hornet* (above). After he crashed, Doolittle (inset) thought the mission was a failure and expected to be court-martialed. Instead, he was promoted to Brigadier General.

victories piled up throughout the winter of 1941 and 1942 in Singapore, the Java Sea, and the Philippines, U.S. Navy and Air Corps planners hatched an audacious scheme to avenge Pearl Harbor and raise American morale: U.S. planes commanded by Lieutenant Colonel James Doolittle would strike a symbolic blow at the enemy capital itself. Sixteen Army B-25 medium-range bombers were loaded aboard the aircraft carrier *Hornet*, which then steamed undetected to within 700 miles of Japan. A Japanese patrol boat, however, spotted the *Hornet* on April 18, forcing Doolittle and his raiders to take off earlier—and 200 miles farther from the target—than planned. Never had aircraft that large taken off from the short, pitching deck of a carrier, but the planes got airborne without a single mishap.

The B-25s bombed industrial targets in Tokyo and three other cities. Lacking the fuel to reach Chiang Kai-shek's airfields in China, most of the flight crews crash-landed or parachuted into China. Eight of the fliers were captured by the Japanese—three were later executed—but Doolittle and 70 others survived. The raid, which caused little physical damage, acutely embarrassed Japan's military leaders, who decided that further expansion of the Empire's borders was necessary to prevent a recurrence.

The Japanese first moved south in an attempt to capture Port Moresby on the strategically important island of New Guinea. Its capture would threaten the supply line between the United States and Australia, leaving the latter ripe for attack. The light carrier *Shoho* guarded the invasion transports, while a separate group comprising the heavy carriers *Shokaku* and *Zuikaku*, both veterans of the Pearl Harbor attack, shielded the invasion force from any American naval forces that attempted to intervene. The Japanese, however, were unaware that U.S. Navy cryptanalysts had deciphered their codes. Admiral Chester Nimitz, commander in chief of the Pacific Fleet, knew their plans and dispatched two carriers to intercept the Japanese.

The ensuing two-day action, known as the Battle of the Coral Sea, made military history. For the first time, two opposing fleets fought a battle without ever sighting each other; carrier-based aircraft inflicted all of the damage.

On the morning of May 7, 1942, Dauntlesses, Devastators, and escorting Wildcats—93 planes in all—from the carriers *Lexington* and *Yorktown* spotted the *Shoho*. The light carrier's Zeroes were too few in number to repel the American air armada; 13 bombs and seven torpedoes slammed into the ship. The *Shoho* sank in half an hour.

The next morning both sides launched large strikes. American planes found the *Shokaku* and scored three bomb hits. Meanwhile, Japanese squadrons spotted the *Lexington* and *Yorktown*; the bombers approached from high altitude as the torpedo planes swooped in at wave-top level. "The water in all directions seemed full of torpedo wakes," wrote Captain Frederick Sherman of the *Lexington*. Maneuvering frantically, the *Yorktown* evaded every torpedo and all but one bomb. The *Lexington* was not so lucky; two torpedoes and two bombs hit her, touching off internal explosions that mortally wounded the great ship.

The first battle fought entirely between carrier forces was over; the Americans lost a top-of-the-line carrier, and the *Yorktown* suffered severe damage that officials estimated would take three months to repair. But the Japanese advance had been stopped. With the *Shoho* destroyed, the invasion ships turned back. New Guinea and Australia were saved, and the initiative in the South Pacific would soon pass to the Allies.

Farther north, however, Admiral Isoroku Yamamoto was already planning an offensive that he hoped would lure the inferior U.S. Pacific Fleet into a decisive showdown. The Japanese objective was Midway, an isolated atoll 1,000 miles northwest of Pearl Harbor. Because the island could provide a base for an invasion of Hawaii, Yamamoto knew that Nimitz would have to mount an all-out defense. But he didn't know that his counterpart was privy to the Japanese plan and timetable and hence able to position his three carriers, the *Enterprise*, *Hornet*, and *Yorktown*—miraculously repaired in a mere 45 hours—in ambush northeast of Midway.

On the morning of June 4, planes from Vice Admiral Chuichi Nagumo's First Air Fleet attacked Midway, inflicting heavy damage. But returning pilots reported that the airfield was still operational. Nagumo, fearing a counterattack by Midway-based aircraft and still unaware that American carriers lurked nearby, ordered his planes loaded with land bombs for another strike on the island. As they reloaded, a Japanese scout plane radioed that it had spotted enemy carriers. The scout didn't realize that planes from those ships were already airborne and searching for the Japanese fleet. Nagumo hesitated before ordering his planes rearmed with torpedoes and armor-piercing bombs, a time-consuming chore.

DAILY NEWS FINAL

TOKIO BOMBED

BULLETIN

Lieutenant Robert Hite (top) is led away blindfolded by his Japanese captors after participating in Doolittle's raid on Tokyo, which the New York *Daily News* trumpeted in its April 18, 1942, edition (inset).

American military installations on Midway Island (top) smolder after a Japanese air attack. U.S. Dauntless dive bombers (inset) eventually located the Japanese carrier fleet.

Meanwhile, U.S. torpedo planes found the Japanese carriers and pressed home their attack with tremendous bravery. Without fighter escort, however, the attackers were easy prey for the nimble Zeroes: 37 of the 41 attackers crashed into the sea without scoring a single hit. A surviving *Yorktown* pilot, Wilhelm Esders, described the slaughter: "Any direction I was able to look, I could see five, six, seven, or more aircraft on fire, spinning down, or simply out of control and flying around crazily." So far, the action had been a total Japanese success. But Nagumo's delay in launching his planes was about to prove disastrous, for at that moment, Best and his comrades appeared high above the crowded Japanese flight decks.

Standing on the carrier *Akagi*'s deck, Captain Mitsuo Fuchida, the aviator who had led the strike on Pearl Harbor, looked up in alarm: "The terrifying scream of the dive bombers reached me first, followed by the crashing explosion of a direct hit." Fuchida staggered to his feet. "Looking around, I was horrified at the destruction that had been wrought in a matter of seconds. Deck plates reeled upward in grotesque configurations. Planes stood tail up, belching livid flame and jet-black smoke. Reluctant tears streamed down my cheeks as I watched the fires spread." More hits on the *Akagi* followed, while other American bombers dove on the *Kaga* and *Soryu*.

Lieutenant Daniel Iverson reported that the *Kaga* threw up "an entire ring of fire from the flight deck." After pulling out of his bombing run, Iverson was attacked by Zeroes. He crash-landed on Midway, where astonished ground crewmen counted 210 holes in his Dauntless.

In a mere five minutes the attack was over and all three Japanese carriers lay dead in the water, blazing from bow to stern. With two broken ankles, Fuchida was evacuated to a nearby cruiser. Meanwhile, the *Hiryu*, the only remaining Japanese carrier, launched its planes, which tailed the *Yorktown*'s bombers on their return flight. "We had determined to sink an enemy ship even if we had to ram her," recalled Lieutenant Commander Takashi Hashiguchi. His revenge-minded pilots scored three bomb and two torpedo hits, forcing the *Yorktown*'s crew to abandon ship. But later that day, planes from the *Enterprise* and *Hornet* found the *Hiryu*; four direct hits sealed her fate.

Although more air strikes were launched the next day, the Battle of Midway had already been decided. At the cost of the twice-damaged *Yorktown* the Americans had sunk four of Japan's finest carriers. The Imperial Navy could never make good the loss of these ships and their experienced aircrews. "The catastrophe of Midway definitely marked the turning of the tide in the Pacific War," wrote Fuchida, "Thenceforward that tide bore Japan inexorably on toward final capitulation."

Survivors of the *Hammann* arrive in Pearl Harbor (above) a few days after Midway. Japanese pilots used a radio compass (below) that was manufactured in Waterbury, Conn.

MISSION ACCOMPLISHED

Colonel James Doolittle (right, center) poses with Chinese officials and fellow U.S. airmen P.J. Leonard, R.E. Cole, and H.A. Potter (left to right) in China following the bombing of Tokyo, a city considered out of range of American bombers. Doolittle returned to the U.S. and eventually participated in the air war in Europe: In 1944, he led the Eighth Army Air Force in massive air attacks on Germany.

BOMBERS AWAY

One of the 16 B-25 bombers that participated in the U.S. raid on Tokyo on April 18, 1942, prepares to take off from the deck of the *Hornet* (left), 700 miles off the coast of Japan. Despite some bungled planning and the remarkable coincidence that Tokyo had scheduled its first air-raid drill for the same day, the attack yielded tremendous psychological, if not tactical, payoffs.

DERRING-DOOLITTLE

Doolittle pilots his B-25 bomber off the deck of the *Hornet* (above), bound for Tokyo in a bold mission to bomb the Japanese capital. The raid stirred panic in the Japanese capital and restored American pride four months after Pearl Harbor.

LADY *LEX*

The glistening calm of the Coral Sea would soon roil with the fallout of battle as the *Lexington* (above), photographed from the deck of the *Yorktown*, prepares to engage the Japanese navy in an unprecedented battle between carriers. One of the U.S. navy's oldest and most beloved warships, the *Lexington* would not survive the historic conflict.

SEA COMMANDER

Admiral Chester Nimitz (left) deployed Task Force 17 to turn back the enemy's thrust at Coral Sea after U.S. intelligence divined Japan's intent to seize Port Moresby—a vital line of supply and communication between the Allies and Australia. Consisting of only two carriers, three cruisers and a few destroyers, Nimitz's Task Force succeeded in halting Japan's southward expansion.

REFUELING UNDER DURESS

The U.S.S. *Neosho* (right), a fleet oiler, withstands the pounding of high seas as it refuels the *Yorktown* before the Battle of Coral Sea. Several days later the *Neosho*, mistaken for a carrier, was destroyed by Japanese fighter pilots—but at some cost to Japan, which lost six planes in the attack.

LAST STAND

A massive explosion rocks the *Lexington* (left) as the *Hammann* backs away after evacuating the doomed ship's crew. The blast, which vaulted a plane overboard, probably occurred when torpedoes in the carrier's starboard-side hangar were detonated by fires on the warship. U.S. destroyers eventually moved in and put the *Lexington*, which had been in service since 1927, out of its misery, sinking it with torpedoes.

UNDER FIRE

One of *Shokaku*'s antiaircraft shells bursts and plunges into the sea (below). The Japanese carrier, which drew fire from more than 40 U.S. planes during the battle, took three bomb hits, one of which destroyed its ability to launch aircraft. The carrier returned to Japan, where it underwent two months of repair work and missed the pivotal Battle of Midway.

EMERGENCY RESCUE

Survivors of the *Lexington* maneuver their lifeboat alongside a rescue ship. Though 216 men were killed in the bombardment of the carrier, more than 2,700, including 150 wounded men (as well as the captain's cocker spaniel, Wags), successfully evacuated the warship and were rescued by U.S. destroyers. Rear Admiral Thomas Kincaid orchestrated the remarkable operation.

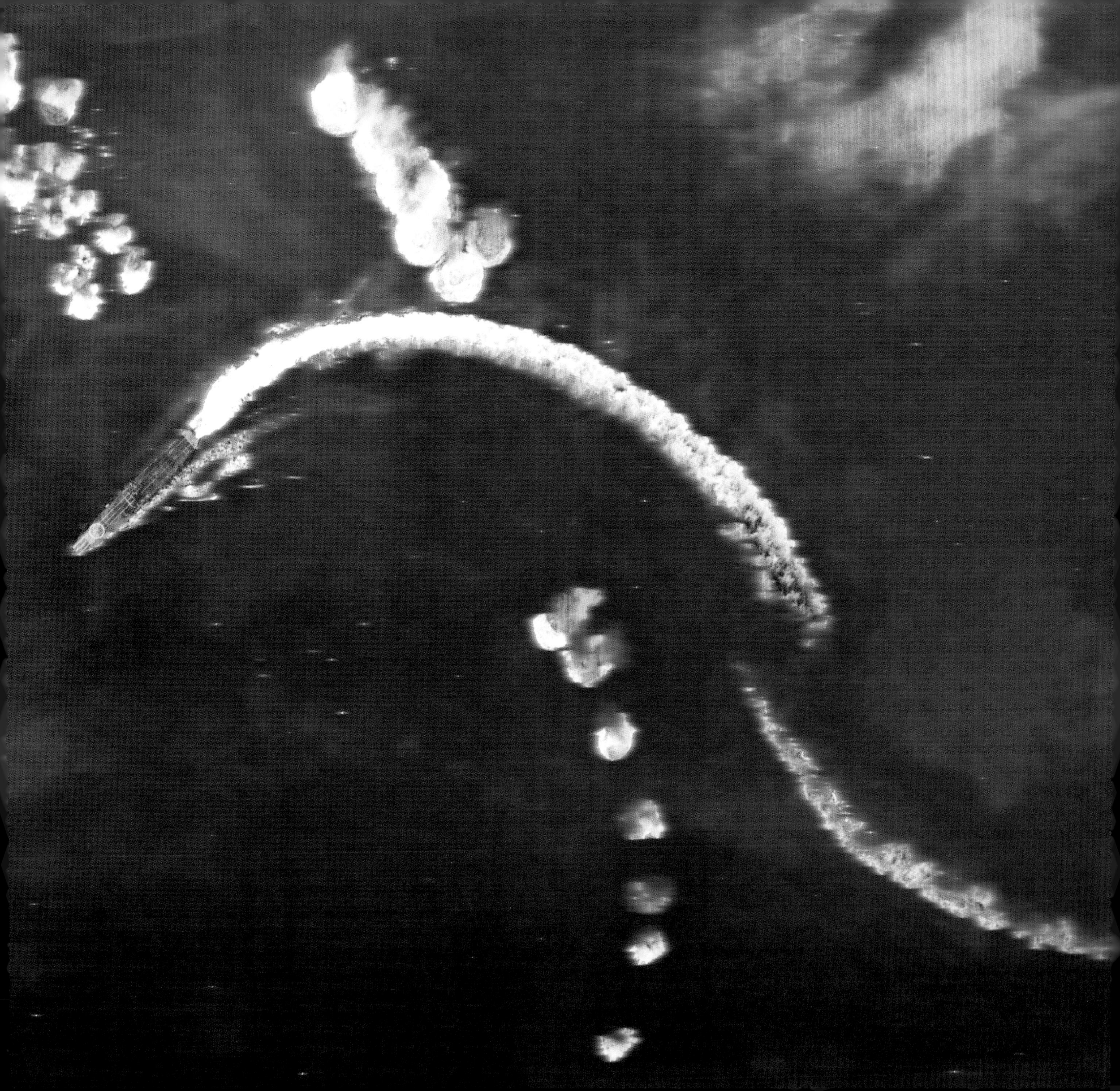

DEVASTATOR DETAIL
Crewmen prepare to launch a squadron of Douglas Devastator torpedo bombers from the deck of the *Enterprise* (above) on June 4, 1942. Named for its location halfway across the Pacific, Midway was a strategic linchpin, and the battle for its two islets was one of the most decisive of the war.

EVASIVE ACTION
Japan's carrier *Akagi* (left) swerves to avoid bombs from U.S. planes near Midway on June 4, 1942. The effort would prove futile as the carrier, the flagship of Japan's Midway strike-force commander, Vice Admiral Chuichi Nagumo, absorbed several direct hits and became engulfed in flames. She sank the next day.

AGAINST ALL ODDS
A victim of bombers from U.S. Task Force 16, the Japanese battleship *Mikuma* (left) lies a smoking wreck off Midway on June 5. Despite being outnumbered 272 to 180 in total bombers and fighters, and eight to three in aircraft carriers, the U.S.—aided by superb codebreaking, deft leadership, and plenty of luck—devastated the Japanese fleet and evened the score in the Pacific. When the fighting stopped, the two countries owned the same number of carriers—a balance which, thanks to U.S. industry, would soon tip America's way.

JOINING THE FIGHT

A Japanese Zero fighter (right) lifts off from a carrier. Japan held a sizeable advantage in firepower at Midway, and indeed struck the first three significant blows. They destroyed dozens of U.S. planes in a damaging attack on the Midway installations and then obliterated two American bomber raids at sea. But when American Dauntless dive bombers finally found the Japanese carriers, the Zeroes were out of position—they had been drawn to lower altitudes by American torpedo bombers—and hence, unable to protect the Japanese fleet.

CRISIS ON THE *YORKTOWN*

Crewmen work furiously to repair damage to the *Yorktown* (left) after the carrier absorbed three bomb hits during the battle. The crew revived the hobbled carrier and even eased her back to a cruising speed of 20 knots—but a second squadron of Japanese fighters, looming only 30 miles to the west, would send her to the bottom.

DIRECT HIT

With the antiaircraft shells of its accompanying destroyers bursting vainly in the sky all around it, the carrier *Yorktown* (right) absorbs a direct hit from a Japanese fighter squadron launched off the deck of the carrier *Hiryu*. The most significant U.S. matériel casualty at Midway, the *Yorktown* sank on June 7. The U.S. also lost the destroyer *Hammann* and 145 airplanes in the battle.

DEATH BLOWS

As the destroyer *Hammann* (above, right) stands nearby in a rescue attempt, the *Yorktown* (above, left) lists to port after being torpedoed by a Japanese submarine on June 6. The *Hammann* was fatally torpedoed for its efforts, and the *Yorktown*, which had withstood several direct bomb hits on June 5 and remained partially functional, finally sank "like a tired colossus, hurt beyond pain" two days later.

STAYING AFLOAT

Crewmen and fliers pick their way along the slanting deck of the crippled *Yorktown* (left). At 2:45 p.m. on June 6, two torpedoes slammed into the carrier's mid-section, and ten minutes later Captain Elliott Buckmaster gave the order to abandon ship. As her crew watched from destroyers, the *Yorktown* drifted on the swells, refusing to sink until the next day.

NARROW ESCAPE

A wounded American soldier (left) is transferred via pulley from one warship to another. While the U.S. victory only turned back Japan's westward thrust and cost the island nation nothing in terms of territory, it would prove to have far-reaching consequences. The Midway atoll was the "keyhole" to the perimeter Japan had established in 1941. Once the Allies breached it, Japan had no choice but to fight defensively for the rest of the war.

ROLE REVERSALS

Women polish the noses of A-20 attack bombers (left). While this job may have suggested "women's work," dozens of stereotypes concerning male and female roles dissolved during the war as women worked as engineers, mechanics, electricians, police officers, lawyers, journalists, cabdrivers, welders, and, yes, riveters.

FAUX ROSIE

J. Howard Miller's 1943 poster (below) for the Westinghouse Corporation, featuring a woman war worker replete with bandana, workshirt, and rouge, mascara, plucked eyebrows, and lipstick, was commonly misidentified as Rosie the Riveter but in fact had no connection to the song or its fictional character.

Rosie
The Riveter

The 1942 song "Rosie the Riveter" became a catchphrase for the six million women who entered the U.S. workforce during the war.

SPARE THE ROD

Workers (above) at a Symington-Gould factory in Buffalo, N.Y., sort rods for reuse in the manufacture of tanks, ships, and railroad parts. Of the six million American women who went to work during World War II, roughly half served as volunteers in the Red Cross. One million were hired by the federal government as clerical workers. Thousands upon thousands took factory jobs or actually joined the military, which included the Women's Air Force Service Pilots (WASP), a female unit that piloted aircraft from production facilities to army bases.

BOLT CUTTERS

Martha Bryant (above, left) and Eulalie Hampden operate a bolt-cutting machine at Todd Erie Basin in 1943. The following year a *National Geographic* article on women in the workforce stated, "As the war goes on, the great feel of it and the great interdependence of it gather strength. It's a man's *and* woman's world."

MASS MOBILIZATION

Beginning as early as 1931, Germany, Japan, and Italy had geared themselves for war while the U.S. sat peacefully unproductive until 1940. Yet by 1942, U.S. production for war equaled that of the three Axis powers combined, generating, among other equipment, 296,429 airplanes, 102,351 tanks and mobile guns, and 87,620 warships. Recruiting posters, such as the one at left, became commonplace.

Cryptology

The greatest weapon in war is information. In World War II both sides made tremendous efforts to secure communications while simultaneously attempting to decipher the enemy's secrets.

COLOSSAL ADVANTAGE
The world's first electronic, programmable computer, the appropriately-named Colossus (top) was housed in Britain's intelligence center at Bletchley Park. The machine helped crack Germany's Lorenz code, which the Wehrmacht thought to be unbreakable, allowing the Allies to read communications between Hitler and his armed forces in the battlefield.

PURPLE PROSE

Using telephone switches and a plugboard, the Japanese Purple cipher device (right) tapped out messages as complexly encrypted as those generated by the German Enigma machine. U.S intelligence, however, solved the Purple code in September 1940, providing a significant advantage at the crucial Battle of Midway in 1942.

ENIGMATIC COMMUNICATION

German general Heinz Guderian (left, standing), commander of the 19th Panzer Corps, surveys the field during the 1940 campaign in France, while his officers (seated) man an Enigma cipher machine. British intelligence solved Enigma in the winter of 1942—too late to save France but in time to influence the battle for the Atlantic.

UNPACKING THE ENIGMA

The battery-powered German Enigma cipher machine (left inset) traveled in a wooden transit case and came equipped with four rotors of code letters and a typewriter-like keyboard. Code-dispatchers usually worked in teams of two: One man pressed the keys, which required some force to advance the rotors, and the other recorded the encoded letters. The message was passed to a radio operator who relayed the orders by Morse code.

BY THE BOOK

Enigma operators aboard ships referred to German navy manuals (above, inset) to adjust the circuitry for their encryption devices. The proper settings varied according to wind, weather and location. The portable Enigmas could go anywhere a field radio went and satisfied the German need for efficient and speedy communications.

ULTIMATE CODE

Private Preston Toledo (above, left) and his cousin Frank, both full-blooded American Navajos, transmit orders in the Pacific in an encrypted version of their native tongue, an unwritten language of great complexity. Philip Johnston, a U.S. veteran who was reared on a reservation, suggested the idea as an unbreakable code. It worked—the Japanese never cracked it.

China-Burma-India

Chiang Kai-shek (below, with Admiral Louis Mountbatten) was a figure of great hope and frustration for the Allies. His giant army represented the best chance to defeat the Japanese, but he was reluctant to unleash it upon anyone but the Chinese Communists.

Allied efforts in the CBI theater began poorly, with Stilwell's long retreat (left), but gradually improved, culminating when the 19th Indian Division—nicknamed the "Dagger Division" (badge, below)—helped capture Mandalay.

The smoke from Japan's devastating attack on Pearl Harbor had scarcely cleared when the Imperial Army launched the next phase of its southern offensive: an audacious campaign in southeast Asia. Japanese forces overwhelmed the Philippines, cut through the jungles of the Malay Peninsula, and plundered the oil-rich Dutch East Indies.

On December 23, 1941, Japanese bombers appeared over the Burmese port city of Rangoon. Since Japan already controlled a broad swath of territory in eastern China, limiting the country's access to foreign aid and supplies, China's only link to its allies was through Burma, a mountainous, jungle-choked nation tucked between India and China. Supplies to China had to be shipped to Rangoon and then sent over the twisting, 681-mile Burma Road into Kunming. By invading Burma, Japan sought to sever China's lone supply route and to establish a base for an eventual invasion of British-occupied India.

The twin-pronged plan got off to an auspicious start as Japanese forces streamed over the border from Thailand and up the tail of Burma. The invaders drove north and quickly pinned the Allies' 17th Indian Division at the Sittang River. Before the British could summon sufficient reinforcements, Japan's ground forces descended upon Rangoon. The battle for the crucial port raged for 75 days, but the outcome was never in doubt. When the shooting stopped, Japan had seized the first rung of the ladder in their conquest of Burma.

At the end of December the Allies had established the China-Burma-India (CBI) theater, splitting its headquarters between Delhi and Chungking, the wartime capital of Generalissimo Chiang Kai-shek's Nationalist government. British lieutenant general Harold Alexander replaced Major General John Smythe, who had overseen the debacle on the banks of the Sittang, as the commander of British forces in the region. The United States sent General Joseph Stilwell to the theater as its top military representative and commander of the few Chinese forces Chiang would allocate to him. A famously crotchety personality, "Vinegar Joe" clashed frequently with the uncompromising Chiang.

The Flying Tigers (right) were in China even before Pearl Harbor. The American Volunteer Group recruited 112 mercenary pilots from the U.S. armed forces in the spring of 1941 to challenge the Japanese with reliable, but obsolete, P-40 fighters. The Tigers flew with patches (inset) that identified them as friends of the Chinese population in case they crashed.

After the fall of Rangoon, the Japanese plunged upcountry once more, driving the British back to the Irrawaddy River. Stilwell and Alexander agreed to establish a defensive perimeter roughly 150 miles north of Rangoon, placing Allied troops in the river valleys between Burma's rugged mountain ranges. Stilwell commanded several divisions of inexperienced Chinese troops near Toungoo on the east flank, while Lieutenant General William Slim positioned the British First Burma Corps along the Irrawaddy near Prome on the west flank. Rather than hold their perimeter and wait for the Japanese, Slim and Stilwell wanted to mount a counteroffensive against Rangoon. But Chiang, reluctant to commit forces that might be used later to fight the Chinese Communists, thwarted the idea. His refusal to grant Stilwell sufficient reinforcements left the 200th Division of the Chinese Fifth Army stranded at Toungoo, crippling any hopes of an Allied offensive.

In the west, Slim's Burma Corps faced a similar rout. Demoralized by the vicious tactics of the enemy—who were reputed to use British captives for bayonet practice—Slim's decimated forces were backed up against the vast oil fields of Yenangyaung. Slim decided to burn the town's 5,000 oil wells, lest they fall into enemy hands. He succeeded in denying the invaders a significant resource, but he and his troops remained trapped. Chiang finally authorized the necessary manpower for escape, allowing Alexander to summon the 38th Chinese Division to rescue the Burma Corps.

With the Allies on the run in the east and the west,

Orde Wingate's Chindit forces (left) were one of the war's best-trained outfits. Named for the fierce sculptured lions that guard Burmese temples (badge, inset), the Chindits wreaked havoc behind enemy lines. Wingate's team helped train the first American combat unit on the Asian mainland, the 5307th Composite Unit (above)—nicknamed Merrill's Marauders after their leader, Brigadier General Frank Merrill. In 11 months of combat, the Marauders fought in 20 engagements and marched more than 600 miles.

general chaos enveloped Burma. Indians who had come to Burma to work under the colonial government streamed back to their homeland, clogging the countryside with hundreds of thousands of refugees. They were routinely attacked by dacoits, ruthless bandits who roamed the war-torn nation and burned every major town within 200 miles of Mandalay.

On April 25 Stilwell and Alexander agreed that the Allies' only course was a headlong retreat. Slim's First Burma Corps began the longest retreat—900 miles—in British military history. Fewer than half of his 25,000 men survived the withdrawal to India.

General Stilwell's division was scattered throughout the Irrawaddy Valley, and he had no choice but to walk out of Burma. Leading a motley column of 114 soldiers, civilians, nurses, and volunteers, the 59-year-old Stilwell slogged 200 miles through jungles, across rivers, and over mountains into India. Dozens of the party's members suffered from disease or heat exhaustion, but they covered as many as 20 miles a day and made it to India in less than a month without a single fatality. "Vinegar Joe" was lauded as a hero when he reached Delhi on May 25, but he would have none of it: "I claim we got a hell of a beating. We got run out of Burma and it is humiliating as hell. I think we ought to find out what caused it, go back, and retake it."

Exactly how to retake Burma became the subject of heated debate. U.S. colonel Claire Chennault, commander of the Flying Tigers, a volunteer air corps that defended southern China against Japanese bombers, believed that air power should be central to any strategy. The flamboyant Tigers—who painted the noses of their planes to look like the snarling mouths of sharks—had achieved some successes against Japan. The victories, however, did more to raise U.S. morale than to inflict actual damage on the

A plain-spoken Brit who spent most of his military career in the deserts of the Middle East, Slim (right) quickly adapted his strategies to the Burmese jungle terrain. He led a successful retreat in April 1942 and returned with the 14th Army (center) to conquer Mandalay in 1945.

Imperial Army. Nevertheless, Chiang and Chennault believed that a small, well-trained air corps could defeat Japan. On the other side of the argument stood Stilwell and the U.S. Army Chiefs of Staff, who firmly believed that only a ground war could repel Japan from Burma and ultimately defeat the island nation.

As the debate continued, the Allies also grappled with China's supply problem. Now that Burma lay in Japanese hands, the Allies had no choice but to fly supplies 500 miles from Assam in India, over the Himalayas, to Kunming in China. The perilous flight traversed the 15,000-foot Santsung Range, nicknamed "the Hump." As Chennault said, "It was as though an air force based in Kansas was supplied from San Francisco to bomb targets from Maine to Florida."

After several conferences and much politicking, a battle plan was agreed upon. The action emphasized Chennault's air power but also called for ground operations in north Burma (by Stilwell's Chinese divisions) and in central Burma (by the British).

Meanwhile, Japan was busy planning two offensives of its own. The first, codenamed U-Go, would open in Burma in March 1944 and would send the Japanese 15th Army, commanded by General Renya Mutaguchi, over the mountains of western Burma and into India to capture the mountainous towns of Kohima and Imphal. After surrounding these strategic targets, the Japanese hoped to march down the mountains and infiltrate the plains of India. From Mutaguchi's point of view, U-Go was actually a preemptive strike. He rightly assumed that the Allies were planning maneuvers to retake Burma, and he had witnessed the modest but surprising successes of British general Orde Wingate's Chindit forces. An irregular outfit that deployed small units and unorthodox tactics, the Chindits had penetrated the Japanese front along the India-Burma border in early 1943. The Chindits' accomplishments amounted to little more than mischief-making behind enemy lines, but they had breached the front and traversed mountainous terrain previously thought impassable to

do so. Larger Allied forces might follow their lead, Mutaguchi reasoned. He planned to invade India before they had the chance. His 15th Army set out on March 6, 1944, and Kohima and Imphal became the sites of some of the fiercest fighting of the war. After more than 80 days of fighting, Mutaguchi reluctantly ordered a retreat. The 15th Army, 85,000 strong, had suffered 65,000 casualties. It was the worst land defeat in Japanese history and the beginning of the end for Japan in Burma.

Japan's other offensive—codenamed Ichi-Go—was a response to Allied naval advances in the central Pacific, which threatened Japanese control of southern Asia. Japan believed that a powerful thrust into China in April 1944 could clear a direct rail route between Nanking and Peking and eliminate Chennault's airfields in southern China. The Ichi-Go offensive greatly concerned Allied leadership after 15 Japanese divisions annihilated 300,000 Chinese troops during a three-week thrust to the Yellow and Yangtze rivers in April. The Allied setback contributed to increasing internal political strife. Stilwell's abrasive behavior had alienated both Chiang and the British, forcing President Roosevelt finally to relieve "Vinegar Joe" in October. Stilwell's position was divided between two new commanders: General Albert Wedemeyer took over in China and General Daniel Sultan assumed control in Burma. The decision was politically motivated, but it paid off on the battlefield. When Wedemeyer's Chinese troops and the American 14th Air Force repelled a Japanese raid on the city of Chihkiang, the Ichi-Go offensive was finally stopped.

In Burma, Sultan coordinated with Slim's forces and swept the Japanese out of Mandalay by March 1945. Rangoon fell to the Allies six weeks later as the panicked Japanese retreated toward Thailand. In an astounding bit of turnabout, British forces trapped the fleeing Japanese 28th Army at the Sittang River. Of the 17,000 Japanese infantrymen who attempted to ford the river, fewer than 6,000 made it across. The Sittang had witnessed Japan's first significant triumph in Burma in 1942. Now it was the site of their final defeat.

Japanese soldiers were taught to choose death rather than surrender, in accordance with the ancient Japanese warriors' code of *Bushido*. Those who were taken prisoner (above) suffered shame unknown to Allied soldiers. The tenacity of the Japanese soldier awed many of the Allied soldiers who experienced it up close. "The strength of the Japanese army lay . . . in the spirit of the individual Japanese soldier," Slim said. "He fought and marched till he died."

FIREFIGHT AT THE SITTANG

British Commonwealth troops (left) crouch in the trenches as they await a Japanese assault from across the Sittang River in 1942. Enemy machine-gun fire soon exploded from only 250 yards away, and the Commonwealth troops suffered heavy losses as the Japanese continued their march on Rangoon.

VINEGAR JOE

Lieutenant General Joseph Stilwell (right) was America's top military representative to Chiang Kai-shek. Although he gained renown for leading the miraculous retreat out of Burma, the outspoken Stilwell quickly grew frustrated with Chiang (and vice-versa). "Stilwell's mission . . . was certainly the toughest diplomatic job thrust upon a professional soldier during the war," said Colonel Claire Chennault, commander of the Flying Tigers.

IMPERIAL MARCH

Japanese forces (left) march into the Burmese town of Maltaban in 1942. Resistance from the natives—who were more fascinated by the Japanese photographer's camera than the display of military might—was negligible, since many Burmese viewed the Japanese as liberators.

BURMA ROAD

With much of eastern China in Japanese hands, the Burma Road (above)—a winding 681-mile lifeline connecting Kunming to Lashio—became China's only avenue of access to the outside world. Supplies were shipped to the southern Burmese port of Rangoon and then sent by rail to Lashio. When the Japanese captured Lashio in April 1942, however, the Burma Road fell under their control.

FLYING THE HUMP

The closing of the Burma Road by the Japanese forced the Allies to supply China via air. Severe winds, monsoons, and plane-shaking turbulence made the 500-mile flight a harrowing trip. Nevertheless, as many as 650 Allied planes (right, near Kunming)—carrying up to four tons of cargo each—made the trip every day.

JUNGLE VISIONARY
General Orde Wingate's plan to create an Allied guerrilla force that could penetrate deep into Japanese territory was highly controversial—as was Wingate himself (above). "Wingate was the most complex character I've ever met," said one of his staff officers. "He was not a lovable person, but he was a great leader."

TOUGH AS NAILS
The Chindits (above) were taught to do more with less than any military outfit in CBI. Armed with only basic military necessities, the 3,000 men of the 77th Indian Infantry Brigade—their official designation—stalked the dark jungles in Japanese-held territory, disrupting enemy communications and lines of supply. By operating behind enemy lines, the Chindits avoided the main concentration of Japanese fighting forces, and their successful raids lowered Japanese morale.

SABOTAGE
A crew of Chindit engineers (right) wires a Burmese railroad line with explosives. Since the Chindits were isolated in the jungle, they could not afford to waste anything of value. After blowing up the bridge, they gathered pieces of the track and railroad ties and used them to reinforce the bunkers in their desolate jungle fortress, ironically nicknamed Broadway.

MISSION FOR MARS

The American 124th Cavalry Regiment (above)—which joined Merrill's Marauders to form the Mars Task Force—crosses a bridge at Pandu Ghat in northern Burma in October 1944. Led by General Daniel Sultan, the long-range penetrating guerrilla force cleared the Japanese from the Burma Road during its drive south.

THE ROAD TO MANDALAY

Chinese soldiers (left) direct an American tank during the Allied effort to retake Burma in 1945. In October 1944 the Allies had succeeded in reopening the Burma Road, and more successes quickly followed.

GOING HOME

Stilwell (left) and Brigadier General Frank Merrill share a laugh not long before Stilwell was recalled by President Roosevelt in October 1944. Stilwell had never seen eye-to-eye with Chiang, and his relationship with the British had deteriorated as well. Despite General George Marshall's unwavering support of Stilwell, Roosevelt relieved "Vinegar Joe" of his command.

HOT SPOT

British soldiers from General William Slim's 14th Army (left) fire 3-inch mortars during the fighting for Meiktila, a major Japanese communications center south of Mandalay. Slim had feinted towards Mandalay, and hit Meiktila hard in February 1945. The British victory won Slim headlines across the world and opened the road to Rangoon for the Allies.

ON THE MOVE

British soldiers (right) storm a Burmese village to search for Japanese soldiers. After the Japanese abandoned their attack on Imphal in July 1944, the Allies went on the offensive and pushed the Japanese out of India and northern Burma.

SOUTHERN SWEEP

As the Allied southern advance continues, Commonwealth troops (above) liberate the railroad town of Prome, near the Irrawaddy River, in 1945. The Allies raced southward in order to reach Rangoon before the monsoon broke. They arrived one day late—on May 2—but managed to enter the city without any opposition.

THE FALL OF RANGOON

Two Gurkha paratroopers (left) make final preparations for their drops into Rangoon in May 1945. An Allied sea-based invasion followed their airborne assault, and the city—which had been evacuated by the Japanese days earlier—peacefully fell into Allied hands.

MOUNTAIN MEN

A Gurkha (left) carries an injured compatriot from the front. The Gurkhas were revered mercenary soldiers from the Himalayan region of Nepal who served in the Indian army under the British. Their lethal efficiency with a *kukri,* a machete-shaped boomerang,was legendary.

Chiang Kai-shek

Franklin Roosevelt championed the Chinese strongman as one of the Allies' greatest assets, but Chiang Kai-shek seemed more concerned with the Chinese Communists than the Japanese.

AMERICAN MADE

Chiang (above, reviewing Chinese officers at an American-run military school in South China) relied on his diplomatic acumen and western ties to remain in power. "The President [Roosevelt] will refuse me nothing," he once bragged. His efforts, combined with those of his American-educated wife and a powerful China lobby in Washington (Chinese propaganda poster, inset), garnered China more than $1.5 billion in Lend-Lease aid.

STRAINED RELATIONS

Chiang, his wife, and Lieutenant General Joseph Stilwell (above) share a rare happy moment on April 19, 1942, one day after the Doolittle Raid on Tokyo. The famously abrasive Stilwell never warmed to the Chiangs. He denounced the generalissimo—whom he mockingly referred to as "Peanut"—as stupid and gutless. For his part, Chiang did his best to have Stilwell removed as his top American advisor.

REVOLUTIONARIES

A young Chiang stands behind his mentor, China's revolutionary leader Sun Yat-sen (above), in 1924, one year before Sun's death. Chiang won a power struggle for leadership of the Nationalist Party and embarked on several "campaigns of extermination" to rid China of communists.

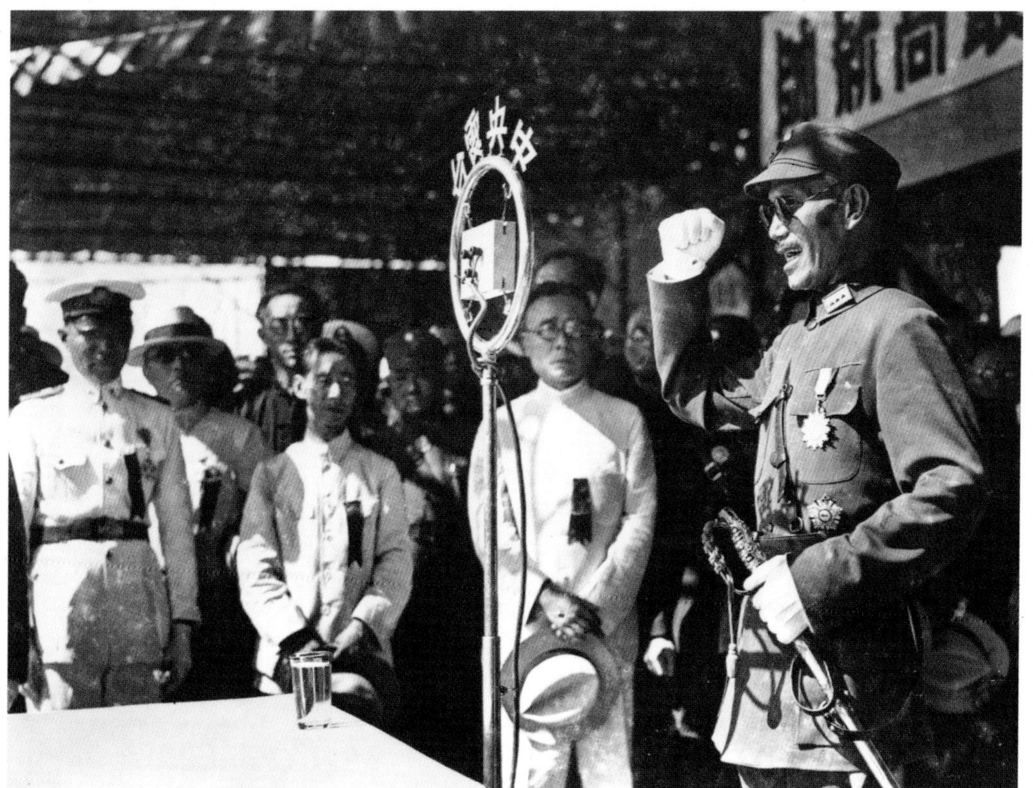

THE GENERALISSIMO

Chiang (left) led a giant army of at least four million soldiers, but when the Japanese invaded in 1937, he ordered them to retreat, exchanging land for time. His goals were survival, rather than victory. The financial and military backing of the Allies allowed that strategy to eventually succeed.

With the mounting worries of the eastern front etched upon his face, Hitler (below) shares a plane with his advisors in late 1942. His invasion of the Soviet Union had devolved into a stalemate, condemning Germany to a prolonged two-front war.

Road to Stalingrad

An officer of the 24th Panzer Division (left) scans the horizon for signs of the Red Army as he and his compatriots surge north to Stalingrad. German tank commanders who recorded 25, 50, 75, or 100 "kills" of enemy armor received medals (below) commemorating the achievement.

On a raw spring day in 1942 Adolf Hitler stood over the conference table in his East Prussian headquarters intently studying a map of the Soviet Union. The war that he had expected to win in a matter of weeks was now in its tenth month. German casualties approached one million men. The Red Army had lost three times that many in prisoners alone, but they refused to capitulate. There was no end in sight. On Hitler's map, the line that marked the front stretched from the Gulf of Finland, just outside Leningrad, south to a point west of Moscow, and then through the Ukraine to the Black Sea, a distance of 1,500 miles.

In June 1941 the Wehrmacht had attacked along the entire front, but owing to grievous losses both in men and in vehicles, such a broad offensive was out of the question in 1942. Examining the map, Hitler pondered three options: His forces could attempt to capture the besieged city of Leningrad; they could renew the advance on Moscow, which had been halted just short of the capital the previous December; or they could concentrate their panzer divisions in the south for a swift thrust into the rich oil fields of the Caucasus.

The rift between Hitler and the generals who stood deferentially around the table with him had grown during the winter, when the Wehrmacht suffered a stunning setback at the hands of the Red Army outside Moscow. He believed that only his refusal to heed their calls for retreat had prevented a catastrophe, and now he seldom bothered to conceal his disdain. "Any logical discussion

was out of the question," wrote General Franz Halder, chief of the army's general staff. "He would foam at the mouth, threaten me with his fists, and scream at the top of his lungs." Although—or perhaps because—his advisors favored another assault on Moscow, Hitler decided to hold in the north and center and strike hard in the south.

Wehrmacht panzer units (top) roll across the vast steppe of southern Russia. Hitler ordered production of a special badge (above) to honor "the heroic achievements of the troops" who served under General von Manstein in the Crimean peninsula.

The operation, codenamed Case Blue, called for Army Group South to advance eastward from Kharkov as far as the Volga, using fast-moving panzer columns to encircle and destroy large pockets of enemy units. Then, with Soviet resistance crushed, the right wing of Army Group South could take the Caucasus. As for the industrial center on the Volga that bore the name of his arch nemesis, Hitler's orders simply stated that Stalingrad should be captured if possible or at least brought "under fire from heavy artillery" to protect the left flank of the advance. But in the coming months the city would become an obsession, dominating the Führer's thoughts and plans. It would cost him an army—and eventually the war.

One of the first goals of the German offensive was to capture the fortified naval base of Sevastopol on the Crimean peninsula. To help neutralize the thickly walled strongpoints that ringed the city, General Erich von Manstein gathered field pieces and heavy mortars of every caliber. "At no other time on the German side in World War II," the general recorded, "can artillery ever have been more formidably massed." Included in this array was the largest cannon ever built, a monstrous railway gun nicknamed "Dora," which required a crew of 4,000 men. With its barrel standing as tall as a 16-story building, Dora could hurl seven-ton shells to a range of 29 miles. One shot penetrated 90 feet of solid rock and detonated a Soviet ammunitions bunker.

But even after the guns had pounded Sevastopol's forts to rubble, German infantry still had to flush out the Soviet garrisons in costly close-range assaults. Stalin had exhorted Sevastopol's 100,000 defenders to fight to the death, and for the most part they did, exhibiting tenacity and courage that impressed the enemy. "Don't believe Ivan is dead just because his legs are blown off [or] someone has stuck a bayonet through his guts," one veteran Wehrmacht officer advised. "If he has an arm left and a rifle within reach, he'll roll over and shoot you in the back as soon as you're past him." The month-long siege finally ended on July 4, when the last remnants of resistance collapsed. For once Hitler was pleased with a general's performance; he promoted Manstein to the rank of field marshal.

To the northeast of the Crimea, Case Blue was proceeding according to plan. In the area between the

At Army Group South headquarters in the Ukraine, Field Marshal Manstein (far left) discusses strategy for the eastern front with Hitler (left, center). The Führer had hoped to quickly seize the oil fields in the Caucasus region of the Soviet Union and use them to finally end the war with the Soviets.

Donets and Don Rivers, Manstein's armies had crushed the Soviet opposition, destroying 1,200 tanks and taking 240,000 prisoners. The Germans then entered the area of the Soviet Union known as the steppe, a vast, treeless plain that, according to one homesick German, offered "no variety, no charm. A single severe tone dominated everything." By July the panzers had reached the great bend of the Don, and Hitler confidently told Halder, "The Russian is finished."

On the left boundary of the German advance was the Sixth Army, commanded by General Friedrich Paulus. By early August he had established bridgeheads across the Don and pushed east toward the Volga, leaving the Romanian Third Army to guard his northwest flank. Within a month panzer units had reached the river to the north and south of Stalingrad, whose defenders had received Stalin's peremptory order, "Not a step back." The separate German columns turned toward the city, and the fight began.

The Battle of Stalingrad was unique in World War II: a five-month-long struggle within the confines of an urban area that stretched some 20 miles along the Volga's banks. From September onward, Luftwaffe air strikes and constant artillery bombardment turned the city into a smoldering, rubble-strewn ruin. After the blitzkrieg of the open steppe, the Sixth Army became embroiled in a *Rattenkrieg*, or war of the rats, in Stalingrad, pitting infantry squads against machine gun nests, and hidden snipers against individual soldiers, among the wreckage of houses and factories. In such confused fighting the front became fluid—the main railway station changed hands at least 15 times. German and Soviet troops often occupied different floors of the same building or even different rooms on the same floor. Progress, in the words of a German officer, was "measured no longer by meters but by corpses."

As autumn progressed, the Sixth Army pushed the outnumbered Soviet 62d Army into an ever-shrinking defensive line. In Stalingrad's northern suburbs, workers at the Dzerzhinski tractor factory drove T-34 tanks off the assembly line straight into battle. By November, nine-tenths of the city was in German hands, but the Red Army still clung stubbornly to a small, shallow perimeter along the Volga.

A Red Army tank crew (above) thanks the agricultural laborers who pooled their savings to finance the manufacture of a tank, aptly labeled *Moscow Farmer*. Russian civilians responded to posters that urged "The Motherland Calls!" (inset), and millions rallied to support the nation in its Great Patriotic War against Germany.

Stalin implored the defenders to hold on just a little longer so that a surprise could be sprung on the besiegers. At dawn on November 19, fresh Soviet reserves led by waves of T-34s slammed into the Romanian Third Army northwest of Stalingrad. The next day additional armored formations smashed through German positions south of the city. The Red Army had turned the tables on the inventors of blitzkrieg; in four days the two pincers met, and Paulus and his 250,000 men were surrounded. "Request freedom of action," he cabled Hitler's headquarters. "Situation might compel abandonment of Stalingrad."

Hitler adamantly refused to consider a withdrawal, promising Paulus that the Luftwaffe would resupply the Sixth Army by airlift. When that effort proved woefully inadequate, he still forbade a breakout, instead ordering Manstein to breach the Soviet ring and relieve the city. In mid-December, Manstein's army fought its way east but could not get closer than 35 miles from the Sixth Army's perimeter. Hitler still denied Paulus permission to attack westward and link up with Manstein's troops. Facing additional Soviet counterattacks along the Don, Manstein was forced to turn back, leaving the doomed Sixth Army to freeze and bleed to death in the devastated city. In a last letter to his family, a 26-year-old officer lamented that he was "one of those who was mighty keen on getting his bars and yelling 'Heil Hitler' with the rest of you; and now it's either die like a dog or off to Siberia."

When he finally realized that all hope of holding Stalingrad was gone, Hitler ordered the troops to fight to the last man. His promotion of Paulus to field marshal sent

Nikita Khrushchev (left, in black hat), the political commissar for Stalingrad, addresses civilians after the liberation of the city. Paulus (above, left) angered Hitler when he chose surrender rather than suicide. "The heroism of so many soldiers," Hitler raged, "is cancelled out by one single characterless weakling."

a clear message since no German field marshal had ever surrendered. But on January 31 Paulus did just that. He and 91,000 starving, ragged troops were marched into captivity. Only 5,000 would ever return to Germany.

The Sixth Army's demise left a gaping hole in the German southern front. The divisions that had advanced into the Caucasus were forced to retreat to avoid being cut off. For the remainder of the winter, the Soviets kept up the pressure, and only Manstein's brilliant tactics of mobile defense, coupled with sharp, local counterattacks, prevented a wholesale rout.

By March 1943 the front had stabilized in almost exactly the same position it had held the previous year. The grand strategy for conquest and decisive victory that Hitler had launched with such high hopes in the spring of 1942 had come to naught. The only tangible result was the addition of millions of new names to the casualty rolls of the costliest war in human history.

Hitler would mount one last offensive in July 1943, an ill-conceived attempt to pinch off the salient around the city of Kursk. But the Soviet high command correctly deduced German intentions, and the Red Army was lying in wait. In the largest tank battle of the war, the Soviets dealt the Wehrmacht a crushing defeat. The initiative and momentum of the conflict passed once and for all to the Soviet Union, and from that moment on, the eastern front moved inexorably westward toward Berlin.

RELOAD

Wehrmacht artillerymen (above) sprint to rearm their massive mortar, which fires one-ton rounds, during the battle for Sevastopol. Case Blue had opened on May 8, with Manstein's 11th Army, achieving a swift victory at Kerch, but the fortified Soviet naval base at Sevastopol held out until early July in a conflict Manstein described as "a bitter struggle for every foot of ground, every pillbox and trench."

SURRENDER
Red Army troops (above) emerge from a railroad tunnel near Sevastopol's North Fort after enduring hours of unrelenting shelling by German artillery. The capture of Sevastopol on July 4 secured the Crimean peninsula for the Germans and covered both the back door to the Caucasus and the southern flank of the forces involved in Case Blue.

FEEDING THE VANQUISHED
After capturing Sevastopol, German troops (left) distribute bread to the city's beleaguered women and children. Made of reinforced concrete and armed with heavy guns, Sevastopol's fortresses presented a daunting challenge to any invader. But the Wehrmacht prevailed by deploying its own enormous guns and fighting with, as one German soldier recalled, "the spirit of madness, the desperation to seize an objective without regard to the cost."

WAR OF THE RATS

As the devastated city smolders around them, German artillerymen (right) fire a howitzer at a distant target in southern Stalingrad. After eighty days of Rattenkrieg, "Stalingrad was no longer a town," said one German officer. "By day it is an enormous cloud of burning, blinding smoke . . . And when night arrives . . . the dogs plunge into the Volga and swim desperately to gain the other bank. . . . Animals flee this hell . . . only men endure."

GUNS ALONG THE VOLGA

A weary German soldier (left) stands oblivious to the raging fire behind him during the ferocious ground fighting on the west bank of the Volga River. "To take Stalingrad is not so difficult for us," one German had written as the battle began in the fall of 1942. "The Führer knows where the Russians' weak point is. Victory is not far away."

AIR STRIKE

A Stuka divebomber (above) heads back to base after bombing a fuel yard on the banks of the Volga. Prior to the late August invasion by Wehrmacht ground troops, the Luftwaffe saturated Stalingrad with bombs. On August 23 more than 600 Luftwaffe planes—half of them carrying firebombs—flew against the sprawling city and reduced its wooden structures to ashes. Some 40,000 civilians died in the fearsome assault.

STALINGRAD'S DEFENDERS

Members of the Soviet 62d Army advance through crumbling, war-torn Stalingrad during street combat against Wehrmacht troops in November 1942. When the German invasion began, the 62d Army—the only Red Army presence in Stalingrad at the time—numbered 50,000 troops and possessed approximately 100 tanks. Against these meager forces the Germans unleashed 100,000 men, 500 tanks, and 1,000 aircraft.

HEADQUARTERS
Red Army officers discuss strategy for the defense of Stalingrad at the command post of Nikolai Batyuk (above, right) in November 1942. The Soviets forced a stalemate in Stalingrad and gained the upper hand when reinforcements finally arrived. Hitler compounded his defeat by transferring forces from positions in the steppe and the Caucasus Mountains to the city, leaving other positions increasingly vulnerable to counterattack.

SNIPER WAR
The crumbling ruins of Stalingrad offer perfect cover for Soviet snipers (right). Opposing snipers mastered this "game" of patience and skill Vasily Zaitsev, a former shepherd from the Ural Mountains, became a Soviet hero for killing 242 Germans at Stalingrad.

STRANDED
Members of Field Marshal Paulus's doomed Sixth Army (right) face a bitter Russian winter as prisoners of war after being captured in Stalingrad. Hitler, who had expected Paulus to fight to the death, heaped additional scorn on the new field marshal when Paulus joined Stalin's Committee of Free German Officers, which discouraged additional German resistance.

WHITE FLIGHT
Soldiers from the German Sixth Army (above) march into captivity in February 1943. Earlier, as Red Army reinforcements came ever nearer Stalingrad, one German soldier wrote, "We could have marched out a long time ago except the grand strategists haven't come to an agreement yet. Soon it will be too late, if it isn't already."

AIR SUPPLY
Hitler's stubbornness left the bulk of the Sixth Army trapped in Stalingrad. The Führer's solution to this "temporary encirclement," as he put it, was to resupply the troops by airlift (right). When he heard of the plan, Luftwaffe general Wolfram von Richthofen said, "In the filthy weather we have here there's not a hope of supplying an army of 250,000 men from the air. It's stark, raving madness!"

АНТОН
ИВАНОВИЧ
СЕРДИТСЯ

BLOCKADED CITY
A Soviet policeman (left) inspects five corpses on a Leningrad street corner during the Wehrmacht's 900-day siege of the city. Rather than repeat the costly street fighting of Stalingrad, Hitler ordered his forces to blockade Leningrad into submission. Starvation, hypothermia, disease, and shelling claimed the lives of nearly one million Russians during the siege.

RED ARMY GUNNERS
Soviet machine gunners (right) defend Leningrad in December 1942. The next month, the Red Army would launch a counterattack to break the Wehrmacht's grip on the city. The Soviet 67th and Second Shock armies, comprising 12 divisions and two armored brigades, drove south from Lake Ladoga and restored Leningrad's supply route.

ROAD OF LIFE
A Soviet truck column (above) traverses the flooded Ladoga Route in January 1942. When frozen, Lake Ladoga provided Leningrad with its only supply route during the German siege. Red Army engineers constructed a railroad 50 miles across the ice in February, and food and supplies slowly trickled into the city. More important, the railway enabled nearly 1 million Leningraders to evacuate the besieged city.

TURNING OF THE TIDE

As shrapnel bursts fill the sky around them, Red Army soldiers (above) follow a pair of tanks into battle during the fighting for Kursk in July 1943. Germany's offensive had exhausted itself, and in the following month the Soviets would take the initiative and force the Wehrmacht back.

CARRYING ON THE FIGHT
While their wounded comrade (above, right) receives medical attention from a military nurse, a Red Army mortar crew bombards German positions during the Battle of Kursk. The Soviets used the momentum of their success at Kursk to recapture Kharkov in August.

DRIVEN BACK
Wehrmacht machine gunners (left) scan the horizon for Soviet troops in Kursk in June 1943. Two months later the Germans were in full retreat. By October the Red Army had regained the most crucial territories they had lost to the Germans in the previous two years. When the Ukrainian city of Dnepr returned to the Soviets in November, the door to eastern Europe lay open to the Red Army.

Warsaw Uprising

Resisting the final round of "resettlements," Jews in the Warsaw Ghetto took up arms against their Nazi tormentors for four weeks in the spring of 1943.

SMOKED OUT

Jewish civilians (above) who had taken cover in an underground bunker are forced out as the Nazis set fire to the entire ghetto. In some cases, Jews "preferred to return to the flames rather than risk being caught by us," wrote Juergen Stroop, an SS officer in Warsaw. Emannuel Ringelblum saved the Oneg Shabbat, documents chronicling the ghetto's history, in a milk can (inset).

CRACKDOWN
A German SS trooper (above) searches a group of Jewish men who work for Warsaw's Brauer armaments factory. After hit-and-run attacks by Jewish paramilitaries forced the Nazis to temporary withdraw, the SS reentered the ghetto with overwhelming force.

CAPTURED
As the ghetto burns behind them, the Neyer family (right)—whose patriarch, Avraham (behind the child), was the only family member to survive the war— is marched by SS troops to the *Umschlagplatz* for deportation to the concentration camps of eastern Europe. The *Umschlagplatz* is now the site of a Holocaust memorial.

WARSAW INFERNO
Strolling nonchalantly past a burning building in Warsaw, SS troops complete the suppression of the Warsaw insurrection. When the Warsaw Ghetto was established by Germany in 1940, 400,000 Jews were walled up in an area, two and one-half miles long and a mile wide. By April 1943 only 60,000 Warsaw Jews remained. When the uprising ended, Juergen Stroop proudly reported that "the Warsaw Ghetto is no more."

YIELDING TO THE INEVITABLE
A resistance figher (above) emerges from his bunker in the Warsaw Ghetto. As the rebellion progressed and the SS resorted to torching the entire ghetto, the city's defenders retreated to the sewers. In the end, some 56,000 Jewish citizens were killed or captured.

Schutzstaffel

Formed to squelch political opposition during Hitler's rise to power, the SS—or protection squad—gradually became the Nazi Party's chief instrument of terror.

PARAMILITARIES

Heinrich Himmler (above, center), the head of the SS, walks with Josef "Sepp" Deitrich (above, right), commander of Hitler's bodyguard, and Ernst Röhm (above, left), Himmler's rival and chief of the *Sturmabteilung* (SA), in 1933. One year later, Röhm was murdered during the Night of the Long Knives, Hitler's two-day purge of SA officers that elevated the SS to supremacy in the Reich. Himmler planned for the SS (longevity medal, left) to evolve into a biologically-superior aristocracy that would defend the Reich.

ENFORCERS
SS soldiers (left) link arms to control the crowd during May Day celebrations in Berlin in 1936. By 1930 Hitler's private armies (SS and SA) outnumbered Germany's own armed forces, and he wasn't afraid to use them. "I will suppress every attempt to disturb the existing order," promised Hitler in 1933.

CRACKDOWN
One week after the Reichstag fire, an SS member (far right) joins a policeman and his german shepherd as they patrol Berlin during the 1933 election—the last democratic election that Germany would enjoy in Hitler's lifetime. SS troops were regularly deployed as auxiliary police during the Nazis' seizure of power, and Himmler eventually became the chief of Germany's national police.

DIVISION OF DEATH
Members of the *Totenkopf*—death's head—Third SS Armored Division (left) rest during fighting in Smolensk. The death's-head insignia (inset) testified to the unit's methods.

"THE BLACK ORDER"
A poster (right) recruits German teenagers to join the Waffen SS, the armed wing of the *Schutzstaffel*. Though it always remained separate from the Wehrmacht, the SS gradually added combat units to its ranks. By 1945, the armed SS totaled 38 divisions.

"Soft Underbelly"

Montgomery (left) salutes victorious British soldiers in the Italian town of Reggio in September 1943. His Eighth Army and Mark Clark's American Fifth Army (insignia, inset) met fierce German resistance as they slowly moved up the Italian peninsula.

"When I assumed command of the Eighth Army I said that the mandate was to destroy Rommel and his army, and that it would be done as soon as we were ready," British lieutenant general Bernard Montgomery announced to his troops on October 23, 1942. "We are ready *now*."

The stern taskmaster had been in charge for only two months, but his arrival coincided with a power shift in North Africa. After 18 months of humiliating defeats and retreat, Allied forces finally rallied near the tiny Egyptian village of El Alamein. German field general Erwin Rommel and his heralded Afrikakorps quite literally had run out of gas on their trek east to Cairo. Their supply lines were stretched thin, and Rommel had pushed himself to the limits of exhaustion; he had returned to Germany in September to receive treatment for a stomach disorder. As Rommel recuperated, Montgomery caught the Germans off-guard with a surprise offensive. Rommel's replacement, General Georg von Stumme, died of a heart attack in the heat of battle, and the overwhelmed German forces fell into disarray. Two days into the Battle of El Alamein, Rommel limped back to the front, but the outcome was already determined. His forces withdrew on November 4 and began a long 2,000-mile retreat west.

Montgomery delivered, shattering the Desert Fox's aura of invincibility. The Germans were on the run, and even worse news awaited Rommel: An Allied force some 100,000 strong led by American general Dwight Eisenhower landed in Morocco and Algeria on November 8.

Operation Torch introduced to the world two of the finest American military minds of the war: General Dwight Eisenhower (below, left) and Lieutenant General George Patton (below, right).

Rommel realized at once that his 70,000 undersupplied, exhausted men were in danger of being trapped between Montgomery's Eighth Army and the fresh troops to the west. "This spelled the end of the army in Africa," he glumly recorded in his diary.

The "soft underbelly" of the European continent—as Winston Churchill labeled operations in and around the Mediterranean—eventually proved anything but for the Allies. The decision to proceed with the Eisenhower-led landings in North Africa, codenamed Torch, tested the strength of the Allied alliance and illustrated the drastically different needs and goals of the "Big Three." Eisen-

Torch was the largest landing operation ever attempted at the time. Some 2,000 Allied vessels (top right) landed in North Africa in November 1942. Aboard the ships, inexperienced American GIs (above) prepare for their first taste of battle.

hower had arrived in England in June 1942 with the intention of planning a cross-channel invasion of France for 1943. But the British insisted that such a plan was premature and refused to endorse the operation, code-named Roundup. They offered Torch—a plan to knock the Italians out of the war—as an alternative strategy, and the Americans eventually relented. If the Americans were disappointed by the postponement of the cross-channel invasion, the Soviets, who were dying in ghastly numbers on the eastern front, were livid. Franklin Roosevelt had promised Josef Stalin a second front by 1942. To the Soviets, an invasion of North Africa not only failed to qualify as a second front but also called into question the western allies' commitment to confront the Wehrmacht at all.

Torch was a cruel baptism for the American troops. The landings on the African coast got off to a rocky start when the occupying French colonial forces, which the Americans had been assured would be friendly, resisted. Only a deal with Vichy France's commander in chief, Admiral Jean Darlan, allowed the landings to continue. More trouble lay ahead. After his lengthy retreat, Rommel received reinforcements and lashed back at his pursuers. While holding off the Eighth Army in southern Tunisia behind a strong defensive position, he launched a sharp counterattack in mid-February against the Allied forces advancing eastward from Algeria.

Rommel's blow fell most heavily on the untried, poorly led units of the United States II Corps defending the Kasserine Pass. The result was a humbling defeat for the American army. The thinly armored, under-gunned American tanks proved no match for German panzers as entire American battalions were wiped out. Casualties among the infantry also ran high, and more than 2,400 GIs, bewildered by the ferocity of the German attack, simply surrendered.

The American high command was shocked by their troops' poor performance. Eisenhower quickly relieved

Rommel's first defeat was celebrated around the Allied world (newspaper, inset). Although his forces jolted the Americans at Kasserine Pass in February 1943, the numerical superiority of the Allied forces, gradually overwhelmed his forces, and Germans began to surrender (left).

How U. S. Aid Reached Egypt In Nick of Time

DETROIT TIMES

DETROIT, MICHIGAN, THURSDAY, DECEMBER 17, 1942 — 42 PAGES — THREE CENTS

Night Edition

ROMMEL ARMY IS CUT IN TWO

Drinking Cut By Canada For Duration

All Sales Curtailed; Liquor Advertising Banned After Feb. 1

A WIFE'S WELCOME FOR CAPTAIN COOL

Capt. Cool Home

U. S. to Ease Meat Quota For Detroit

Wickard's Order to Permit Drawing on 1943 Allotment

Fierce Islanders Fight for U. S.

Polynesians in Only Native Unit Serving Under American Flag

Afrika Korps Now Facing Annihilation

Brilliant British Blow Splits Axis Column West of El Agheila

CAIRO, Dec. 17 (UP)—British forces in Libya have cut Field Marshal Erwin Rommel's fleeing Axis army in two, a middle eastern command communique said today.

Roosevelt Mum on Brown

The Weather

Miss Victory Puts Job First

RAF Raids Reich, Also Mines Sea

The War Fronts

Robert Taylor, Wife Ask Names Legalized

Zoot Suit Youths Held

Three Believed Linked to Early Morning Holdups of War Factory Workers, Possibly Killing

In the Times TODAY

Lansing, Pontiac, Saginaw, Bay City, Flint, Ft. Custer News on Page 33

Major General Lloyd Fredendall, commander of the demoralized II Corps, and replaced him with Major General George Patton, who soon whipped the corps into fighting shape. The Americans learned from their trial-by-fire experiences in North Africa, and the Allies soon regained the initiative. In April 1943 the Allies cornered Rommel's army in a small pocket near the coastal cities of Bizerte and Tunis. Rommel himself was not on hand for the subsequent denouement; Hitler had secretly ordered the popular commander home to avoid the mortification of having him captured. But Hitler stubbornly refused to withdraw Rommel's men. Some 275,000 veteran troops fell into Allied hands in Tunisia in early May.

At the Casablanca Conference in January 1943, Roosevelt and Churchill had agreed upon the next Allied offensive: an invasion of Sicily—codenamed Husky—scheduled for the summer of 1943. At dawn on July 10, elements of the U.S. Seventh Army—led by Patton—and Montgomery's Eighth Army waded ashore on five separate beaches along the south coast. For the first time in history, an amphibious invasion was supported by large-scale airborne landings as the U.S. 82d Airborne Division parachuted into drop zones behind enemy lines.

A beachhead was secured within a day by some 80,000 Allied troops, and Patton turned his divisions west toward Palermo while Montgomery started up the eastern coast. As the campaign slowly gained momentum, a personal rivalry developed between Patton and Montgomery. The two men could hardly have been more different, but they did share one characteristic: a love of publicity.

Yet their problems were tame compared to the tensions between the two Axis armies. Some Italian units fought tenaciously, while others surrendered or deserted en masse. "Ninety percent of the Italian army are cowards and do not want to fight," one German division commander said. The Germans at times found themselves defending sectors of the front entirely on their own.

On July 22, Patton's Third Infantry Division triggered a political crisis in Italy when it captured Palermo, Sicily's largest city. King Victor Emmanuel III subsequently demanded Benito Mussolini's resignation, adding, "At this moment you are the most hated man in Italy." The Duce, Italy's dictator for 21 years, was quickly

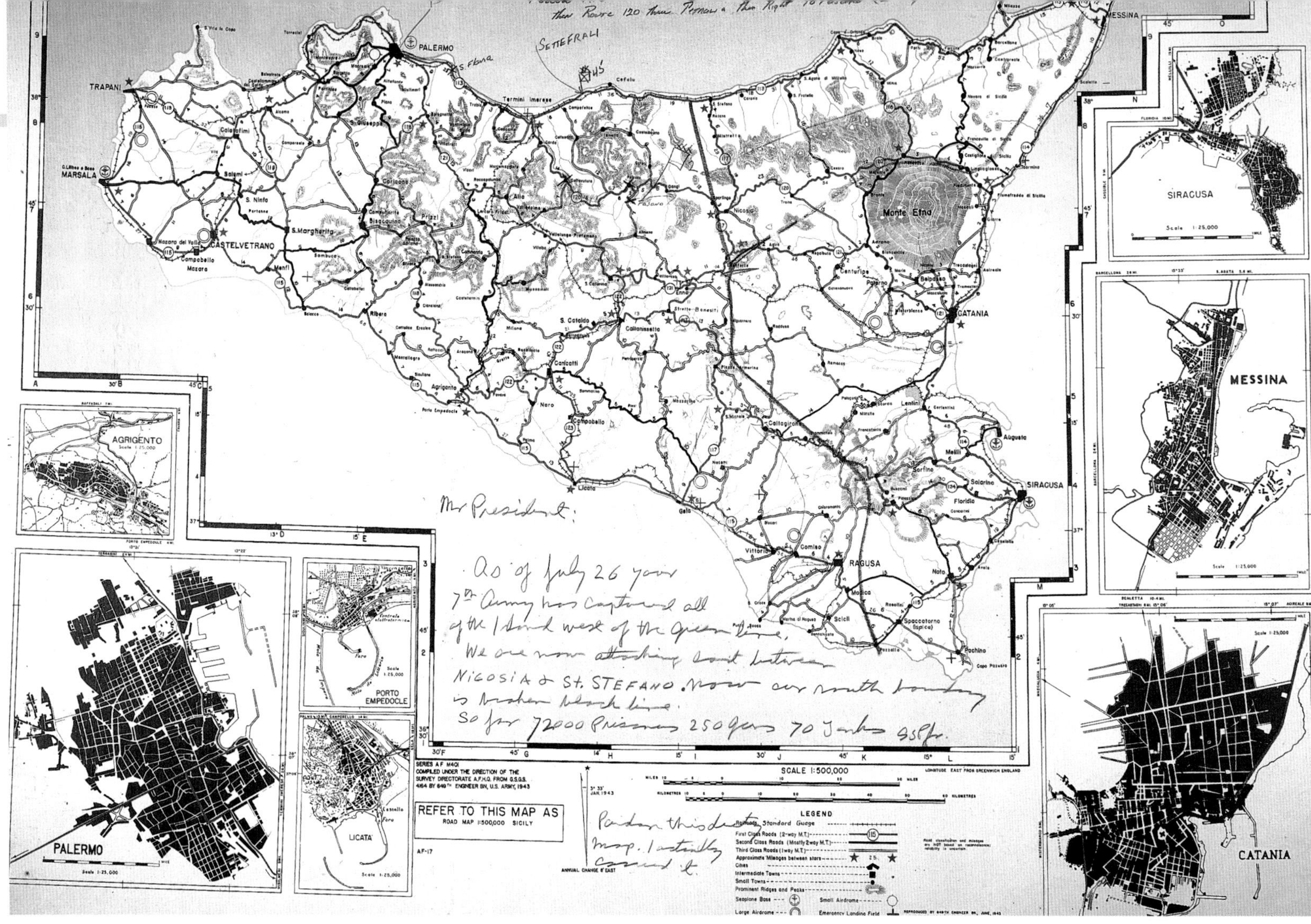

Under Patton's command, the American Seventh Army became a formidable fighting force during Operation Husky—the Allied invasion of Sicily. Patton was so proud of his men that he wrote a glowing progress report to President Roosevelt on a map of the island (above).

arrested and interned on the island of Ponza. Many Italians were jubilant—"Finally we can say what we think," a Roman resident rejoiced. "We can breathe." Adolf Hitler, however, was furious at the political chaos in Rome and threatened to assume civil and military control of the country. Only when the new Italian government pledged to remain in the war did Hitler's threats subside.

As German prospects diminished in Sicily, the Führer authorized Field Marshal Albert Kesselring, the commander in chief of the Southern Theater, to conduct a fighting retreat to the northern tip of the island. On August 8 Kesselring tempted Hitler's wrath by ordering an evacuation across the two-mile-wide Straits of Messina to the toe of the Italian boot. Surprisingly, Hitler allowed the operation to proceed. When it was finished, 40,000 German troops and their equipment, 10,000 vehicles, and some 70,000 loyal Italian soldiers had escaped to safety. To much fanfare, Patton beat Montgomery to the city of Messina (by a few hours), but the two commanders, in their zeal to outdo one another, had simply chased the Germans off the island rather than capturing them. Sicily was secure, but the German troops who escaped to the Italian mainland took up strong defensive positions and awaited the next Allied amphibious assault.

In spite of its promise to Hitler, the Italian government was eager to make peace with the Allies. Suspecting treachery, Hitler sent German reinforcements and advised Wehrmacht units throughout Italy to be prepared to disarm their Italian comrades in the event an armistice should be announced. Kesselring put his addi-

tional forces to good use. He shrewdly deduced that the likeliest Allied invasion spot on the Italian mainland would be via the Gulf of Salerno and stationed the 16th Panzer Division in defensive positions near the coast.

Landing on the morning of September 9, exactly where Kesselring had predicted, General Mark Clark's U.S. Fifth Army met fierce resistance. Three days later a strong German counterattack, spearheaded by tanks, almost broke through to the invasion beaches. "Enemy resistance is collapsing," the German commander on the spot cabled Kesselring. Clark considered withdrawing from the beaches, and Berlin boasted of a "second Dunkirk." But concentrated Allied naval gunfire bombarded the Germans with 11,000 tons of shells and helped drive the Wehrmacht back. The relentless naval and air assault gradually weakened Kesselring's forces, and with the British Eighth Army advancing north from their landing site in the Gulf of Taranto, Kesselring pulled his troops back on September 15.

One week earlier Italy had signed an armistice with the Allies. But Allied soldiers who thought the war in Italy was over were grossly mistaken. Germany, disgusted by its ally's double-cross, quickly seized control of Rome.

Although Germany was now at war with Italy, Hitler refused to turn his back on Mussolini. He ordered German commandos to rescue the Duce from his mountaintop chalet. They spirited him away to a warm reunion with Hitler, who installed him as the head of a fascist regime in northern Italy. The once-haughty Mussolini, now a broken man scorned by his own people, would rule this rump domain as a Nazi puppet for the next year and a half.

The Allies, meanwhile, faced a slow, grinding advance up the Italian boot. The Germans were entrenched behind a seemingly endless series of river lines and mountain ranges, and they had also gained a new ally—the Italian weather. Autumn rains turned the region's inadequate roads into impassable quagmires. "Our troops were living in almost inconceivable misery," wrote famed war correspondent Ernie Pyle. "Thousands had not been dry for weeks. Other thousands lay at night in the high mountains with the temperature below freezing and the thin snow sifting over them." The grueling campaign for Rome would drag on for another eight months.

Italy's sudden collapse (newspaper, inset) exposed the instability of Mussolini's regime. The Allies landed in Italy on September 3, and Marshal Pietro Badoglio (above, with Eisenhower) agreed to an armistice only five days later. Mussolini would be rescued (top left) by German troops, but his political credibility was destroyed.

DESERT SHOWDOWN
Two British soldiers accept the surrender of a German panzer crew (above) at El Alamein, a railway station about 60 miles west of Alexandria. Montgomery, who had twice as many troops and tanks under his command as Rommel, forced the Desert Fox to fight a static, set-piece battle that limited the panzers' mobility.

ROAD TO RETREAT
German soldiers (right) reload a long-range 88-mm antitank gun. German artillery failed to hold off the Allied thrust at El Alamein, but deadly minefields—nicknamed "Devil's gardens" by the Germans who laid them—slowed the advance and helped allow Rommel's beaten army to escape.

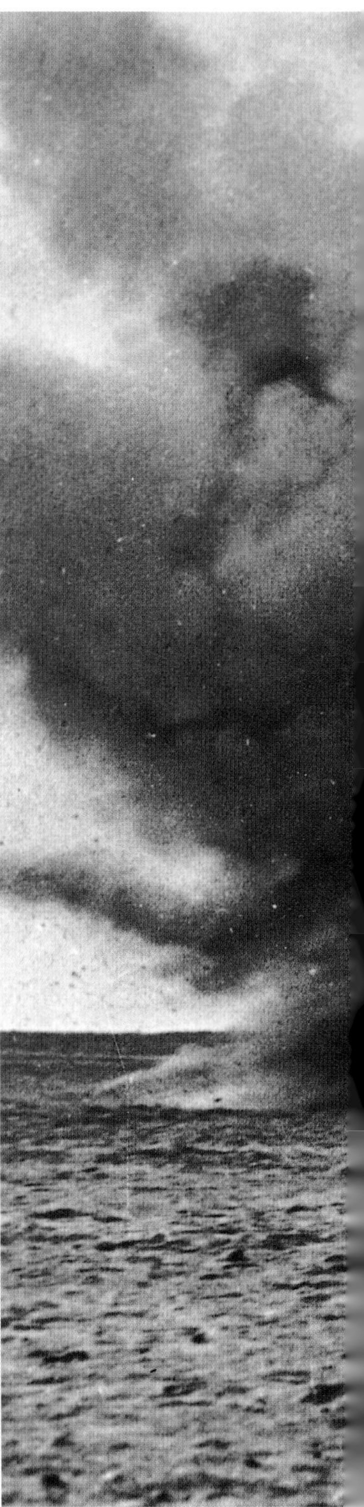

GUARDED ADVANCE
British soldiers (above) take cover behind a deserted German panzer. Rommel abandoned many tanks and other vehicles during his retreat because he simply didn't have the fuel to move them. Montgomery's cautious pursuit spared the fleeing army but cemented the battle's verdict. "Before Alamein we survived," Churchill said. "After Alamein we conquered."

NIGHT FIGHT
Commonwealth troops (left) fire at German positions near the Mareth Line on March 16, 1943. The Mareth Line was a 25-mile chain of forts and barricades built by the French in 1939 to guard against Italian aggression from Libya. When the Germans finally retreated from the Line on March 26, there was nothing left to stop the Allies from racing north into Tunisia.

TEAMWORK
After chasing the Axis up the Tunisian coastal plain, crewmen of an American Sherman tank (below) joyfully greet the crew of a British armored vehicle near Kairouan in April 1943. "It's good to see somebody besides a Nazi," said one American soldier.

WESTWARD PURSUIT
A pack of British Crusader tanks (left) sweeps across the North African desert after the victory at El Alamein. Rommel had begun to withdraw when an order from Hitler arrived, commanding his forces to hold. Once the retreat started, however, the exodus became impossible for Rommel to halt. In the end, 30,000 Axis soldiers surrendered to the Allies.

OVER HILL

A battalion of U.S. Rangers (above) marches over mountainous terrain in North Africa in January 1943. Three months after the Torch landings, the Anglo-American invasion forces were still learning how to fight as a cohesive unit. Internal political crises—especially after the North African French forces joined the Allies—were just as troubling as military difficulties. On the battlefield, however, American soldiers proved themselves quick studies.

NEXT STOP: TUNIS

American sergeants George McGray and Bernard Haber (right) consult a map of Tunisia in April 1943 during the Allies' final drive toward Tunis. By May 13 they had taken the port city and permanently evicted Axis forces from North Africa.

HEADCOUNT
American soldiers (left) add to a collection of German helmets gathered during the North African campaign. In addition to the 275,000 POWs, approximately 40,000 Axis soldiers were killed in the defense of Tunisia. As Axis resistance diminished in North Africa, Mussolini's quest for an African empire vanished.

SICILIAN WELCOME
General Patton's troops (left) roll through Palermo on July 23, 1943. The liberation of the northwestern Sicilian city won headlines for Patton but did little to further the strategic objective of the Allied mission: the capture of Messina on the northeast coast.

BRIT GRIT
Soldiers of the Sixth Battalion, the Royal Innsikilling Fusiliers (above), storm a dwelling in the eastern Sicilian town of Centuripe. While the Americans drove northwest against inferior Italian opposition, the British faced elite German forces on the east coast of the island. Hitler had no intention of giving up. "Sicily must be made into a Stalingrad," he said. "We must hold out."

BLOOD BROTHERS
An American medical officer (right) attends to a wounded soldier as sympathetic Sicilian women watch. The Allies suffered 19,000 casualties during the 38-day campaign to capture the island. However, those numbers could have been worse, had most Italians felt less cordial toward the Americans. "In the very remotest and most ancient town," wrote war correspondent Ernie Pyle, "we found that half the people had relatives in America."

383

NO PLACE TO HIDE
Four American GIs (above) attempt to take cover on a mesh landing mat as Luftwaffe bombs burst in the Gulf of Salerno behind them. The day before the invasion, the Allies had heard news of Italy's surrender—an announcement that touched off celebrations aboard the invasion ships. This, as one historian put it, was "a psychological disaster" since the Germans would defend Italy ferociously, regardless of the armistice.

OPERATION AVALANCHE
With their landing craft creating a smokescreen, Allied soldiers (left) unload gear during the launch of Operation Avalanche, the code-name for the Allies' amphibious assault on mainland Italy. The steep gradient of the beaches at Salerno made it possible for the large landing craft to run up on the sand and unload troops directly onto shore.

HEAVY GUNNERS
Members of the British Shropshire Yeomanry man their 5.5-inch howitzer in Italy on September 22, 1943. In the first nine days of the Allied assault on mainland Italy, the invaders were nearly thrust back into the sea and suffered heavy casualties. British general Sir Harold Alexander praised the Allied resistance under the German counterattack, saying, "It was an impressive example of stubborn doggedness in defense."

SWEET RELIEF

Having traversed the rugged terrain south of the city, weary Allied advance units are greeted by streams of grateful Neapolitans (left) on October 1, 1943. German field marshal Kesselring and his forces had occupied Naples for two weeks, carrying out a systematic demolition of the city that spared only monasteries, churches, museums, hospitals, and historic buildings. Anything that might benefit the Allies was destroyed.

KEEPING WATCH

Allied soldiers (right) scan the horizon for enemy activity during the Allied invasion of Italy. Most Italian soldiers had quit their arms and given up the fight, but the German occupiers resisted fiercely. The Allies suffered nearly 10,000 casualties in the first 10 days of the invasion but successfully completed the war's first large-scale opposed landing in Europe.

INLAND ADVANCE

Under smokescreen, U.S. Rangers (left) breach a rise in the mountains outside Naples. As they fought their way inland over increasingly rugged and roadless terrain, the Allies were forced to rely on packtrains of mules to carry their supplies. The U.S. Army sent out a desperate call at home for mule shoes, nails, halters, and packs, as well as for blacksmiths, veterinarians, and mule skinners who knew how to operate packtrains and manage the animals.

Bernard Montgomery

Highly meticulous, fiercely determined, and slightly eccentric, the maverick "Monty" seized the international spotlight with his victory over Rommel at El Alamein—and never relinquished it.

OUTFOXING ROMMEL

Sporting his trademark beret (inset) and standing in the turret of his Grant tank, Montgomery (top) watches the beginning of the Wehrmacht retreat from El Alamein. A set-piece battle—Montgomery's specialty—the conflict was the first defeat for German commander Erwin Rommel and sent the Desert Fox scurrying in retreat out of western Egypt. Montgomery chased him across Libya and into Tunisia—a pursuit of 2,000 miles—earning Montgomery a knighthood and a promotion to General.

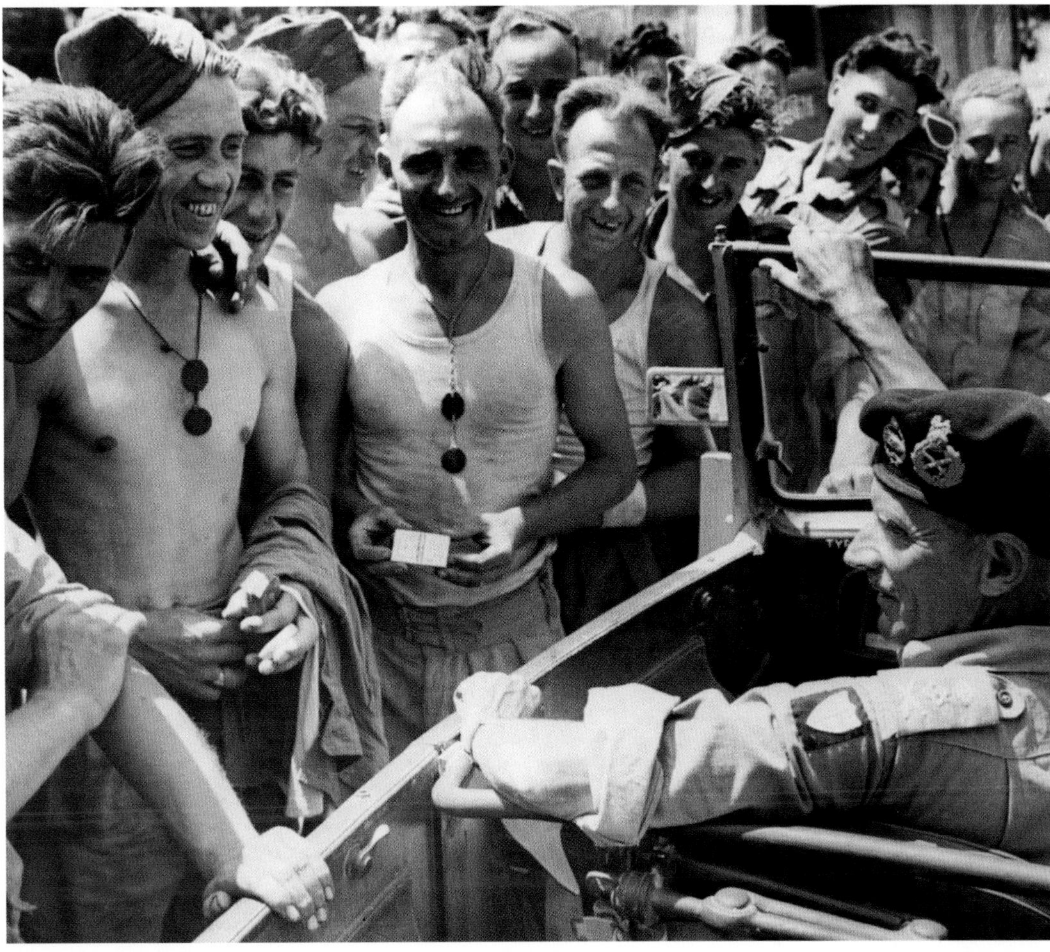

MAJOR MONTGOMERY
Commissioned into the Royal Warwickshire Regiment in 1908, Montgomery (above, right) was wounded in October 1914 during the World War I battle of the Aisne. After being hospitalized in England, he returned to the front in early 1916 as a brigade major.

THE COMMON TOUCH
British "sappers," or demolition experts, greet Montgomery (above, in car) warmly near the front line in Sicily. Though often prickly with men of his rank or higher, Montgomery was famous for his ability to win the confidence of soldiers. As E. T. Williams, Montgomery's intelligence chief, wrote, "Most awkward to serve alongside, impossible to serve over, [Montgomery] was an excellent man to serve under."

COUNTDOWN TO BATTLE
Montgomery (right, pointing) reviews a map and discusses tactics with officers of his Eighth Army prior to encountering Rommel in the North African desert. Remaking the defeated and demoralized Eighth in his own image, Montgomery purged most of its officers and replaced them with men in whom he placed complete trust and confidence.

PERSONALITY CLASH
While the cocky and egomaniacal Montgomery (above, right) clashed most famously with U.S. general George Patton, he irritated almost everyone of rank that he came in contact with. British prime minister Winston Churchill (above, left) described Montgomery as "indomitable in retreat, invincible in advance, insufferable in victory."

Segregation

African Americans in the military faced the same shameful policies of discrimination that generally prevailed in American society during World War II.

BLACK AND WHITE
A poster (inset) calls for cooperation between blacks and whites in the domestic war effort. It is one of the ugly ironies of the U.S. war effort, which vanquished history's most notorious racist, that African Americans were denied basic rights and relegated mostly to support roles in the military. Even those who distinguished themselves in battle, like the famed Tuskegee Airmen (above), returned to a postwar America that still judged a person by the color of his or her skin.

NOT INVITED
Many skilled African-American laborers (above) were excluded from the prosperous wartime economy. Of the 100,000 employers in the aircraft industry in 1940, only 240 were African Americans.

SEPARATE AND SECONDARY
Members of an engineering battalion in Algeria (above) line up for lunch. Like most of the African Americans in the war, these men lived, worked, ate, and slept in segregated units, and they never saw combat. In the U.S. Navy, 95 percent of African Americans were employed as messmen.

STARPOWER
Heavyweight boxing champion Joe Louis (right), who was the first black American hero embraced by all races, lent his name and image to help mobilize African Americans for the war. Louis volunteered for the army in 1942, helped raise money for the war effort, and visited soldiers in military hospitals. Thousands of African Americans were eager to enlist to prove their equality and affirm their status as citizens, deserving of all rights.

INSPECTING THE TROOPS
At a ceremony near Reggio, Italy, Lieutenant General Mark Clark, commander of the Fifth Army, surveys the ranks of the all-African-American 92d Division. Joining the Fifth in the bloody battle for Italy, the 92d excelled; its members received more than 12,000 decorations, including 95 Silver Stars for bravery in action.

Island Fighting

Although the Second Marine Division (badge, below) had gained experience at Guadalcanal, nothing could have prepared them for the carnage that awaited at Tarawa. Marines (left) who landed on the heavily fortified island encountered fierce Japanese resistance.

"I remember exactly the way it looked the day we came up on deck to go ashore," novelist James Jones reminisced about the South Pacific island of Guadalcanal. "The delicious sparkling tropic sea, the long beautiful beach, the minute palms of the copra plantation waving in the sea breeze, the dark green band of jungle, and the dun mass and power of the mountains rising behind it to rocky peaks." But Jones and the thousands of other United States Marines and Army infantrymen who served on Guadalcanal soon discovered that behind the postcard facade of a tropical paradise lay a pestilential hellhole of stifling, disease-ridden jungle and muck-filled swamps inhabited by an extensive menagerie of venomous creatures and insects. Guadalcanal would have been a dangerous place even without a war going on.

When the United States launched its first offensive of World War II against this insignificant speck in the far-off Solomon Islands, few Americans had ever heard of Guadalcanal. It gained importance only because the Japanese were constructing an airstrip there, from which they could threaten the Allied supply line to Australia. The First Marine Division expected a fanatical defense, but to their surprise they landed almost unopposed on August 7, 1942. The few Japanese defenders in the area quickly retreated into the jungle. By the next evening 11,000 Marines had captured the targeted airstrip—which they renamed Henderson Field, after a Marine aviator killed at Midway—along with large quantities of equipment and supplies.

Only a handful of Japanese (below) surrendered on Tarawa. Their suicidal tactics on the island prompted Admiral Nimitz to reconsider Allied strategy for island warfare.

But a Japanese counterattack was already underway. On the night of August 8, seven cruisers and a lone destroyer steamed southeast through the narrow passage known as "the Slot," which ran down the middle of the Solomons. Emerging undetected from a rain squall into the sheltered waters between Guadalcanal and tiny Savo Island, the Japanese column took the American invasion fleet by complete surprise. With superior night-fighting tactics, accurate gunnery, and effective long-range torpedoes, Japanese ships sank four cruisers—killing more than 1,000 sailors—before withdrawing back up the Slot. Four more naval battles during the fall

ALBUQUERQUE JOURNAL

October 27, 1942

Price 5 Cents

Japs Strike on Sea, Land, Air In Battle for Guadalcanal

Allies Increase Grip on Desert Line

Flyers Blast Enemy Ships; U.S. Destroyer Sunk; Plane Carrier Wasp Lost Sept. 15

Willkie Renews Plea for Second Front in Europe

Condemns Censorship That Makes Military, Civil Leaders Supreme

RAPS IMPERIALISM

Reports to the Nation On Trip to War Zones; Fears Loss of Allies

Stalingrad Fight Remains Centered In Factory Area

German Airplanes Kill at Least Eight In Raids on England

TAKE 1450 PRISONERS

Gains in Egypt Being Solidified; Await Tank Clash

City Will Honor U.S. Navy Today

Navy Reports Land Fighting Is 'Heavy'; Dive Bombers and Fortresses Strike Tokyo Cruisers; 22 Planes Shot Down Near Big Airport

When Torpedoes Hit It's Like Earthquake, Say Wasp Survivors

Poll Tax Dealt Committee Blow

Six Go On Trial In Treason Case

American airmen (above) gather for final instructions at Henderson Field, the central objective on Guadalcanal. Fighting for the island was so taxing on pilots that they were cycled out after thirty days of duty. Despite a major offensive in October 1942 (headline, inset) the Japanese withdrew from Guadalcanal in February 1943.

of 1942 produced so many sunken ships that this part of the Slot earned the nickname "Iron Bottom Sound."

Meanwhile, Japanese naval transports landed fresh troops on Guadalcanal, and the beleaguered Americans were fighting desperately to defend a perimeter around Henderson Field. It was the first time that American Marines encountered the enemy face-to-face, and his tenacity, ruthlessness, and utter disregard for the "accepted" rules of war shocked them. Hospital tents, clearly marked with the Red Cross insignia, were bombed and strafed. Japanese soldiers rarely took prisoners and committed suicide rather than be captured themselves. For both sides, Guadalcanal was a brutal, dehumanizing campaign fought under the most horrendous conditions that sapped men's strength and hardened their resolve.

While this battle raged, another campaign was being fought on the large island of New Guinea, 500 miles to the northwest. Japanese units under General Tomitaro Horii, an experienced jungle fighter, accomplished what Allied commanders had thought impossible. The Japanese crossed the Owen Stanley Range, one of the most rugged, forbidding mountain ranges on earth, and advanced to within 32 miles of Port Moresby, a key position in the defense of Australia. Australian troops, with American reinforcements, bravely counterattacked and drove the Japanese back over the mountains to Buna, on New Guinea's north coast. Thousands of Japanese died of starvation and sickness during the retreat; Horii himself drowned while crossing a swollen jungle river. But the mountain range made any Allied offensive almost impossible, and the Japanese dug in and recuperated. General Douglas MacArthur, the supreme commander of Allied forces in the Southwest Pacific, grew impatient, and in November he ordered Lieutenant General Robert Eichelberger "to take Buna or not come back alive."

Eichelberger was one general who led his men from the front. During an attack on Buna, he left a regimen-

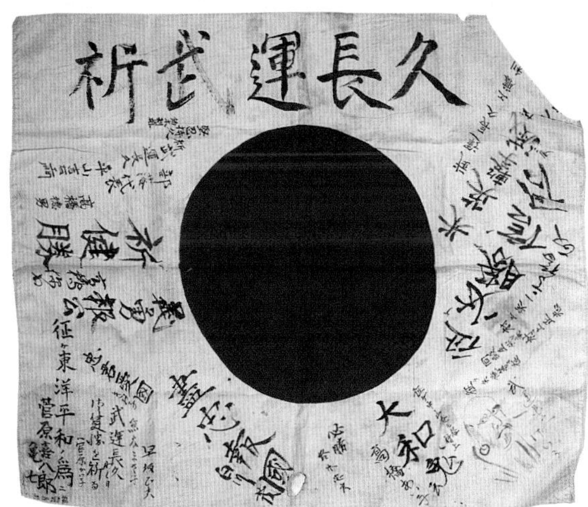

Despite dwindling supplies, the Japanese (above) fought to the end of their endurance on Guadalcanal. Even when defeat was imminent, Japanese officers ordered desperate frontal assaults that forced stunned Americans to slaughter waves of Japanese soldiers (middle). Gifts from home, such as patriotic flags adorned with prayers and slogans (left), urged Japanese soldiers to remember their loyalty to their emperor.

tal command post to move forward among an infantry company that had bogged down. "When I arrived at Buna," he later wrote, "there was a rule against officers wearing insignia of rank at the front because this might draw enemy fire. I was glad on that particular day that there were three stars on my collar, which glittered in the sun. How else would those sick and cast-down soldiers have known their commander was in there with them? They knew, being sensible men, that a bullet is no respecter of rank." After a vicious and costly two-month struggle, Eichelberger's troops took Buna.

Back on Guadalcanal, a climactic naval engagement in November finally turned the tide of the land battle there. The U.S. Navy gained control of the Slot, thus denying supplies and reinforcements to the Japanese forces ashore. Army units relieved the decimated First Marine Division and pushed the Japanese into the far northwest corner of the island. During the first week of February 1943, Japanese destroyers furtively evacuated more than 13,000 emaciated survivors of the Guadalcanal garrison. Those too feeble to make the trip were given hand grenades to blow themselves up when the Americans approached. Altogether, 24,000 Japanese and more than 1,500 Americans died on the hellish island.

One surviving Japanese officer commented bitterly, "We lost the battle. And Japan lost the war." But the victors of Guadalcanal and Buna were not feeling so sanguine in the wake of their success. Tokyo was still 3,000 miles away, and as Lieutenant General George Kenney, commander of the Allied air forces in the southwest Pacific put it, "There are hundreds of Bunas ahead of

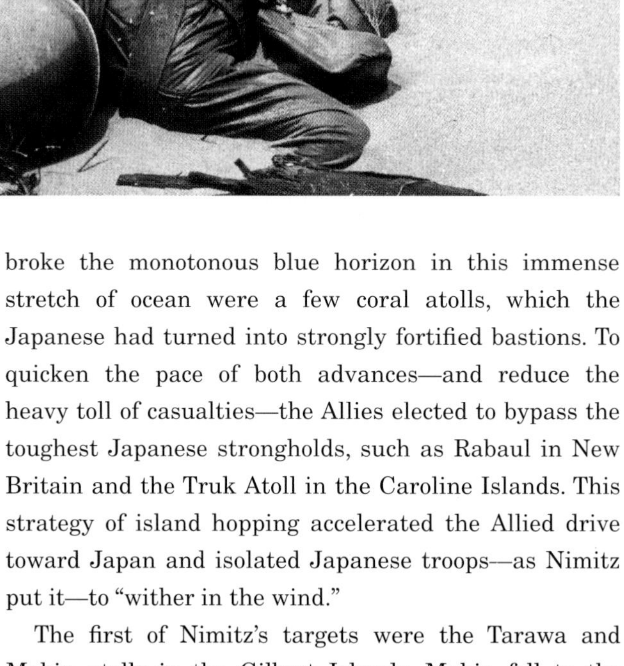

Japan sought to exploit the physical and emotional fatigue of Allied soldiers by dropping leaflets (above) that emphasized the futility of the Allies' struggle for New Guinea. The fight for Buna alone cost the Allies more than 3,000 men, and photographs of dead U.S. soldiers (right) brought Americans at home "directly and without words into the presence of their own dead," according to LIFE magazine.

us." The Japanese had demonstrated dogged determination. "Fortitude is admirable under any flag," Eichelberger acknowledged, "and those Japanese soldiers had it." Kenney added, "The emperor told them to hold, and, believe me, they have held! As to their morale—they still yell out to our troops, 'What's the matter, Yanks? Are you yellow? Why don't you come in and fight?' A few Japanese snipers, asked to surrender after being surrounded, called back, 'If you bastards think you are good enough, come and get us!' "

Nonetheless, the Allies had gained the initiative, and the remainder of the Pacific war would be defined by two separate Allied offensives. The first was led by the flamboyant, publicity-conscious MacArthur. His forces would continue pushing along the north coast of New Guinea from Buna in a series of amphibious end-runs around Japanese defensive positions, while simultaneously climbing the Solomons chain, island by island. The other main thrust, under the command of Admiral Chester Nimitz, would press westward from Hawaii across the vast reaches of the central Pacific toward Japan. All that broke the monotonous blue horizon in this immense stretch of ocean were a few coral atolls, which the Japanese had turned into strongly fortified bastions. To quicken the pace of both advances—and reduce the heavy toll of casualties—the Allies elected to bypass the toughest Japanese strongholds, such as Rabaul in New Britain and the Truk Atoll in the Caroline Islands. This strategy of island hopping accelerated the Allied drive toward Japan and isolated Japanese troops—as Nimitz put it—to "wither in the wind."

The first of Nimitz's targets were the Tarawa and Makin atolls in the Gilbert Islands. Makin fell to the Allies with little resistance, but Tarawa—a few acres of low-lying sand and palm trees surrounded by a coral

reef—was a different story. Admiral Keiji Shibasaki, commander of the garrison's 5,000 crack troops, boasted, "A million men cannot take Tarawa in a hundred years." Nevertheless, the American Second Marine Division came ashore on November 20, 1943. Almost immediately, the operation went terribly wrong. The preinvasion naval bombardment had hardly touched the defenders in their deep concrete bunkers. The Japanese emerged and began blasting the advancing boats with artillery fire. Worse still, American planners had misjudged the tides, and the flat-bottomed landing crafts got hung up on the reef. The Marines had to disembark and wade through hundreds of yards of open water, while exposed to machine-gun fire, just to reach dry land. About half of the soldiers in the first wave were hit before they even made it to the beach.

So many wounded and dead Marines lay strewn along the landing beach that an American tank commander refused to drive his tanks over the carnage. But when he backed his platoon into the water to look for another route ashore, four of the tanks sank into shell holes, drowning the crews; the other two were quickly knocked out by Japanese guns. Those Marines who made it safely ashore began assaulting the Japanese bunkers, one by one. Inching forward in small groups, they methodically demolished them with high explosives or burned the occupants alive with flamethrowers.

Although the fighting was bloody and the costs atrocious, it took three days—not a hundred years—to subdue Japanese resistance on Tarawa. Admiral Shibasaki sent a last radio message to Tokyo before he was killed in his command post, "Our weapons have been destroyed and from now on everyone is attempting a final charge . . . May Japan exist for ten thousand years!" When the firing finally stopped, only 17 Japanese soldiers were alive.

At an appalling price, the U.S. Navy and Marine Corps had learned many hard lessons at Tarawa about the proper way to conduct an amphibious assault against a heavily defended beach. Furthermore, they learned that the Japanese soldier would not give an inch defending his territory and his emperor. Both MacArthur and Nimitz would have many opportunities to make use of these lessons in the coming campaigns.

Lieutenant General Robert Eichelberger (above, near left, in Papua with General Sir Thomas Blamey of Australia) apparently did his job in New Guinea too well. MacArthur shelved him after the Allied victory in Buna because he felt Eichelberger received too much of the credit. In Gona, a Commonwealth chaplain (above) marks the grave of one of the hundreds of dead Allied soldiers. During the fighting, "rotting bodies, sometime week old," wrote British war correspondent Ian Morrison, "formed part of the fortifications."

NATURAL RESOURCES

An Australian soldier (above) uses the stump of a palm tree to steady his aim at Japanese pillboxes during the assault on Buna on January 2, 1943. Control of New Guinea's northern coast was crucial to the Allied strategy in the Pacific. The Japanese were deeply entrenched, and the final drive was bloody and difficult. Although the battle for Buna-Gona did not receive as much attention as Guadalcanal, the fighting was equally savage.

HEIGHT ADVANTAGE

Lieutenant W. M. Finley (left) climbs a tree to operate a new 25-pound gun that had been airlifted to the weary Allied troops in Gona. Although the mountainous jungle of New Guinea posed extreme challenges, Allied troops quickly learned to take advantage of the terrain.

POINT BLANK
An American GI (left) cautiously examines the body of a Japanese sniper moments after exchanging fire at Buna. The Allies secured Buna on January 2, 1943, but it took the Allied infantry nearly two weeks to clean out the extensive network of Japanese bunkers and evacuate the few survivors. Tenacious, honor-bound Japanese soldiers fought to the bitter end, some lying among piles of corpses and shooting at passing Allied patrols. As a precaution, Allied troops took to bayonetting each enemy corpse.

DON'T LOOK BACK

On the deck of a U.S. aircraft carrier, a sign (right) alerts departing pilots, "Proceed: Without *Hornet*." The U.S.S. *Hornet* was sunk by Japanese destroyers during the Battle of Santa Cruz while its own planes were bombarding Japanese carriers. The carrier *Enterprise* was also badly damaged at Santa Cruz but managed to limp home. The naval battles around Guadalcanal were called "a rough school for the U.S. Navy" by one American historian; nevertheless, American naval forces ultimately managed to repulse the Japanese navy.

SINKING PROSPECTS

The efforts of both sides to reinforce and supply their men in the Solomon Islands led to several major battles at sea. The Japanese had gained naval superiority when they won the Battle of Savo Island in August 1942, and they used their advantage to begin landing troops on the larger island of Guadalcanal. After the Allies gained control of the surrounding waters, however, Japanese vessels (left) were sent to the bottom of "Iron Bottom Sound" in increasing numbers.

SPECTACULAR END

The carrier U.S.S. *Wasp* (right) burns in the South Pacific, after she was hit by enemy submarine torpedoes on September 15, 1942. A victim of the protracted battle for control of supply lanes near Guadalcanal, the *Wasp* was escorting ships and supplies when she was hit. Five epic naval clashes occurred near the Solomons between August and November 1942.

JAP CV
PROCEED
WITHOUT
HORNET

WATCH AND WAIT

Admiral Harry Hill and his staff (above) watch the invasion of Betio, the Tarawa Atoll's largest island, from the bridge of the U.S.S. *Maryland*. Bombers from American carriers assaulted the Japanese positions on the morning of the landing, and the *Maryland* and other battleships hurled 3,000 tons of explosives on the beaches during the day. The Second Marine Division landed believing that the enemy had been decimated by the assault, but the Japanese had created virtually impenetrable concrete bunkers and were poised to repel the American assault.

PROCEEDING WITH CAUTION

The 27th Infantry Division (right) wades ashore the burning island of Butaritari, in the Makin Atoll. Though a probing raid a few months earlier had met little resistance and the invasion force outnumbered the Japanese defenders 20-to-1, it took four days for the Allies to clear the island.

HELLISH WASTELAND

A squad of Marines (left) gathers behind a pack howitzer during the fierce fighting for Tarawa. Reports of the savage struggle (note the two bullet holes in the helmet of the standing GI) on the jungle atoll and photos of dead Allied soldiers appalled many Americans back in the United States. Admiral Nimitz received several letters from the parents of dead soldiers and sailors that blamed him for the "Tarawa fiasco."

LONE SURVIVOR

American GIs lead a Japanese soldier (right) into captivity on Tarawa. Japanese POWs were often stripped of their clothes and gear both to expose hidden grenades and to prevent attempted suicides. Of the nearly 5,000 Japanese soldiers who defended the "hornets' nest" on Tarawa, only 17 survived a series of Japanese suicide charges. Lieutenant Norman Thomas radioed his commanding officer, "We are killing them as fast as they come at us."

CLOSE COMBAT
Rear Admiral Howard Kingman, who commanded the bombardment of Betio prior to the Marine invasion, told his troops "We will not neutralize Betio. . . . We will obliterate it!" But 1,000 Japanese construction workers and 1,200 Korean laborers had spent more than a year creating bunkers dug into the coral, with eight-foot walls and with concrete and steel roofs. The bunkers were virtually unscathed by the bombing, and it turned out that the only way to take the pillboxes was to climb on top of them and drop explosives inside (above).

FROZEN FATE

American soldiers pass a Japanese corpse (left) near Holtz Bay on the island of Attu. The Japanese had invaded the western Aleutian island in June 1942. Their presence was intolerable to the American military, but weather conditions and a shortage of manpower delayed a counterinvasion until May 1943. The outnumbered Japanese soldiers held the Americans off for three weeks, but at the cost of virtually its entire 2,300-man force. Only 29 Japanese survived.

CLEAN-UP CREW

American soldiers hunt for holdouts on Attu (right). After 20 days of fighting, the northern branch of the landing force gained the high ground and isolated the Japanese on the narrow eastern end of the island. Rather than surrender or retreat, the Japanese dug an extensive system of trenches, which they defended to the death.

MASSACRE BAY

Members of the Seventh Infantry Division (left) board a transport bound for Massacre Bay, on the southern side of Attu. Unremitting fog stalled the Allied landing and veiled a Japanese counterattack. Nevertheless, the entire Allied operation was completed in three weeks.

Between world wars, Japan fell under the influence of militants who believed their nation's *Yamato Damashii*—its unique spiritual strength—would allow them to overcome superior enemy forces.

PATRIOTIC ZEAL

The potent, almost religious nationalism that drove the Japanese war effort had deep roots in the country's history. In the tradition of samurai warriors, who were early practitioners of Buddhism, even Buddhist monks (left) were able to reconcile their non-violent religious beliefs with the armed defense of the homeland.

The Spirit of Japan

URBAN FARMING

Japanese students (left) plant rice in Ueno Park, Tokyo. Every arable inch of Japan was planted with crops in an effort to relieve food shortages. In some cases, entire schools were transferred to the countryside so that students could help farm the land.

CHILD'S PLAY

Japanese girls (above) learn how to operate lathes so that they can replace older workers who are more valuable to the nation's defense. The inexperience of the youths, however, and the gradual decline in nutrition limited their contributions.

HOMEFRONT

Women (right) of Japan's *Tonarigumi*—neighborhood associations—prepare parcels to be sent to their soldiers at the front. In 1943, the Japanese government relaxed some of the nation's most sacred traditions in order to fuel its war effort. Women, who historically did not work outside the home, were encouraged to join the workforce. Those who did not participate were branded unpatriotic.

PRIDE OF PLACE

A woman (left) scans the sky for American bombers during an air raid drill in Kawasaki. Local associations, which numbered more than a million by 1944, organized Japan's civil defense and helped to heighten national pride and unity.

Hollywood at War

Even before Pearl Harbor, Hollywood realized that patriotism was profitable. America's entry into the war ushered in a wave of propaganda films that reassured the nation that her cause was just.

NAZI TRAMP

Charlie Chaplin (above) was one of the first filmmakers to attack Europe's fascist regimes. "The Great Dictator" (poster, inset) was a satire that took on a whole different meaning by the time it was released in October 1940. Hollywood, however, still had to defend itself against those who accused films of "war-mongering." Darryl Zanuck, head of Twentieth Century-Fox was unapologetic. "If you accuse us of producing films in the interest of preparedness and national defense . . . you are right."

BRIT GRIT

In the Academy Award-winning film "Mrs. Miniver" (1942), Greer Garson and Walter Pidgeon (above) personified the quiet heroism that allowed Great Britain to endure the German blitz.

MR. CAPRA GOES TO WAR

Colonel Frank Capra (above, right)—of "It's a Wonderful Life" fame—made several propaganda films, including "Tunisian Victory," which told the story of the North African campaign.

PLAY IT AGAIN

In "Casablanca" (1942; poster, right), Humphrey Bogart's Rick abandons his deep-rooted sense of indifference and neutrality and joins the struggle against Nazi oppression.

HALT HITLER

Warner Brothers's "Confessions of a Nazi Spy" (1939) was a heavy-handed anti-Nazi film that was eventually banned by several countries who didn't want to offend Germany. German diplomats were portrayed as violent war-mongerers who were so evil that Edward G. Robinson was actually believable as the good guy.

THE COLOR OF BATAAN

Although most war movies of the time made special effort to include characters representing every ethnicity, African Americans were often ignored. It wasn't until 1943's "Bataan" that an African American (played by Kenneth Spencer, left) was credited with contributing in the battlefield to the American war effort.

Air Front: Europe

A B-17 (left) of the American Eighth Air Force (patch, below) carries out a precision bombing raid on a Focke-Wulf airplane plant in Marienburg, Germany, in January 1943. Such raids were fraught with danger as Allied planes had to contend with both enemy fighters and antiaircraft flak.

At midnight on May 30, 1942, two British Stirling bombers approached the German city of Cologne. The Rhine River shimmered 15,000 feet below in the light of a full moon, pointing the way to the center of the ancient city. The Stirlings were pathfinders, aircraft whose incendiary bombs would mark the way for an air raid of unprecedented magnitude. Behind the pathfinders stretched three "bomber streams"—a fleet of over 1,000 aircraft—nearly the entire Royal Air Force Bomber Command. British planners hoped to overwhelm Germany's air defenses and deal a pulverizing blow, not only to Cologne's industrial facilities, but also to the workers who manned them.

At 12:47 a.m., as the pathfinders released their bombs over the center of Cologne, they were met by searchlight-guided antiaircraft fire. When the first wave of heavy bombers arrived, the German defenders found themselves increasingly unable to cope with the overwhelming number of targets. The heart of Cologne was already ablaze by the time the second wave of British heavies arrived carrying loads of high-explosive bombs. The city had been under savage bombardment for more than an hour when the third and final wave of Lancaster and Halifax bombers arrived at 2:25. As they dropped their payload and turned for home, British aircrews witnessed a sea of fire over three miles long and two miles wide. The column of smoke from the burning city rose to 15,000 feet, and the glow of the fires was visible as far away as the Dutch coast, some 125 miles away.

A British ground crew (below) reviews a series of photos from a night sortie against Germany. At the start of the war the RAF attempted daylight bombings but soon found night raids to be more effective.

At dawn, residents of Germany's third-largest city emerged from the debris to find a scene of nightmarish devastation. More than 600 acres of Cologne lay in ruins. Nearly 500 residents were dead and at least 45,000 were homeless. Some 250 factories—central to the German war effort—were destroyed or badly damaged. As refugees streamed out of the city, German authorities were powerless to censor the news of the terrible raid. The cost was surprisingly light for the RAF—only 39 of the 1,046 bombers deployed in the raid were lost.

British Lancaster bombers (above) fly in formation on a daylight mission. The most heavily used bombers in the RAF, Lancasters flew more than 156,000 missions during the war. On January 1, 1944, the RAF began a series of massive bombing raids on the German capital of Berlin (center). By the end of March 6,000 Berliners had been killed and some 1.5 million were left homeless.

The architect of Operation Millennium—as the raid on Cologne was called—was Air Chief Marshal Arthur Harris. Harris had been appointed to lead the RAF Bomber Command in February 1942, at a time when Britain's strategic bombing offensive against Germany suffered from a lack of effective aircraft and poor operational experience. The heroic performance of the RAF in the Battle of Britain had not translated to success in the skies over Germany. Heavy losses in planes and aircrews convinced the British that daylight raids, unescorted by fighter aircraft, stood little chance of success against determined enemy fighters and antiaircraft defenses. Even when it confined operations to nighttime raids, the RAF seemed to be fighting a losing battle.

To penetrate Germany's territory and strike at industrial targets, British aircraft had to penetrate the Kammhuber Line, a twenty-mile-wide barrier of searchlight batteries and fighter squadrons that stretched from Denmark to the Franco-Swiss border. When they were alerted to an air raid, searchlight crews would lock their beams onto a bomber and guide waiting Luftwaffe double-engine fighters to individual targets. The introduction of radar-controlled searchlights and the powerful ground-based Würzburg radar system made the Kammhuber Line even more formidable. Even if a bomber survived the Line's defenses, the crew still faced the batteries of antiaircraft guns that ringed German cities.

By November 1941, RAF casualties had reached unacceptable levels, and by early 1942, Bomber Command had been reduced to fewer than 378 operational aircraft, of which only 70 were modern heavy bombers. But Prime Minister Winston Churchill remained convinced that strategic bombing would win the war. "There is one thing that will bring [Hitler] down, and that is an absolutely devastating exterminating attack by very heavy bombers from this country upon the Nazi homeland," he wrote in 1941. With his urging, British planners initiated a devel-

RAF commander Arthur "Bomber" Harris (above, left) welcomes home a Halifax bomber crew that was rescued after 16 hours in a dinghy in the North Sea.

In every country, victory abroad directly depended upon conservation at home. The British poster at right reminded citizens of the importance of coal to the war effort.

opment program that promised the delivery of 3,500 new bombers by the spring of 1942.

Along with improved weaponry, the government presented Harris with a new operational directive. The Air Ministry authorized him to carry out his bombing missions "without restraint." Bomber Command's new objective was to be "focused on the morale of the enemy civil population and in particular of industrial workers." Harris didn't hesitate. On March 28 a force of over 200 planes firebombed the historic Baltic port of Lübeck, destroying over half of the city. In the following month the RAF flattened the nearby Heinkel assembly plant at Rostock. In June the RAF launched a 900-plane raid on the submarine facilities at Bremen.

For all the destruction wrought by the RAF—Harris claimed that his bombers were destroying two German cities a month—the Germans proved to be remarkably resilient. Within a month of the RAF firebomb attack, Cologne's industry returned to normal production. German defenses also improved. In the spring of 1942 the Germans assigned additional fighter squadrons and installed a double line of powerful Freya early warning radars to the western front.

The arrival of the United States' Eighth Army Air Force, however, helped to lessen the mounting British losses and intensified the pressure on German cities. Commanded by General Ira Eaker, the Eighth Army Air Force had been slowly gathering strength in England since the winter of 1942. But U.S. and British commands faced a fundamental difference of opinion. Despite the RAF's failed attempts, Eaker believed high-level daylight bombing was the key to destroying Germany's

Crew of the U.S. Eighth Air Force (above) don their "Mae West" life preservers before boarding their B-17. The life preservers were nicknamed for the busty actress because of their shape once inflated. The "flying fortress," noted for its long range and heavy defensive armament, was developed as a self-defending bomber; German fighters quickly proved otherwise.

industrial might. The critical piece of equipment for such bombing, he maintained, was the formidable B-17 "Flying Fortress." The massive, 65,000-pound "Fort" was powered by four 1,200-horsepower engines capable of lifting a 6,000-pound bomb load to altitudes as high as 26,000 feet. The Americans were confident that the "Forts," teamed with B-24 Liberators and operating in tight formations, could defend themselves against anything that the Germans could throw at them.

Initial American efforts were not encouraging. A dozen daytime raids against targets in Belgium, France, and the Netherlands yielded limited results, and a single attempt to destroy German U-boat bases on the French coast cost the Americans nearly 100 aircraft. Despite British criticism of the Americans' "poor showing," Churchill approved plans for more daylight raids. "By bombing the devils around the clock," he said, "we can prevent the German defenses from getting any rest." Accordingly, on January 27, 1943, the Americans launched their first mission over Germany, a costly raid against submarine manufacturing centers in the North Sea port of Wilhelmshaven.

By March an improved automatic flight system that gave the bombardier control of the aircraft during the bombing run allowed American airmen to damage seven U-boats at the Vegesack shipyard. But losses remained high. Eaker pestered Washington with demands for more planes. Finally, convinced by Eaker's projections of potential operations, Washington promised him an additional 944 bombers and replacement personnel by the summer.

As the Americans built up their strength, the RAF launched attacks against German industrial targets in the Ruhr Valley. Beginning in the spring RAF bombers attacked the Krupp steel works at Essen and continued with raids on Mulheim, Oberhausen, and Duisburg. Aircraft using specially designed "skip bombs" destroyed two dams and damaged another on the Ruhr River.

In the summer Harris turned his sights on Hamburg. On July 24, 740 RAF bombers lit up the city with fires that still raged when the planes returned two days later. The second attack caused a firestorm that incinerated the city, creating hurricane-force winds that drove temperatures to more than 1,800 degrees Fahrenheit. In four raids between July and August, more than 43,000 Hamburg civilians were killed.

As the Allies improved the teamwork and efficiency of their double-fisted bombing campaigns, they decided to strike at the nerve center of Nazi Germany: Berlin. Although it had been attacked once in January 1942 in response to a German Blitz attack on London, Berlin had been left relatively unscathed by the Brits because of its formidable air defenses. The gruesome successes in Hamburg, however, encouraged the Allies to target the German capital as their next major operation. In November 1943, Harris ordered the first of 16 devastating raids that combined to level 2000 acres of Berlin by the end of the campaign in March 1944.

When Harris took control of Bomber Command in February 1942 he told an interviewer, "There are a lot of people who say that bombing cannot win the war. My reply is that it has never been tried yet. We shall see." Although the round-the-clock raids by the combined British and American air forces wrought unprecedented damage upon German cities, German capacity to wage war never seriously suffered. Five months after the horrific Hamburg raid, industrial production in the region returned to 80 percent of normal. By the end of 1943 American and British air force commanders were compelled to recognize that their massive air campaign, conducted at the cost of so many men and machines, had failed to destroy German morale and war production.

The waist-gunner of a B-17 (above, left) keeps a sharp lookout for enemy fighters. Though known for their heavy armor, B-17s still needed fighter escorts for dangerous day missions. Flying at high altitudes, American crews were kept warm by special uniform equipment (above), including shearling jackets and pants, non-regulation shearling mittens, and winter flying boots.

HAMMERED

The German port city of Hamburg (left) absorbed repeated Allied bombings in 1943. During one four-night raid in late July, 62,000 acres of the city were destroyed in a firestorm. Later bombing missions would cause even greater destruction to the city.

DELIVERING THE PAYLOAD

An Allied ground crew worker (right) examines the munitions destined for Hamburg, a center of German U-boat construction. While the pilots and their flight crews won all the glory, ground crew members worked tirelessly, transporting the bombs to the airfield and then loading them onto the planes.

LIGHT SHOW

On the night of January 30, 1943, an RAF Lancaster soars high above Hamburg (right) amid the beautiful but deadly streams of German antiaircraft fire. It was the early success of the Hamburg missions which gave "Bomber" Harris and the RAF the confidence to set their sights on Berlin.

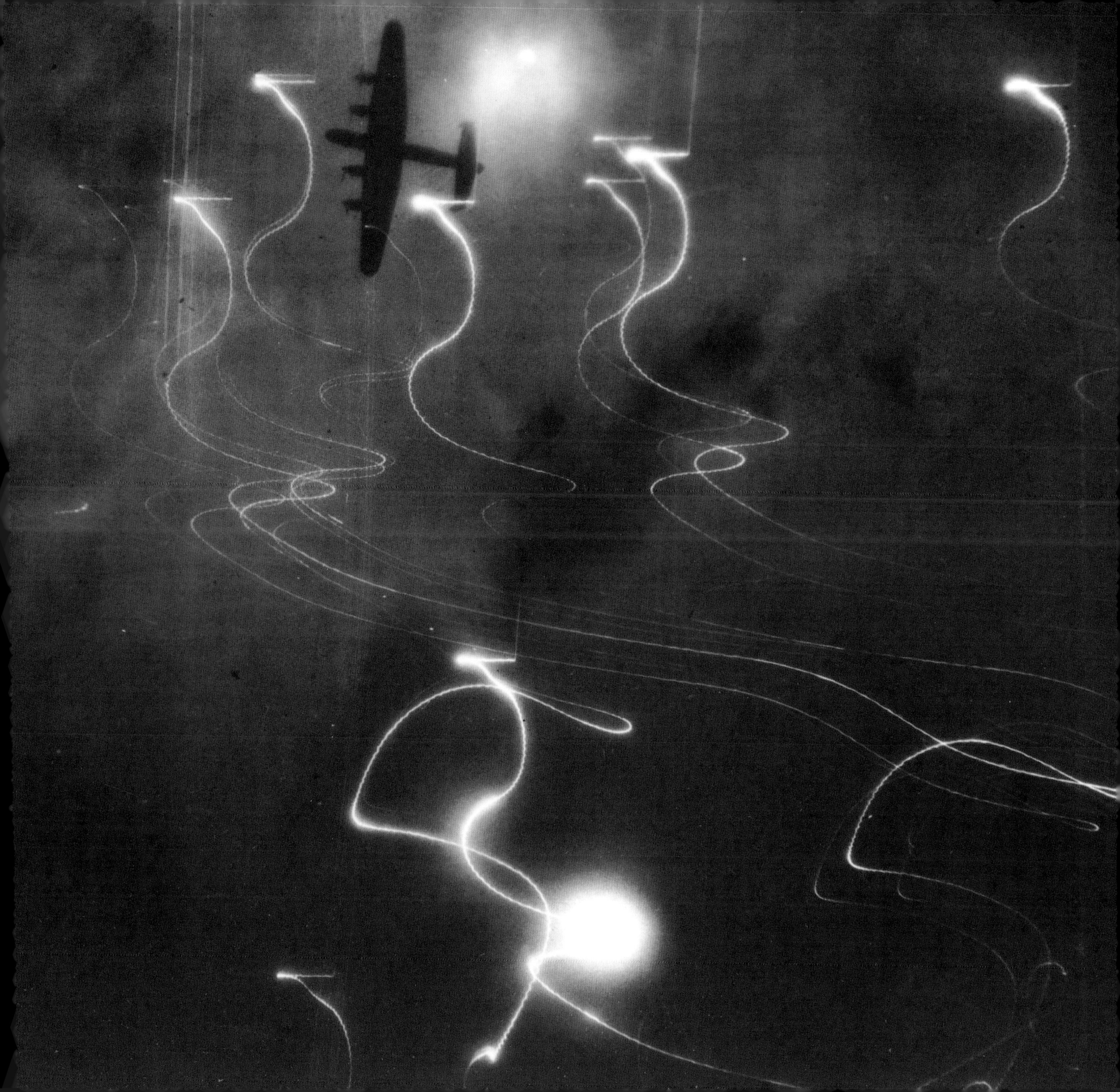

GRISLY AFTERMATH

In a Berlin gymnasium decorated with Christmas trees, victims (above) are laid out for identification after an Allied bombing raid in December 1943. An estimated 600,000 Germans died as a result of Allied strategic bombings.

BERLIN BURNS

When news of the Hamburg raids reached other German cities, one Luftwaffe officer reported, "In every large town people said, 'What happened to Hamburg yesterday can happen to us tomorrow.'" On the night of November 18, 1943, those fears were realized in Berlin. Joseph Goebbels convinced upwards of one million Berliners to leave before the heaviest bombings began; those who remained saw much of their city reduced to rubble (left).

SURVIVAL

Berliners (left) who survived an August 1943 Allied bombing raid stand in line for a hot meal. Despite the constant bombardment, the city's public services and transportation remained functioning through April 1945.

LONG-DISTANCE LANCASTERS

During a rare daylight raid in October 1942, RAF Avro Lancasters buzz in low over Le Creusot, France. The target of this mission was the Schneider munitions works located in the Burgundy region. The Avro, which debuted in March 1942, boasted heavy defenses and was capable of carrying large bomb loads over great distances.

SHELL-SHOCKED

A soldier helps a dazed and disheartened family through the rubble of Mannheim, Germany. The first British raids on Mannheim occurred in late December 1940. In an apparent retaliation for the German bombing of Coventry one month earlier, 134 RAF bombers were ordered to drop their payloads in the center of the south-western German city rather than on specific industrial targets. The civilian casulties totaled 568.

DISSECTING A MISSION

An intelligence officer debriefs a bomber crew (above) after its mission. Pre-flight preparation and postflight intelligence meetings accounted for a large portion of a crew's time when not in the air. Successful raids went a long way toward keeping spirits high. As one English airman ebulliently exclaimed after an effective assault, "When those Germans start putting those fires out they won't have enough water to make a good pot of tea."

HAPPY LANDING

Safe and sound in southern England, an American bomber crew (left) takes time for a post-mission photo in front of their B-17. American fliers arrived in England in the summer of 1942. Though their service was welcome, their brash tactics and cocksure attitudes prompted some Britons to lament, "The trouble with the Yanks is they're overpaid, oversexed, and over here."

KNOWING YOUR ENEMY
A German flak unit stationed in Norway (above) carefully reviews diagrams of various Allied bombers. German antiaircraft guns were known as *Fliegerabwehrkanonen*—"flak" for short. By December 1942, German flak units in Europe had downed more than 8,000 enemy aircraft.

SET THE NIGHT ON FIRE
A German 88-mm antiaircraft battery (right) fires at British bombers during a night raid. Large guns like these were generally used on waves of bombers rather than targeting individual aircraft. One American military observer likened the process of heavy bombers trying to evade flak to that of "an elephant trying to waltz on rollerskates."

PATHS OF RESISTANCE

French resistance fighters (left) brazenly display their weapons as they walk down a Paris street. Less bold members of the resistance were more likely to carry small arms, like this American-made Liberator pistol (inset) that was dropped by parachute to Allied supporters in Nazi-occupied Europe. Charles de Gaulle set the tone for these brave fighters in an impassioned 1940 radio address, saying, "Whatever happens, the flame of French resistance must not and shall not be extinguished."

Resistance

Brave men and women throughout Europe continued to fight for freedom even during German occupation. Their actions came at great personal risk, and many courageous patriots paid with their lives.

BOOK COVERS CAN BE DECEIVING

Subterfuge was an important strategy for resistants everywhere. A hollowed-out children's book (inset, left) was used by a Dutch resistant to conceal a revolver. One Norwegian dental assistant who was a POW in Germany built a radio into a fellow inmate's dentures so that they could hear BBC's European service programs.

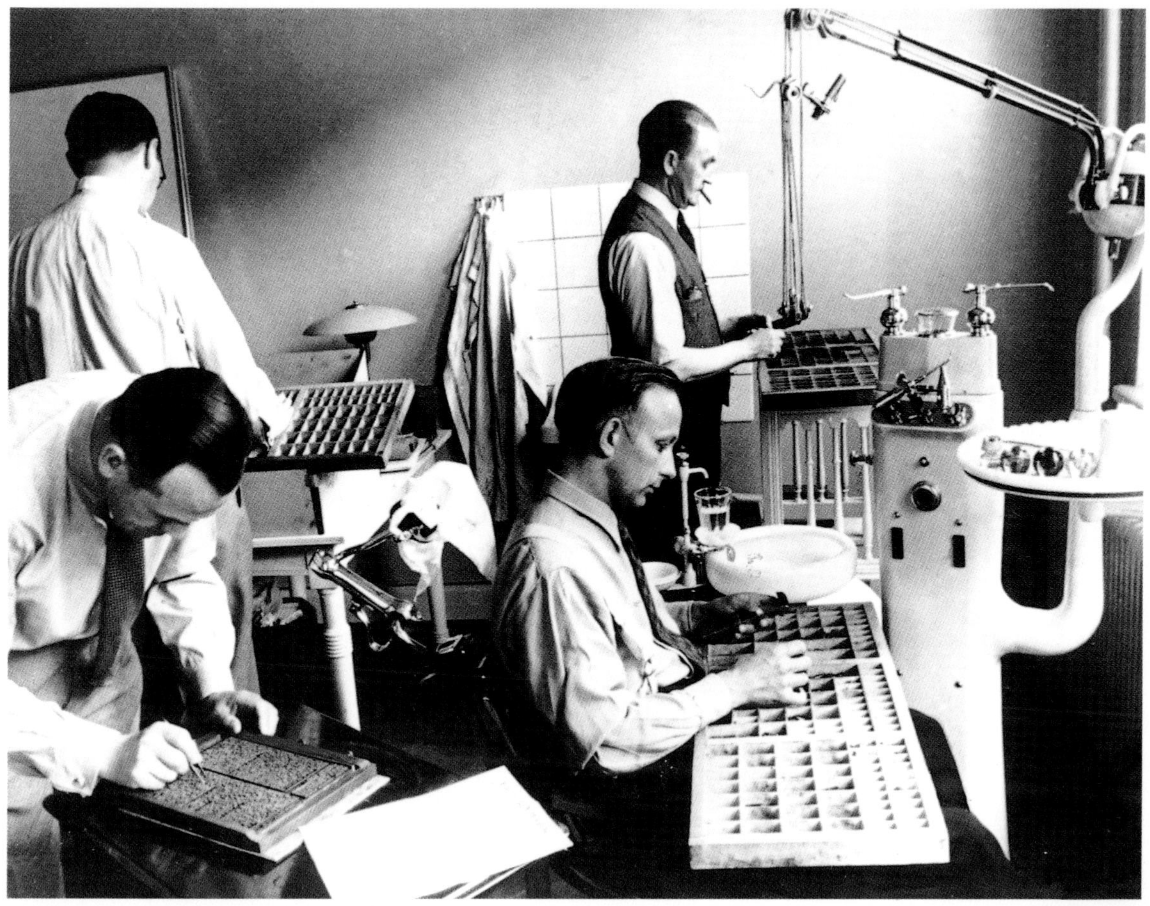

ADVERTISING THE CAUSE
A poster (above) celebrates the French resistance. Resistance networks throughout Europe did their best to keep citizens aware of their cause. In Denmark 17-year-old student Arne Sejr created what he called "Ten Commandments for the Danes" and placed copies in neighborhood mailboxes. The commandments included, "Do worthless work for the Germans, work slowly for the Germans, destroy everything useful to the Germans, join the fight for Denmark's freedom!"

SECRET PRESSES
Typesetters in the cramped quarters of a dentist's office (above) prepare the monthly editon of the resistance newspaper *Free Denmark*. In the event of a raid, all printing plates and trays of type could be hidden quickly inside secret cabinets. Another Dutch publisher concealed his printing shop within a hollowed-out haystack.

GOING UNDERGROUND
Members of the Polish Home Army, like the two radio operatives above, created one of the war's most efficient intelligence networks. It harbored escaped Allied POWs and provided the Allies with information on Germany's rocket weapons.

DEFIANT TO THE END
A member of the French resistance (left) smiles at his German executioners as they take aim. German retribution for the resistance's infractions was swift and lethal. When one of their own was killed, the Germans sometimes executed as many as 50 Frenchmen in retaliation.

PUPPET MASTERS
Adolf Hitler (left) and his minister of propaganda Joseph Goebbels (on Hitler's left), used movies to communicate their ideas to the German populace, which bought 1 billion movie tickets at the country's 5,000 theaters in 1942. An avid film fan himself, Goebbels was responsible for the production of hundreds of films, including the 1940 documentary "The Eternal Jew" (inset). The film contributed to the growing anti-Semitic violence throughout Germany.

German Propaganda

Promoting Aryan supremacy and spewing anti-Semitic venom, Nazi ceremonies and propaganda films proved powerful tools in swaying the German people.

HITLER'S MOVIE MADAME

Leni Riefenstahl (right) peers through a camera during the filming of the 1934 Nazi Party Congress at Nuremberg. "Triumph of the Will "depicted massive stadium rallies and the Führer's hypnotic oratory and was acclaimed around the world as the greatest documentary ever made. Two years later Riefenstahl shot a million feet of film for "Olympia", her documentary on the 1936 Olympic Games in Berlin.

BERLIN 1936

The 1936 Olympic Games (poster above) were a triumph of German propaganda. Hitler hoped the Games would showcase a revitalized Germany, and he left nothing to chance. Even the torch relay from Athens to Berlin was adroitly choreographed—and filmed by Riefenstahl—to glorify Hitler and the Reich. Tens of thousands of Nazis lined the torch's route in Austria and Germany. Only Jesse Owens managed to ruin the lavish Nazi spectacle. The African-American sprinter defied the myth of Aryan supremacy by winning four gold medals.

PROPAGANDA

German films helped rationalize Germany's invasions of Poland and the Soviet Union by portraying Germanic peoples in those countries as victims of the terrible brutality of the "subhuman" Slavic populations. In "Homecoming"(left), a Pole rips a swastika necklace from a helpless German woman. In the war thriller "Bomber Squadron Lützow"(below left), German bomber crews save the day by mowing down the evil Polish guards who threaten the helpless German refugees.

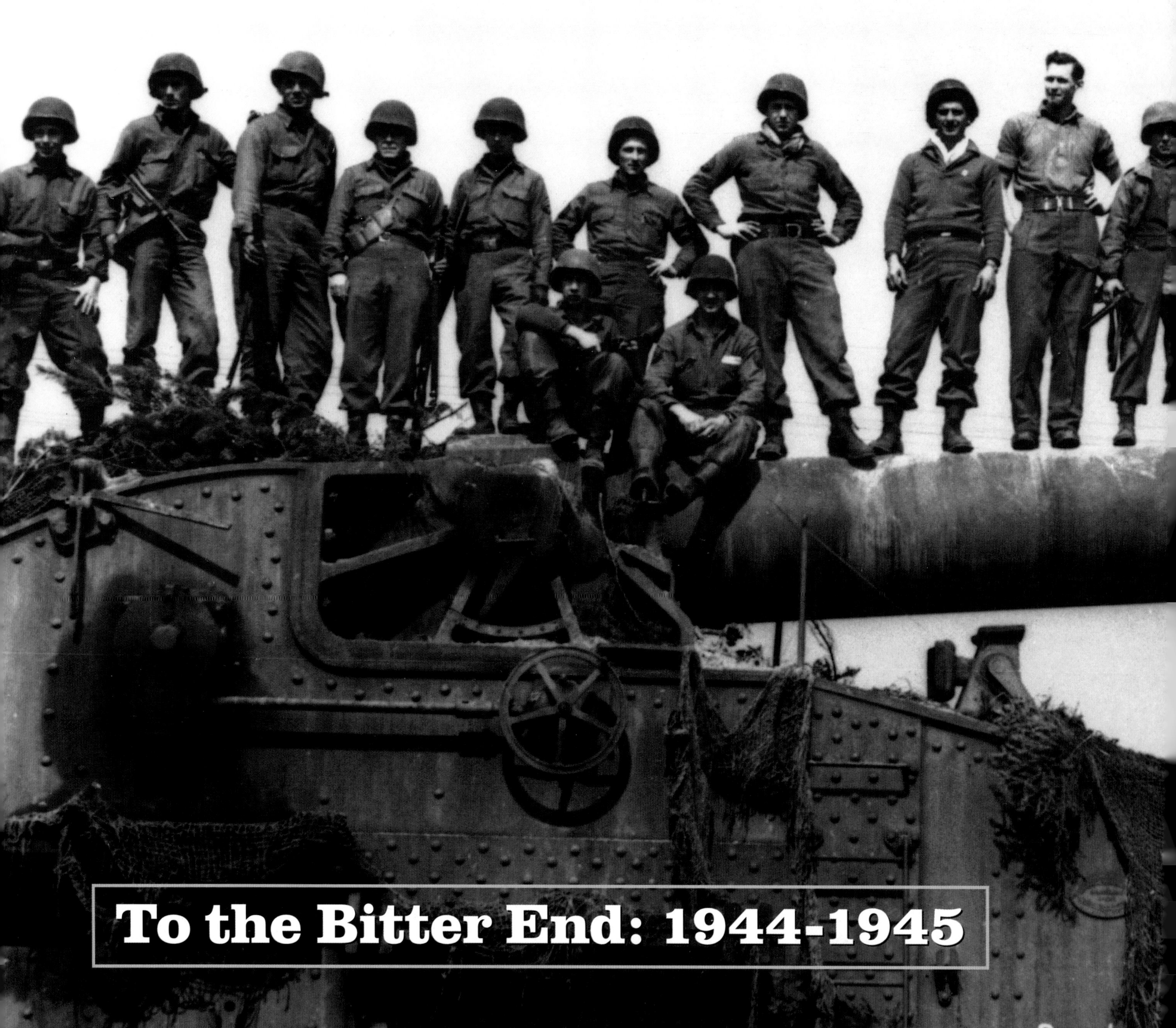

To the Bitter End: 1944-1945

To the Bitter End: 1944-1945

On December 6, 1943, one week after the first "Big Three" conference in Tehran, General George Marshall met privately in Cairo with President Franklin Roosevelt. In Iran, Roosevelt and Winston Churchill had guaranteed Josef Stalin a second front in Europe by May 1944. Stalin, who had received similar promises in 1942 and 1943, was skeptical. He demanded to know who would lead the cross-Channel invasion, code-named Overlord. "Nothing will come of these operations," Stalin said, "until someone is appointed to lead." Roosevelt hesitated but promised he would name the commander for Overlord in two weeks. His decision would be one of the toughest of his career, affecting not just the futures of two great men, but the postwar fortunes of the United States.

Marshall had earned the right to the command. As architect of the American war effort, he had transformed an "army" of 174,000 men in 1939 into a ferocious military machine that was simultaneously waging two separate wars on opposite sides of the globe. It pained Roosevelt to think that the man most responsible for an American victory would not receive the credit he deserved. "I hate to think that 50 years from now practically nobody will know who George Marshall is," Roosevelt explained. But Marshall had grown too important to Roosevelt and to the country. As the president admitted to Marshall in Cairo after he informed the proud general that Dwight Eisenhower would lead the Overlord invasion, "I feel I could not sleep at night with you out of the country." Eisenhower would eventually ride the glory of D-Day to the White House, but if Marshall was disappointed by Roosevelt's decision, he never showed it.

The Tehran conference had been contentious but productive. Roosevelt and Churchill had conferred often during the war, but this was their first joint meeting with the wily Stalin. Although Roosevelt found

Timeline: 1944-1945

1944

June 4

The U.S. Ninth Army captures Rome.

June 6

D-Day: Allied forces storm the beaches of Normandy, France.

New York Post

INVASION

SMASHING AHEAD!

Nazis Say We're 10 Miles In; Sky Troops Far Beyond Lines

July 20

Adolf Hitler survives an assassination attempt when a bomb explodes during a meeting in East Prussia.

August 1

Polish patriots band together in Warsaw and revolt against the Nazi occupation.

August 25

The Allies march into Paris.

October 20

U.S. troops, led by General Douglas MacArthur, "return" to the Philippines, landing on the island of Leyte.

Stalin to be a man who "gets things done," Churchill's contempt for the Soviet dictator was surpassed only by his opposition to Hitler. (If Hitler invaded hell, Churchill had remarked in defending his alliance with the Soviets, he would back the devil himself against the demon in Berlin.)

For now, the need to preserve a united front against Hitler led Churchill and Stalin to set aside their quarrel. As Churchill opined, "The only thing worse than fighting a war with allies was fighting a war without them." Although Churchill had doubts about a cross-Channel invasion of France—his confidence in amphibious invasions had been shaken by his role in the ill-fated assault on Gallipoli in 1915—the Allied leaders left Tehran agreed that there would be no backing down from Overlord and no peace until Germany was beaten.

While the Big Three were smoothing over their differences, the Axis leaders continued to pursue separate paths. Hitler had never liked consulting with his allies, and his pact with Italy and Japan made no provision for strategic coordination. From the beginning, Germany had towered over Italy militarily, and Benito Mussolini had proven to be more of a liability than an asset to Hitler. In North Africa, the Balkans, and Italy itself, German forces had been forced to bail out front-line Italian forces so poorly commanded and ill-equipped that the Duce's mystique of leadership had at last been shattered. Still, Hitler had rescued the fallen dictator from captivity and used him to prop up fascism in northern Italy—a last-ditch attempt by the Führer to salvage something from his costly partnership with Mussolini.

Japanese forces, meanwhile, might have helped Hitler's cause immeasurably had they attacked the Soviet Union from Manchuria as the Germans approached Moscow in 1941, thus preventing Stalin from shifting forces from Siberia to defend his capital. Nothing in the Axis

December 16

The Battle of the Bulge: Germany launches a massive counteroffensive in the Ardennes.

1945

February 4/11

Roosevelt, Churchill, and Stalin meet at Yalta to discuss Allied strategy.

February 19

U.S. Marines land at Iwo Jima and are met by heavy Japanese resistance.

March 4

U.S. and Filipino forces complete the liberation of Manila.

March 7

The Allies occupy Cologne and capture the Remagen Bridge, which spans the Rhine River.

agreement obliged Tokyo to support a German offensive, however, and Japan's interests lay elsewhere. Having pursued their separate agendas, the two major Axis powers now found themselves on the defensive, and neither was in any position to help the other. Japan's plight in the Pacific was even worse than Hitler's situation in Europe, for the Japanese war effort depended on shipments that were being decimated by American submarines. Only one-tenth of the oil produced at Japanese-controlled sources reached its destination after 1943. Short on supplies, reinforcements, and air support, Japanese units in the Pacific suffered ruinous losses but kept on fighting with a fierce determination that made island warfare sheer hell for American forces.

Even as Germany and Japan waged separate struggles against mounting odds, they continued to act like partners and share intelligence, thus providing a bonanza for Allied codebreakers. In late 1943, for example, Japan's ambassador to Germany toured the coast of France with German officers and sent a coded cable to Tokyo detailing the defenses there. Intercepted and deciphered by American intelligence, the cable confirmed that the Germans were expecting an invasion at Calais and had left Normandy lightly defended. The Allies encouraged such German thinking, feigning a build-up across from Calais while preparing for the real landing at Normandy.

Hitler, who had long prided himself on dictating events, was now increasingly at the mercy of forces beyond his knowledge or control. While his Nazi enforcers continued to hunt down Jews and send them to death camps, he himself was the target of a growing number of conspirators who hoped to eliminate him before he brought Germany to ruin. While he prepared to rain terror on Britain with new rocket weapons that could level buildings, the Allies were refining ways of incinerating entire cities. German rockets may have been a revolutionary weapon whose technology would one day send a man to the moon, but their effect in World War II was negligible when compared to the amounts of explosives being dropped on Germany by Allied bombers: Twelve American Flying Fortresses alone could deliver the same firepower as 30 German rockets.

Timeline: 1944-1945

1945

March 9	April 1	April 12	April 28	April 30	May 2
U.S. B-29s fire-bomb Tokyo.	The U.S. 10th Army lands on Okinawa.	President Roosevelt dies; Harry Truman is sworn in as president.	Italian partisans execute Mussolini in Milan.	Hitler commits suicide in Berlin.	Berlin falls to the Soviet Army.

Germany wasn't the only country investing heavily in the development of revolutionary weapons. The Allies may have been years behind in rocket research, but they were ahead of the Germans in the race to harness atomic energy. In 1939, Albert Einstein had warned Roosevelt that German scientists may be working on the creation of an atomic bomb and urged the United States to begin its own research. The horrible possibility of an atomic bomb in the hands of Hitler motivated the Allies to form their own top-secret atomic program, codenamed the Manhattan Project. Not knowing the extent of German progress, the Allied team raced through development. On December 2, 1942, Italian émigré Enrico Fermi had achieved a controlled chain reaction at the University of Chicago, confirming that an atomic bomb was possible. The Allies gathered the greatest scientific minds of the free world and poured billions of dollars into the project. By 1945, 120,000 people were employed at such top-secret installations as Oak Ridge, Hanford, and Los Alamos. On July 16, 1945, a team of scientists in New Mexico led by Robert Oppenheimer successfully tested the first atomic bomb.

Hitler's demise and Germany's capitulation in April 1945 spared the German people a fate worse than "unconditional surrender." (Records revealed that the German atomic program was still in its infancy.) But Japan, although already beaten in many respects, refused to adhere to the Allies' surrender demands and defended their diminishing perimeter with increasing ferocity. Japan would not surrender, even after the strangulation of the islands created mass starvation, and even after the Allies had firebombed Tokyo in March, killing 89,000 civilians.

The U.S.'s decision to use atomic weapons continues to be debated. The horrors of Hiroshima and Nagasaki revealed the atom to be a source of destruction unknown even to the scientists who mastered it. The two blasts, however, accomplished their mission: the war ended. The bombs saved thousands of American lives that certainly would have been lost during an invasion of Japan, and they spared the lives of an equal number of Japanese who would have fought to the death in its defense. World War II was over, but the travails of peace, now complicated by the weapons of a nascent nuclear age, would prove equally challenging.

May 7

Germany surrenders unconditionally to the Allies in Rheims.

July 16

The U.S. tests first atomic bomb in New Mexico.

August 6

The *Enola Gay* drops atomic bomb on Hiroshima.

August 9

One day after the Soviets declare war on Japan, the U.S. drops a second atomic bomb on Nagasaki.

August 14

Japan agrees to the Allied surrender terms.

My Girl

War in the Air: East & West

A crewman directs a P-51 Mustang (left) to take off from Iwo Jima in 1945. The Mustang was the most effective American fighter of the war and provided escort for the U.S. 20th Army Air Force (patch, below) in bombing raids on Japan.

"I wanted my crews to be well 'blooded,'" said Air Marshal Arthur Harris of RAF Bomber Command—well "blooded," indeed. By 1944 the Allied precision air raids of the first years of the war had given way to massive, saturation attacks. Allied bombers operated virtually unopposed in enemy air space, obliterating military, industrial, and civilian targets and raising new strategic and moral questions about the practice of aerial warfare.

When the war began, the effectiveness of air power was still debatable. In 1918, Great Britain had dropped a mere 534 tons of bombs on Germany, but rapid technological advances pushed air power through an accelerated adolescence during the interwar years. In the early days of World War II, the Luftwaffe proved the strength of air power in the skies above Poland, Scandinavia, and France. German airplanes outclassed the Allied opposition in such an overwhelming fashion that Hermann Göring, the chief of the Luftwaffe, had every reason to brag in 1939, "If bombs [ever] drop on Germany, my name is Meyer." In the Pacific, the Japanese adapted German aerial blitzkrieg techniques and used them to attack Pearl Harbor and the Philippines.

By 1944, however, the tables had turned. The U.S. alone was producing more aircraft per year than Germany and Japan combined. This growing numerical disparity in the skies radically tipped the balance of power in both theaters, as the Allies continued attempts to club the Axis into submission.

When General Curtis LeMay (below, with cigar) arrived in the Pacific theater in 1944, he introduced the low-altitude incendiary bombing tactics that he had utilized to devastating effect in Europe.

The Royal Air Force had been bombing German positions in Europe since 1940, and the American Eighth Army Air Force had joined them in 1942. "If one were to recount all the sorrow that these bombing nights have brought, one could fill whole libraries," wrote Joseph Goebbels, the Nazi propaganda minister, in 1944. "But in spite of this, life goes on." Life did go on for the German people after the initial shock of the Allied bombing raids—and so did the war.

Although the Allies had failed to end the war with air power alone, the costs to the German people and

Workers (top) move a 108-gallon drop tank at an airfield in England. The tanks, which fit neatly beneath the wings of P-51 Mustangs (top right), could be jettisoned when necessary, allowing the U.S. Strategic Air Force (patch, above) to bomb targets deep inside the Reich.

the Reich's war effort were devastating. On paper, however, that did not seem to be the case. In April 1944, German fighter plane production increased 186 percent in only five months, despite constant aerial bombardment. Other German production figures also refuted the effectiveness of Allied air power. But contrary to the remarkable resilience of German industry, the Allies' air offensive was slowly crippling the Reich. Even if the Germans could replace lost planes, they had a difficult time finding men who could fly them. During a four-month span in 1944, the Luftwaffe lost more than 1,000 pilots. "The only raw material that cannot be restored in the foreseeable future is human blood," said Field Marshal Erhard Milch, Göring's chief deputy.

Since the beginning of combined bombing offensives in 1943, the Allies had developed new planes, techniques, and innovations that enhanced the success of bombing raids. Unescorted bombers—even the B-17 Flying Fortress, which was reputed to be "self-defending"—were easy targets for German fighters. It wasn't until the Allies began using P-47 Thunderbolts, P-38 Lightnings, and P-51 Mustangs as escorts that Allied fortunes changed. These fighters were equipped with "drop tanks" of extra fuel, which substantially extended the planes' range. The Mustangs—called "Little Friends" by grateful Allied bomber crews—fended off German fighters while the heavies delivered their destructive payload with increased effectiveness.

As Allied bombing experiments yielded greater successes, air force leadership increased the boldness and magnitude of the raids. As General "Hap" Arnold told his air commanders in January 1944, the new mission was to "destroy the enemy air force wherever you find them, in the air, on the ground, and in the factories." Between February 20-26, the RAF and U.S. Army Air Force ordered a massive assault on German aircraft factories and synthetic-oil plants. The "Big Week" raids targeted factories and plants in Leipzig, Regensburg, Augsburg, Fürth, and Stuttgart. In six days and nights, 6,100 Allied bombers—escorted by thousands of fighters—dropped 10,000 tons of bombs on the Reich and destroyed or damaged more than half of the production facilities of Germany's aircraft industry.

Preparations for the Allied invasion of France, tentatively scheduled for May, also involved the use of air power. Beginning in March, U.S. and British bombers targeted railway yards and repair centers in Belgium and northern France with the intention of creating a "railway desert" around the Normandy beaches. This systematic bombing of railway targets, dubbed the Transportation Plan, would effectively strand the Ger-

man forces at Normandy, cutting them off from reinforcements and supplies. By early June, Allied pilots had flown some 200,000 sorties, chopped up France's rail system beyond recognition, destroyed 1,500 locomotives, and severed all 24 bridges over the Seine between Paris and the English Channel. General Dwight Eisenhower was so pleased with the success of the Transportation Plan and so confident of Allied air superiority that he assured his troops before D-Day, "If you see fighting aircraft over you, they will be ours."

Once the Transportation Plan was completed, the Allies redoubled the combined bomber offensive, pounding Germany's cities with 24-hour raids. The Reich was hammered mercilessly—some 600,000 German civilians were killed and 800,000 injured by Allied air power. Göring's once proud Luftwaffe was no longer a factor. Some German soldiers morbidly joked after D-Day, "If the plane is blue it is British, if it is silver it is American, and if it is invisible it is ours." Still, Germany refused to surrender, and the Allied bombing rampages continued.

Adolf Hitler refused to visit his destroyed cities—as Churchill had in 1940—and hoped that a new arsenal of secret weapons could still save Germany. He ordered the mass production of unpiloted aircraft, such as the V-1 flying bomb and the V-2 rocket, history's first ballistic missiles. Between September 1944 and March 1945, the new German wonder weapons killed more than 2,000 Londoners, but the revolutionary missiles were too inaccurate to make a decisive impact. Hitler may have been better served manufacturing Messerschmitt-262s, the world's first jet aircraft that began production in the summer of 1944, but a shortage of pilots and fuel supplies convinced him otherwise.

The targeting of civilians had always been a contro-

B-29 fuselages and tailpieces (above) on the floor of the Boeing Plant near Seattle, Washington, await further components and assembly. Boeing was a key contributor to the booming U.S. war machine. In 1944 the U.S. manufactured 96,000 aircraft, 94,000 more than it had produced in 1940.

A statue atop a Dresden church (above, right) seems to gesture forlornly at the devastation wrought by Allied pilots (above). "The enemy sees your light! Make it dark!" orders a German poster (inset) designed to protect the Reich from Allied bombers.

versial—if accepted—aspect of the Allied strategic bombing philosophy. The February 1945 destruction of Dresden, an historic city rich in culture but of minor military significance, renewed the moral debate regarding such raids. Eight hundred RAF bombers set the defenseless city ablaze during the night of February 13, and 300 American B-17s arrived during the day to continue the slaughter. Dresden was consumed by a firestorm that lasted for four days, killing 35,000 German civilians. The attack sparked outrage in Germany, as well as in the Allied world, where citizens of the western democracies were shocked to learn that their governments engaged in "terror bombing." As horrible as the destruction of Dresden was, it proved the inadequacy of Allied terror tactics, because the Germans still refused to surrender. Churchill, for one, was unapologetic. "Air power was the weapon which both the marauding States selected as their main tool of conquest. . . . This was the method by which the nations were to be subjugated to their rule. I shall not moralise further than to say that there is a strange, stern justice in the long swing of events."

In the Pacific, Japan had long been protected by the expansive perimeter the Imperial Army had established in the early days of the war and by the vast dimensions of the region itself. With the exception of Doolittle's daring raid on Tokyo in 1942, the Allies settled for air bases in China and India, thousands of miles from the Japanese islands. The B-29, therefore, was the ultimate American weapon in the Pacific theater. Originally designed to strike Germany from North America—and costing more to develop than the Manhattan Project—the massive "Superfortress" could fly 4,200 miles and had a bomb capacity of 10 tons of explosives—four tons more than a B-17. With its superior range, the B-29 allowed the U.S. to strike directly at the Japanese homeland from bases in Chengtu in south central China.

The American B-29 raids got off to a rocky start, but by June 1944 the Superfortresses were hitting Japan. The campaign received two additional boosts during the summer. In August 1944, Major General Curtis LeMay, formerly of the Eighth Army Air Force in Europe, took command of the B-29s. LeMay brought with him from

Europe a strong belief that the war could be won with air power. Only 38 years old, LeMay aggressively confronted the B-29's problems and limitations. He personally participated in a raid on Manchuria to get a better idea of the plane's capabilities. Upon returning, he revamped bombing strategies and retrained B-29 pilots. At about the same time, American forces secured airfields in the Mariana Islands, 1,300 miles south of Tokyo. By November more than 100 B-29s were operating from Saipan, ending the tactical and supply difficulties associated with the Chinese airfields. From these new air bases, American B-29s could fix Tokyo squarely in their cross-hairs.

On November 1, 1944, Captain Ralph Steakley piloted his B-29, the *Tokyo Rose*, 32,000 feet above Tokyo. Steakley eluded Japan's air defenses, snapped 7,000 reconnaissance photos of potential targets in the Japanese capital, and flew back to the island of Saipan. His appearance over Tokyo would be one of the last times that the sight of an American bomber over Japan was not immediately followed by hellish devastation.

In March, hordes of B-29s descended on Tokyo and torched 16 square miles of the city's center, killing an astonishing 89,000 people. The subsequent firestorm generated enough heat to boil the waters of the city's canals. The offensive continued and reached its peak during the spring and summer. Scores of Superfortresses, armed with firebombs, unleashed destruction such as the world had never seen. Raids on Nagoya, Kobe, Osaka, Yokohama, and Kawasaki—whose buildings were composed primarily of wood—left 260,000 people dead and some 10 million people homeless.

Waves of B-29s took off twice a week, annihilating three or four cities in each outing. Japanese cities were completely erased from the map. LeMay warned Arnold that if things continued at their current pace and the Japanese refused to capitulate by October, he would run out of targets to attack. Only four major Japanese centers had been spared: Niigata, Kokura, Hiroshima, and Nagasaki. The exemption of these cities, as a few men in the highest offices of the U.S. government knew, was not an oversight.

With its four 16-foot propellers churning, a B-29 Superfortress (above) prepares for takeoff from a U.S. airbase in Chengtu, China, on its way to bomb Japan. Beginning in late 1944, the Superforts flew essentially unopposed over Japan.

TARGETING THE RAILS

Clouds of smoke billow into the air above Liege, Belgium (above), after B-17 Flying Fortresses from the Eighth Air Force bombed several railroad targets. The raid was part of the Allied effort to hamstring German forces on the Atlantic coast by cutting off their ability to resupply and relocate troops.

ROUEN RUINS

The highway bridge in Rouen, France (above), lies shattered in the Seine, in the shadow of the unscathed Rouen Cathedral, after being hit by U.S. bombers on May 27, 1944. The bridge was one of 24 bridges across the Seine that were destroyed by Allied bombs during the execution of the Transportation Plan.

ANTIAIRCRAFT FIRE

A trio of B-26 Marauders from the Ninth Army Air Force (above) braves heavy flak to bomb targets in Dieppe, France. The lead plane (left) absorbed the heaviest German fire; its bombardier suffered mortal injuries and its gunner was gravely wounded. Before succumbing to his wounds, the bombardier released his ordnance, and the plane safely returned to base.

BOMBER COMMAND
Using a floor map of Japan, a status board, and radio communications equipment, mission controllers (right) monitor a raid on Japan from the XXI Bomber Command operations room on Guam. After witnessing the horrific damage that the B-29s inflicted on Japan, U.S. general Joseph Stilwell, who had doubted the effectiveness of air power, said, "I recognize now the terrible military virtues of strategic bombardment."

FINISHING TOUCHES
Seated in the bomb bay of a B-29, a munitions worker (below, right) installs a fuse in a 500-pound demolition bomb. Most of the B-29s that attacked Japan, however, were loaded with incendiary bombs, which were set to detonate 100 feet above the target and release containers of jellied gasoline, or napalm, which burst into flame on contact.

NEW BASE
Recently relocated from the China-Burma-India theater, three Superfortresses taxi across an airfield on Tinian. The island would serve as a base for B-29 raids on Japan from October 1944 onward. The planes were part of the 58th Bombardment Wing, commanded by Major General Curtis LeMay, at 38 the youngest two-star general in the Army Air Forces. After LeMay took command, the number of B-29s that hit their primary targets in Japan rose from 36 to 91 percent. One senior officer remarked that "LeMay is an operator; the rest of us are just planners."

53

BOMBS OVER KOBE

As a dense cloud of smoke smothers the city, U.S. incendiary bombs plummet toward the port of Kobe (right). Nearly 500 B-29s destroyed more than 50 percent of the city on June 4, 1945. By August, Superfortresses had razed almost half of the aggregate area of 66 Japanese cities—178 square miles of destruction.

GHASTLY SCIENCE

A pair of U.S. B-29 bombers bound for Japan (left) cruise over the Mariana Islands. The Superforts unleashed their destruction in three stages: The first formation of planes dropped napalm; the second wave released hundreds of oil containers, which showered fuel on the napalm fires; and the third group dropped magnesium-thermite bombs, which mixed with the oil and napalm to produce fires of raging intensity.

REFUGEES

In the wake of an incendiary-bomb attack on their city in May 1945, residents of Kobe (above) haul their possessions on their way to find new shelter. In many cases, the Americans dropped leaflets on the Japanese populace to warn them of the imminent danger. "Attention, Japanese people! Read this carefully as it may save your life or the life of a relative or friend," one leaflet began. "We are determined to destroy all the tools of the military clique, which they are using to prolong this useless war. But unfortunately, bombs have no eyes. . . . Evacuate these cities and save your lives."

SAFE AND SOUND

A group of rescued airmen poses atop the submarine U.S.S. *Tigrone* (right), which saved them in late June 1945. The *Tigrone* rescued 31 fliers in the Pacific, more than any other American submarine.

RESCUE MISSION

An airman (left) scans the horizon from the nose of a B-17 bomber on air-sea rescue duty. To improve the military's rescue operations, the Navy contributed PBY Catalinas and PBM Mariners, slow but reliable flying boats that could land in the water to retrieve pilots. Equipped with lifesaving gear, the awkward-looking machines were affectionately nicknamed "Dumbos" after the flying elephant of movie fame.

LIFELINE

Floating in the Pacific in his one-man dinghy, Sergeant Karl Wright (right), a radio operator who had bailed out of a B-29 bomber, reaches out for a line from a rescue ship. Searching for missing pilots in vast stretches of the Pacific Ocean was often a futile business, but rescuers learned to look for a reflection, a wisp of smoke, or a piece of wreckage to guide them to downed fliers.

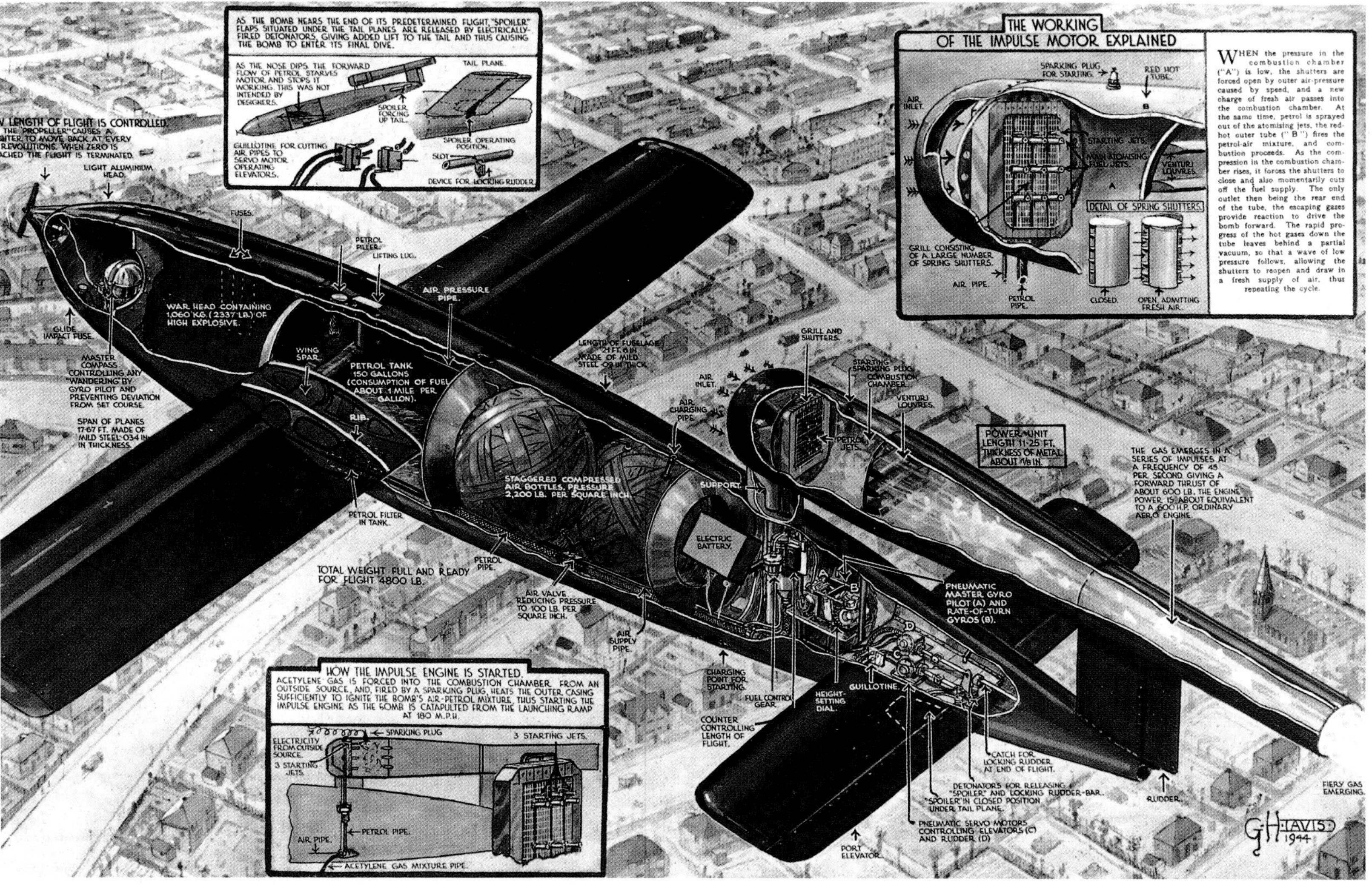

V-Weapons

While the Allies labored to develop their own revolutionary weapons, Hitler hoped that *Vergeltungswaffen*—"weapons of reprisal" such as the V-1 pilotless aircraft and the V-2 rocket—could reverse Germany's dwindling fortunes.

"SECRETS OF THE FLYING BOMB REVEALED"
On October 7, 1944, *The Illustrated London News* contained a cross-section of one of Germany's pilotless, remote-controlled V-1 bombs (above)—"drawn from details obtained from a captured flying bomb." History's first cruise missiles, the V-1s were nicknamed "buzz bombs" by the British citizens they terrorized. Although more than 6,000 Londoners died from V-1 attacks between June and September 1944, almost half of the 9,000 missiles that were launched toward Britain were destroyed by antiaircraft fire or fighter intervention.

ROCKET SCIENTISTS
German workers put the finishing touches on a V-2 guided missile (left), the brainchild of Werner von Braun (below), a pioneer of rocketry who handled the technical aspects, and Walter Dornberger, a World War I veteran who outlined the practical considerations for the weapon. When Hitler saw a film of one of their early missiles, he declared it the "decisive weapon of the war."

PREPARING THE WARHEAD
While a forced laborer (above, right) performs some of the menial work, German technicians test various systems of a V-2 rocket before the weapon is deployed.

TERROR IN CLAPHAM
Residents of London's Clapham district transport a victim from the wreckage of a V-1 attack on June 17, 1944. The flying bombs may have been introduced earlier if not for an August 1943 attack by British Bomber Command on the Baltic island of Peenemünde, where the V-1 and V-2 programs were headquartered.

Death Camps

In January 1942 the Nazis approved the "Final Solution," authorizing the transfer of millions of Jews and other "undesirables" to six specialized camps with the sole purpose of systematic extermination.

AUSCHWITZ

A group of Jewish women and children (above) waits in line outside the Auschwitz concentration camp in the summer of 1944. Awaiting inside the camp's walls was death by Zyklon B poison gas, whose skull-and-crossbones label (inset) warned "Poison Gas! Cyanide Preparation!" At the height of its activity, Auschwitz's giant gas chambers murdered 8,000 people per day.

MENGELE'S MADNESS

Drawing from a vast pool of "volunteers," Reich doctors recklessly experimented on concentration camp inmates. The grotesquely sadistic Dr. Josef Mengele conducted numerous medical experiments at Auschwitz, including investigating the effects of starvation on infants and children (below).

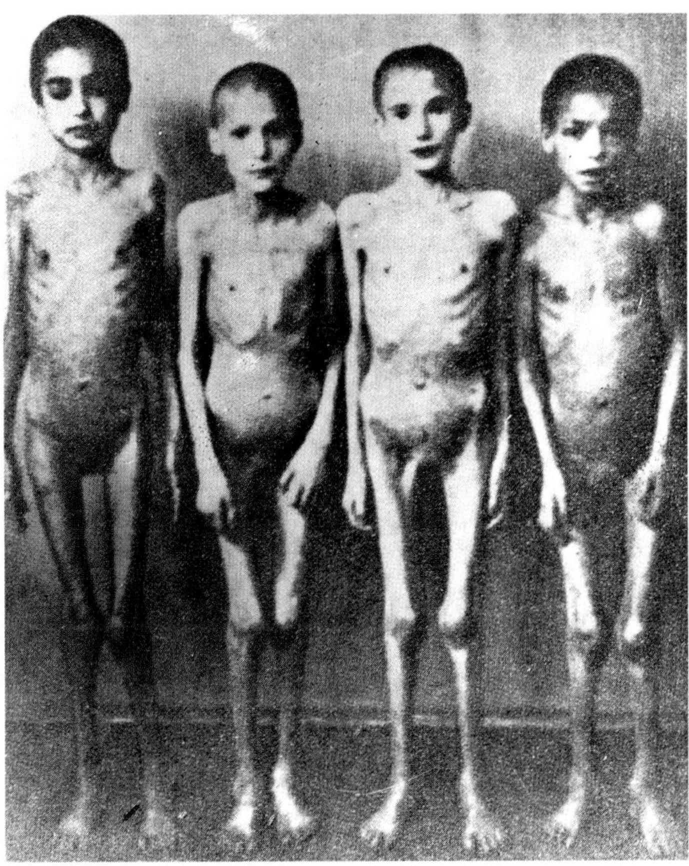

ATROCITY

The remains of women cremated at Buchenwald (above) were found by the U.S. Third Army in April 1945. Although not technically a death camp, Buchenwald was the site of mass killings in early 1945 as the SS assigned special units to eliminate the "evidence" by cremating the corpses of the gassed prisoners before Allied troops arrived.

WAITING TO DIE

A group of Jewish men (left) await death at Chelmno—the first Nazi extermination camp to be opened. About half of the six million Jews who died during the Holocaust were killed at one of the six death camps: Auschwitz, Belzec, Chelmno, Majdanek, Sobibor, and Treblinka.

BUCHENWALD BUTCHERS

SS Colonel Karl Koch (left), commandant of the Buchenwald camp, poses with his family. His wife, Ilsa (far left), gained notoriety for her own brutality; she was tried for war crimes at Nuremberg and committed suicide in prison.

67

General MacArthur (below) triumphantly wades ashore at Leyte Island on October 20, 1944, fulfilling his promise to the Philippines. Upon landing he proclaimed: "I have returned. By the grace of Almighty God our forces stand on Philippine soil. . . . Rally to me."

Return to the Philippines

U.S. troops, tanks, and construction crews (left) land on Noemfoor Island, just north of New Guinea, in July 1944. In four days, the island and its three airfields were in Allied hands. Navy Construction Battalions—or Seabees (patch, inset)—built bases in forward areas such as Noemfoor at break-neck speed. Their motto: "Can Do!"

In early July 1944, General Douglas MacArthur received an urgent message from his immediate superior, General George Marshall, ordering MacArthur to Pearl Harbor on July 26. The message offered no explanation, but MacArthur, whose troops had recently secured the island of Noemfoor, off the northwest coast of New Guinea, guessed that Marshall would pull him away from the war at this crucial moment for only one reason. President Roosevelt was coming to the Pacific.

Unlike the unified command structure of the European theater, Allied military operations in the Pacific were divided between two commands. In the spring of 1942 MacArthur had argued that the primary route for the rapid defeat of Japan should be through the Philippine Islands. The recapture of the Philippines, using New Guinea as the springboard, would sever Japanese lines of communication with the Dutch East Indies and their vital resources of oil and other war matériel. Admiral Chester Nimitz and his naval strategists—who didn't share MacArthur's personal commitment to the Philippines—had proposed a drive across the central Pacific using the Navy's aircraft carriers to cover the seizure of strategic island bases on Japan's vulnerable eastern flank. Control of these islands would provide vital landing strips that would allow bombing missions against the Japanese home islands and limit the operations of enemy naval forces. If the island of Formosa were then captured, the Navy insisted, the Philippines could be bypassed or more effectively attacked from the central Pacific.

The U.S. Army and Navy's mutual dislike and mistrust of each other had forced the Allies into a reluctant compromise in July 1942. For two years, the system of dual commands had succeeded in spite of itself. MacArthur's forces had launched successful thrusts northward from Australia through New Guinea, and Nimitz's fleet had advanced through the central Pacific along the far-flung island chains of Micronesia—the Gilberts, the Marshalls, the Carolines, and finally the Marianas. By July 1944,

As Allied landing craft race toward shore, an Allied plane keeps a watchful eye over Tanahmerah Bay, on the north coast of New Guinea (above), in April 1944. Surprised by the attack, Japanese forces guarding this portion of the coast uncharacteristically turned tail and fled into the jungle.

however, a decision had to be made—the Philippines or Formosa? President Franklin Roosevelt, recently nominated for a fourth term, sailed from San Diego to meet with his two chief Pacific strategists. MacArthur argued passionately that the U.S. had a responsibility to liberate the Philippines first, while Nimitz offered a sound, objective reasoning for attacking Formosa. MacArthur, who had been the Army's chief of staff under Roosevelt in the 1930s, sensed he had won over the president. On his flight back to the front, MacArthur couldn't control his enthusiasm. "We've sold it!" he told an aide.

The two-pronged Allied advance that gradually rolled back the Japanese gains of 1941 and 1942 was a series of bloody island battles. After securing the Gilbert Islands in November 1943, Admiral Raymond Spruance, commander of the Fifth Fleet, targeted the Marshall Island chain, 600 miles to the northwest, where the Japanese had determined to make a stand. Following a massive naval bombardment on January 31, 1944, U.S. forces landed on Kwajalein Atoll and moved on to capture Eniwetok two weeks later. In support of their invasion of the Marshalls, the American fleet's carrier-based aircraft attacked the Japanese base at Truk in the Caroline Islands, sinking over 200,000 tons of Japanese merchant shipping and destroying 200 aircraft.

The U.S. fleet quickly turned toward the Mariana Islands, 1,000 miles west of the Marshalls, in the Philippine Sea. In June the Marines landed on Saipan as a preparatory operation for the invasion of Guam. Some 30,000 Japanese defenders, under Lieutenant General Yoshitsugu Saito, manned the garrison on Saipan, and the men of the U.S. Second and Fourth Marine Divisions were forced to root the enemy out of a maze of fortified bunkers. The battle ended on July 7 when U.S. forces defeated the largest banzai attack of the war—3,000 Japanese troops died when they fearlessly charged American lines.

At sea, Admiral Jisaburo Ozawa's Combined Fleet challenged Spruance's fleet west of the Marianas in the

Battle of the Philippine Sea. Ozawa tried to lure the superior Allied naval forces into a Midway-esque confrontation, but his attempts to reverse Japanese fortunes in the Pacific failed. In one of the great carrier battles of the war, the Japanese lost over 400 aircraft and three carriers before being forced to retire toward Okinawa. The decisive defeat cost the Japanese almost half of their carrier strength and two-thirds of their aircraft, allowing the Americans to occupy the neighboring island of Tinian on August 1 and Guam on August 11.

Farther south, MacArthur had taken his first step toward the Philippines in mid-1943 by isolating Rabaul, a major Japanese naval base in the Bismarck Archipelago off the northwest coast of New Guinea. Allied forces under Admiral William "Bull" Halsey—a rare naval officer in that he got along with MacArthur—opened a series of operations in October with New Zealand forces, capturing the Treasury Islands. On November 1 a task-force under Rear Admiral Aaron Stanton landed U.S. Army and Marine forces at Empress Augusta Bay on Bougainville, the largest of the Solomon Islands. Fierce fighting lasted until the Japanese defenders, under General Haruyoshi Hyakutake, were defeated in April. Seven thousand Japanese soldiers and more than 1,000 Americans died for Bougainville.

MacArthur, meanwhile, began a series of "leap-frog" landings in western New Guinea to suppress the increasingly-isolated Japanese forces. Beginning in January 1944, U.S. and Australian forces secured the Huon peninsula and pushed along the coast. In April the Allies captured the Japanese airbases at Hollandia. The following month an American force landed on Biak, an island guarding the entrance to Geelvink Bay, but the Japanese defenders stubbornly held out until August. After capturing Aitape, east of Hollandia, the Allies successfully fought off a series of determined counterattacks in August by over 20,000 Japanese troops based at Wewak. With the northern coast of New Guinea

Admiral Chester Nimitz (top) rose from submarine commander of the Atlantic Fleet in 1912 to commander of the Pacific Fleet during World War II. He sent Marines (above, left) to take the Kwajalein Atoll in the Marshall Islands in February 1944. Marine Corps Raider Battalions (patch, inset) took part in several of Nimitz's perilous amphibious raids in the Pacific.

Crewmen of the U.S.S. *Birmingham* blast water onto the burning carrier U.S.S. *Princeton* (above), which was hit by a Japanese dive-bomber in the Battle of Leyte Gulf. After the fire was brought under control, disaster struck both ships when a torpedo magazine on the *Princeton* exploded, sending debris onto the deck of the *Birmingham* that killed 229 American sailors.

secure, the Allies began construction of a major base at Hollandia, from which they could dominate the southern half of the Philippine Sea.

After the president and the joint chiefs of staff finally authorized MacArthur's return to the Philippines in September, his forces in New Guinea took Morotai in the Moluccas as a stepping stone to Mindanao, the southernmost of the Philippine Islands. The Allies, however, decided against invading Mindanao after carrier-based aircraft encountered only light resistance. Instead, they targeted the east coast of Leyte, a smaller island north of Mindanao. In October, a massive American landing force, consisting of Halsey's Third Fleet and Vice Admiral Thomas Kinkaid's Seventh Fleet, converged on the Surigao Strait. The Japanese high command, aware that losing the Philippines would allow the Allies to attempt a direct invasion of the Japanese main islands, devised a complicated operation—codenamed Sho-Go—to repel the Allied landings. On Leyte, General Tomoyuki Yamashita was to hold his 14th Army inland and await the American landings. While Japanese air units attacked the landing force, a carrier taskforce under Vice Admiral Ozawa aimed to lure Halsey's carriers away from the invasion zone. This would pave the way for a formidable naval surface fleet from Brunei Bay, built around the powerful battleships *Yamato* and *Musashi*, which would

With MacArthur's return to the Philippines, America believed that victory was imminent (cartoon, left). But Japanese resistance on Luzon proved otherwise. The XI Corps of the U.S. Eighth Army (patch, inset) clashed with stubborn Japanese forces at ZigZag Pass, a narrow path in the Zambales Mountains of Luzon. Casualties on both sides were high, and Japanese forces under General Tomoyuki Yamashita (far left) would hold out until Japan's final surrender in September 1945.

split into two taskforces and destroy the unprotected Allied landing craft in the Leyte Gulf.

The operation began with disaster for the Japanese. On October 23, U.S. submarines detected and attacked Vice Admiral Shoji Nishimura's taskforce off Palawan, an island that forms the western boundary of the Sulu Sea. The next day, in the Sibuyan Sea southeast of Mindoro Island, American carrier-based aircraft sank the *Musashi* and three other warships. One part of Sho-Go did go well for the Japanese, however. Halsey diverted forces to pursue Ozawa's carriers to the north and Vice Admiral Takeo Kurita's attack fleet was able to pass unopposed through the San Bernardino Strait. As he turned toward Leyte Gulf, Kurita's fleet surprised a force of American escort carriers. Although Kurita sank five U.S. ships, a spirited defense by the overmatched Americans and reports that Nishimura's fleet had been annihilated convinced Kurita to break off the action and withdraw.

The Battle of Leyte Gulf, the largest naval engagement in history, cost the Americans one fast carrier, two escort carriers, and three destroyers. Several other Allied ships were damaged by a terrible new Japanese weapon: kamikaze pilots. But for Japan, Leyte Gulf was catastrophic. The Imperial Fleet lost three battleships, four aircraft carriers, six heavy cruisers, three light cruisers, and 10 destroyers. Japan would never again test the American fleet in the Pacific.

Despite their defeat at sea, the Japanese still managed to land reinforcements on Leyte, and their stubborn resistance in the island's rugged interior delayed the American capture of the island until Christmas. The struggle for the main island of Luzon and the capital city of Manila would last until April 1945, but to many, the battle had been won on October 20, when General MacArthur gloriously waded ashore and announced, "People of the Philippines, I have returned."

WADING GAME

Holding their rifles over their heads, U.S. Marines (left) wade ashore at Cape Gloucester, New Britain, in December 1943. The purpose of this landing and others along New Britain, New Guinea, and the Solomon Island chain was to isolate the large Japanese base of Rabaul, which was located on the northern tip of New Britain.

BIRD OF PREY

A B-29 bomber (right), its nose painted to resemble a falcon, glides in low during a strafing run on Japanese positions near Boram, New Guinea. The operation was part of Admiral Halsey's overall strategy to "change the name of Rabaul to Rubble."

AGONIZING EXIT

Clutching his face in pain, a wounded U.S. Marine (right) is lifted from a landing craft onto a large transport during the invasion of Bougainville. The Japanese operated five airfields on the southern part of the island, which—if captured—the Allies could use to launch a final assault on Rabaul. The commander of the Japanese Sixth Division ordered his men not to rest "until our bastard foes are battered, and bowed in shame—till their bright red blood adds yet more luster to the badge of the Sixth Division."

JUNGLE ADVANCE

Soldiers of the 37th Division (right) cautiously follow the lead of an American tank during the fierce battle for Bougainville in March 1944. The 37th, which had gained experience during the fight for New Georgia, joined the Third Marine Dision in the assault on Torokina, a cape halfway up the island's west coast.

REINFORCEMENTS

Army troops (left) trudge through the surf en route to the shores of Arare, New Guinea, in May 1944, during MacArthur's final drive to eliminate Japanese resistance on the northern coast of the island. Army forces also landed on the nearby island of Wakde to capture a Japanese airfield. Within 24 hours of the landing, MacArthur announced "the practical end of the New Guinea campaign," but hostilities persisted until August.

HELL OF A FIGHTER

An F6F Hellcat fighter (left) awaits takeoff clearance from the deck of the U.S.S. *Lexington*. Carrier-based aircraft distracted Japanese naval forces in the Marshalls while the Marines stormed Kwajalein Atoll. Pilots referred to the Hellcat as the "Aluminum Tank." With six Browning machine guns, the F6F struck fear into the hearts of enemy pilots. At war's end, the Hellcat had shot down 5,156 enemy planes in air-to-air combat and achieved a 19:1 kill ratio.

WAR COUNCIL

Having safely eluded enemy fire during the initial assault of Roi Island in the Marshalls, U.S. Marines (right) confer about their next move. Though many of these islands were heavily garrisoned, Allied casualties were surprisingly light. In the end, the Allies captured enough of the Marshalls to isolate several enemy strongholds.

END GAME

American soldiers (right) coax hungry and frightened civilians out of the caves where they had been hiding during the fighting for Saipan. The island was secured in early July, but Saipan's population feared Allied occupation. Depite reassurances from the Americans that they would not harm captives, hundreds of civilians and Japanese troops committed suicide by holding grenades or jumping off of cliffs.

"HELL IS ON US"

A wounded Marine (below) receives a plasma drip from a Navy corpsman on Saipan. In less than a month of fighting, the U.S. lost over 2,000 men and more than 12,000 were wounded. Casualties on the Japanese side were far heavier, with 29,000 dead. When news of the Allied victory at Saipan reached Tokyo, Emperor Hirohito exclaimed: "Hell is on us." Prime Minister Hideki Tojo called it "an unprecedentedly great national crisis" and resigned his post in shame.

FIGHT TO THE DEATH

Silhouetted against Saipan's jungle backdrop, an American soldier (right) points his rifle into a bunker. Although Guam was his primary objective, Admiral Nimitz chose to invade Saipan first because it was closer to Japan. Controlled by the Japanese for 30 years, Saipan was defended by 30,000 troops when it was invaded by the U.S. Marines on June 15, 1944. Fanatical banzai charges stunned the Americans but hastened the Japanese's demise. "The Japs just kept coming and coming," said one American soldier. "I didn't think they'd ever stop."

SEA SUPERIORITY
A U.S. destroyer comes astern of an American carrier (above) in the Philippine Sea, where American naval forces dealt Japan's First Mobile Fleet another defeat. Task Force 58, composed of 15 American carriers and seven battleships, annihilated the aircraft from nine Japanese carriers in what was later called the "Great Marianas Turkey Shoot."

BLAZING DEFEAT
Spewing fire and smoke, a Japanese plane (left) plummets out of the sky toward the U.S.S. *Kitkun Bay*. The American assault on the Marianas prompted Vice Admiral Jisaburo Ozawa and the Japanese navy to attack the American Fifth Fleet, in what would be the last great carrier battle of the war.

THE FIRST STEP
Two American A-20 attack aircraft (above) carry out a strafing run on a Japanese rail line on Luzon. The Japanese, unlike the U.S. in 1941, had heavily bolstered their Filipino defenses with 350,000 troops, and the road to Manila would be a slow and costly path for the Americans.

WELCOME BACK
A Filipino civilian directs an American tank (right) toward Japanese positions during the fighting on Leyte Island in October 1944. Although the Japanese had made great efforts to befriend the Filipinos during the occupation, oppressive measures turned hundreds of civilians into guerrilla soldiers who welcomed the return of the Americans.

PATH OF LEAST RESISTANCE
U.S. soldiers from the Tradewind Task Force (right) board a transport bound for the tiny, lightly defended island of Morotai. MacArthur invaded the island, located midway between western New Guinea and the Philippines, in September 1944 to build an airfield that could be used to protect the Allied landings on the Philippines.

HOUSE TO HOUSE

American soldiers (above), with rifles at the ready, conduct house-to-house searches for Japanese within Manila's "Walled City." When the Americans reached the *Intra Muros*, they found hundreds of Japanese soldiers holed up in the rubble, holding some 4,000 civilians hostage.

BOMBS AWAY

A 2,000-pound bomb (right) falls upon Japanese shore installations in Manila Harbor. As MacArthur's forces moved inland, he prohibited air attacks in order to spare many of Manila's 700,000 citizens from wholesale carnage. Sadly, MacArthur's attempts to preserve the capital failed, as Japanese resistance required artillery shelling.

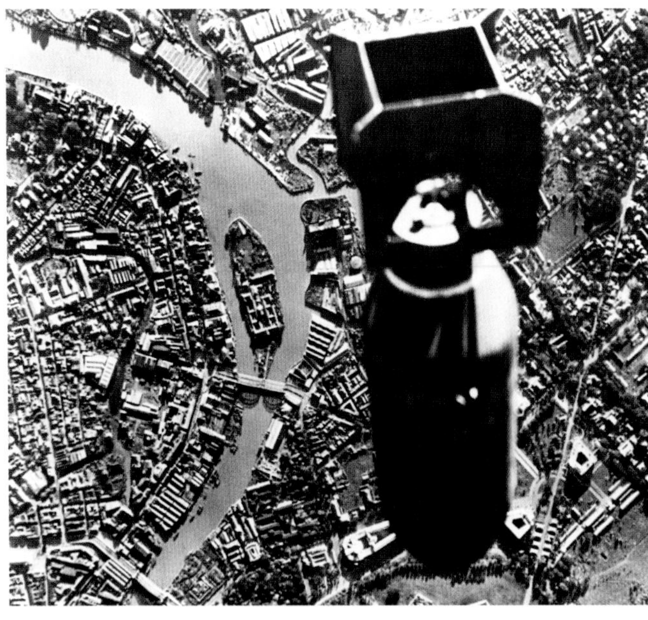

SURVIVING THE SIEGE

American soldiers (right) help women and children hostages from the rubble of two Manila churches. One survivor of the ordeal recalled, "Dreadful darkness filled the interior of the church. We trampled on the dead bodies lying everywhere." After the siege ended on February 23, 3,000 of the 4,000 hostages were liberated; the others had been killed.

Douglas MacArthur

Controversial, contradictory, flamboyant, and bombastic, MacArthur fulfilled his promise to the Philippines, but his political ambitions prevented him from quietly fading away.

AMERICAN CAESAR
Rarely photographed during the war without his trademark corn cob pipe, sunglasses, and Filipino field marshal cap (inset), MacArthur (above) experienced both glorious victory and devastating defeat in the Pacific. Questions still remain as to why MacArthur's forces at Clark Field in the Philippines were caught unprepared by the Japanese the day after Pearl Harbor.

FINAL SURRENDER

MacArthur (above) presides over Japan's unconditional surrender on September 2, 1945, aboard the U.S.S. *Missouri* in Tokyo Bay. MacArthur, who earned his share of medals (like the Silver Star, inset) and titles in his 52 years of military service, was named supreme commander for the Allied forces in 1945.

TWO KINGS

MacArthur (above, left) and Emperor Hirohito pose together after Japan's surrender. The photograph was widely circulated in Japan to reassure the Japanese people that the Allies would not punish or remove their "divine" leader.

HEIR TO THE THRONE?

Although MacArthur (below, left) did not share Roosevelt's politics, he served loyally as Army chief of staff until 1935. "I think that you are our best general," Roosevelt reportedly told him. "But I believe you would be our worst politician."

THE CHIEF

MacArthur (above, in France with General Maxime Weygand in 1931) became the youngest four-star general in the history of the U.S. Army when he was named Army chief of staff in 1930. During World War I, the famously flamboyant general had earned the nicknames, "Beau Brummell of the 42nd" and "d'Artagnan of the Western Front," as much for his impeccable appearance as for his battlefield acumen.

Invasion of Western Europe

Life's Robert Capa photographed the first waves of infantry assault at Omaha Beach (left). A darkroom error ruined 98 of his 106 pictures, and the salvaged eight were blurred, inadvertantly enhancing the horrific chaos of D-Day. The 101st Airborne (insignia below) was dropped behind enemy lines to keep German reinforcements away from the invasion beaches.

"The war will be won or lost on the beaches. The first 24 hours of the invasion will be decisive." That was the judicious assessment of Field Marshal Erwin Rommel, the brilliant German commander who had frustrated the Allies in North Africa and to whom—along with Field Marshal Gerd von Rundstedt—Hitler had entrusted the job of crushing any assault on Fortress Europe. In spring 1944 the German high command knew the Allies were coming, but one crucial question remained: Where would they land? Unable to defend every mile of coastline between Holland and the Bay of Biscay, Germany reinforced its defenses at the most likely invasion areas: near Calais, which offered the shortest water crossing and closest path to Germany, and the French ports facing the English Channel.

Rommel accelerated work on the so-called Atlantic Wall, a massive construction project begun in 1942. Under his direction, millions of mines and obstacles were added to obstruct invading troops at the waterline, and reinforced concrete gun emplacements—along with an interlocking chain of bunkers—were installed to pin the enemy on the beaches. Vast low-lying inland areas were flooded to trap airborne troops. With these defenses in place, Rommel's plan was to move up his Panzer reserves and drive the Allies back into the sea. Worn out by the strain of nonstop preparation, and with a period of stormy weather predicted for early June, Rommel decided to return to Germany for a quick family visit. He hoped to surprise his wife on her birthday, June 6.

General George Patton (below, left) and General Bernard Montgomery (below, right) exchange pleasantries on July 7, 1944, as General Omar Bradley looks on. While Bradley and Montgomery helped plan the invasion, Patton was assigned to lead the fictitious Operation Fortitude.

Across the Channel, southern England was practically sinking under the weight of three million Allied soldiers, sailors, and airmen, and two million tons of matériel stockpiled for the invasion. Supreme Allied Commander Dwight Eisenhower and his staff had decided to sidestep the strongest German fortifications by landing on the coast of Normandy between the mouth of the Seine and Cherbourg. This 60-mile strip of shoreline contained no suitable port, but Allied planners had come up with an ingenious solution. Old ships and specially-constructed barges would be towed across the channel and scuttled in shallow water off the beaches to create two artificial

Paratroopers (above) display signs of eager bravado as their C-47 idles on the runway in England. American airborne troops faced the "$10,000 jump": The GI's were made to buy life-insurance policies for that amount in the event they did not survive the leap into the French night.

harbors. To keep the true landing site secret, the Allies hatched an equally ambitious plan: Operation Fortitude. Rubber tanks and planes, phantom armies, and fake radio messages—all designed for German consumption—indicated an Allied attack along the Pas de Calais, led by hard-charging American general George Patton.

By the end of May final preparations for Operation Overlord, as the actual Normandy invasion was named, were complete. "The mighty host was tense as a coiled spring," Eisenhower wrote, "a great human spring, coiled for the moment when its energy should be released and it would vault the English Channel in the greatest amphibious assault ever attempted." After a one-day postponement due to poor weather, D-Day began shortly after midnight on June 6, 1944.

Specially trained pathfinders parachuted into France to mark drop zones for the three airborne divisions—the U.S. 82d and 101st, and the British Sixth—that followed on their heels. But as the transports approached the drop zones, the tight formations of C-47s were broken up by cloud cover and antiaircraft fire. Rather than landing in large, cohesive units, 20,000 paratroopers were scattered all over the countryside. Many drowned in the flooded areas; others became tangled in trees. Finding a mere handful of enlisted men around him, Major General Maxwell Taylor of the 101st Airborne wryly told his staff, "Never have so few been commanded by so many."

The bungled drop would have been a complete catastrophe if it hadn't also contributed to German confusion. The scattering of Allied airborne forces actually helped disguise the primary objectives of Overlord and caused the Germans to hesitate in ordering counterattacks to the beaches. As one American D-Day veteran described it: "The Germans knew where they were, but didn't know what was going on, while the paratroopers knew what was going on, but had no idea where they were."

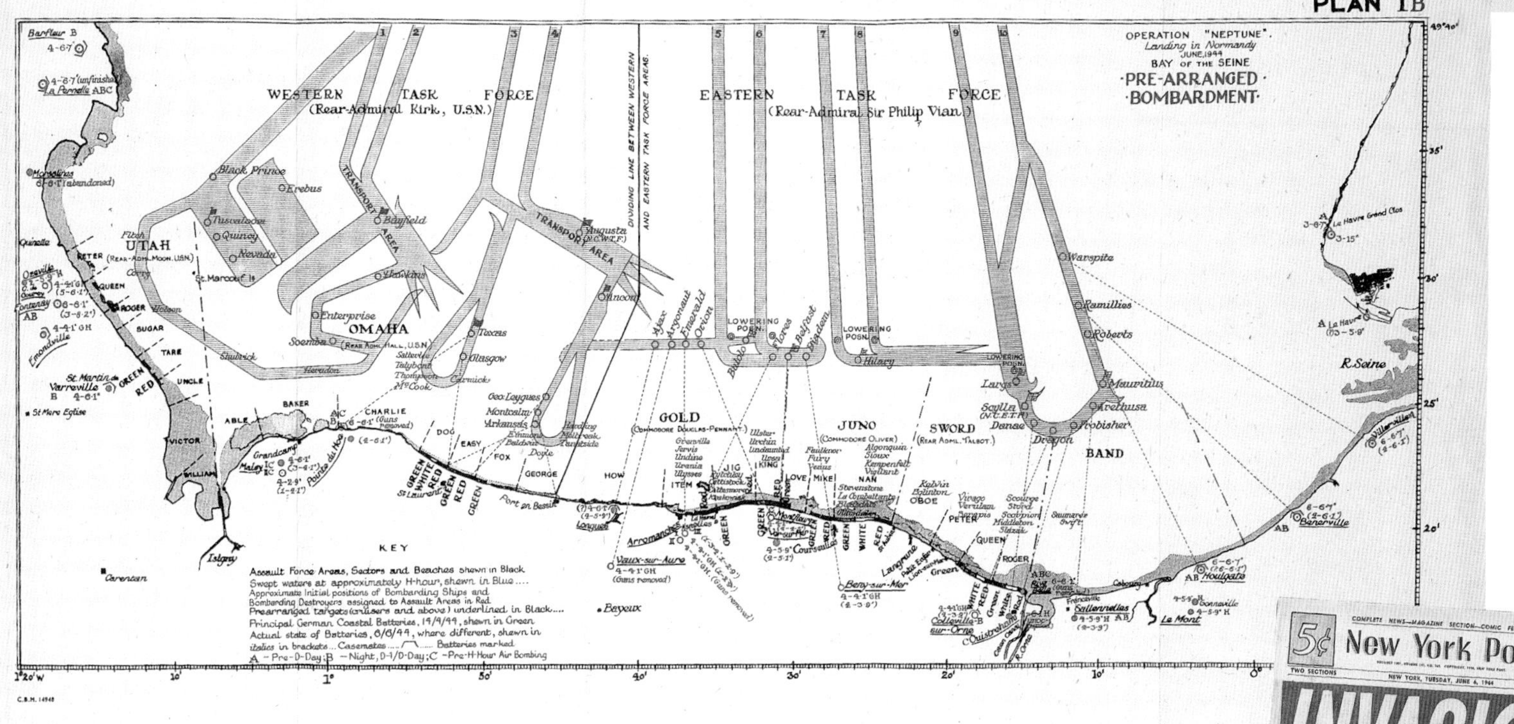

New York Post

5¢

NEW YORK, TUESDAY, JUNE 6, 1944

INVASION

SMASHING AHEAD!

Nazis Say We're 10 Miles In; Sky Troops Far Beyond Lines

The massive invasion's intricate planning, shown in the map above, paid off: German defenders were taken mostly by surprise, and when the sun set on June 6, some 156,000 Allied troops had landed in Normandy. The D-Day headline from the *New York Post* (inset) announced the news in the U.S.

As a chilly gray dawn broke, the greatest armada in history—nearly 5,000 vessels of every size and shape—materialized out of the offshore mist, while 12,000 Allied planes swept the skies overhead. A thunderous air and naval bombardment saturated the German coastal positions. Swarms of small landing craft and amphibious tanks churned through swells and heavy surf toward five separate code-named beaches: British and Canadian troops landed on Gold, Juno, and Sword, while American infantry assaulted Utah and Omaha. Though opposition was sometimes heavy, Allied troops cleared the first four beaches in quick order and began moving inland.

Omaha Beach, however, proved much more difficult to clear than anticipated. Allied intelligence failed to detect a crack enemy infantry division that had recently transferred to the area. One-hundred-foot bluffs above the beach gave German gunners an unobstructed field of fire against soldiers of the 29th and First Infantry Divisions as they poured from their landing craft. "We got out of the boat and started wading and then I saw men falling and had to push past their bodies," wrote LIFE photographer Robert Capa, who landed in the first wave. "The water was cold, and the beach still more than a hundred yards away. The bullets tore holes in the water around me." Capa took cover behind a steel beach obstacle, "and I felt safe enough to take pictures of the other guys hiding just like I was."

Pinned down for hours in a murderous crossfire of machine guns, mortars, and artillery, the American troops finally rallied. "Two kinds of people are staying on this beach," Colonel George Taylor exhorted his dazed and frightened men. "The dead and those who are going to die—now let's get the hell out of here." Singly and in small groups, the soldiers edged forward through the onslaught. By early afternoon they had cleared the high ground and secured the beach.

When Rommel received word of the landings, he rushed back to his headquarters. But the crucial hours when the invasion forces were most vulnerable had slipped away. To make matters worse, Hitler had been misled by the Fortitude campaign and believed that Normandy was merely a feint to cover the main land-

SS Lieutenant Colonel Max Wünsche (above, right) drives injured Lieutenant Rudolf von Ribbentrop (left)—son of the Nazi foreign minister—to an aid station near Falaise. Despite a swift and disciplined escape, an estimated 50,000 Germans surrendered to the Allies at the Falaise "pocket."

ings yet to come near Calais. He initially refused appeals to release the Panzer reserves, and any chance of overrunning the invasion beaches disappeared. "The first phase of the invasion," Rommel's chief of staff Hans Speidel glumly noted, "ended with an obvious military, political, and psychological success for the Allies."

But the cost, especially at Omaha, where more than 2,200 American soldiers were killed, wounded, or reported missing, was sobering. Strewn on the beach was a vast panorama of wreckage and death. "There were trucks tipped half over and swamped," war correspondent Ernie Pyle wrote, "and small landing craft half submerged. There were tanks that had only just made the beach before being knocked out. There were jeeps that had burned to a dull gray.... On the beach lay, expended, sufficient men and mechanism for a small war. They were gone forever now."

Although the seaborne forces had achieved a firm foothold—and linked up with the paratroopers in many areas—by the end of D-Day, not all of the preinvasion objectives had been reached. Field Marshal Bernard Montgomery, for example, was supposed to occupy Caen before nightfall. Six weeks later, his divisions were still stalled outside the city, facing fierce German resistance. In the American sector, the infantrymen and tankers found themselves struggling through thick, tall hedgerows that lined every farmer's field and provided almost impregnable positions for German defenders. An enterprising American sergeant devised a serrated blade that could be welded to the front of a tank, allow-

ing it to plow through the stiff, tangled undergrowth. Still, daily progress was often measured in yards, and casualties ran high.

Finally, on July 25 the Americans launched Operation Cobra against the German divisions manning the St. Lô sector of the front. B-24 heavy bombers obliterated miles of enemy trenches—killing or burying troops alive—and pulverized tanks and guns. The stunned survivors offered little resistance as American infantry poured into the breach to open a path for the armored columns of Patton's newly activated Third Army. Cobra enabled the Allies to breakout from the Normandy beachhead. Sherman tanks and halftracks raced forward, ignoring their flanks and often outrunning their supplies.

Hitler foolishly ordered a counterattack, which only prevented the German formations that remained relatively intact from withdrawing to defensible positions. Instead, they were snared in what came to be known as the Falaise "pocket," a vast death-trap for thousands of German troops. Two whole German armies found themselves cornered. After an organized but costly retreat, German resistance south of the Seine River collapsed and the road to Paris lay open. Eisenhower gave the Second Free French Armored Division the honor of leading Allied forces into the capital on August 25. After four years of occupation, Parisians exuberantly feted their liberators with hoarded champagne and heartfelt embraces.

By mid-September—one month after General Alexander Patch's Seventh Army had landed on the Riviera in southern France against only scattered German opposition—France had been liberated, and the Wehrmacht was in full retreat toward the German border. Common sentiment in the Allied camp held that the war would be over by Christmas. Little did anyone suspect what long and costly battles still lay ahead.

German leadership was split on the role of tanks, such as Tigers (above, left), in the defense of Fortress Europe. Rommel wanted the tanks near the beaches to crush the initial assault. He worried that the millions of mines, including the Teller model (inset, with poster illustrating its components), would merely slow an invasion. Rundstedt preferred to hold the tanks in reserve for a decisive counterattack.

INSPECTING THE WALL

Field Marshal Erwin Rommel (above, center) inspects western Europe's coastal defenses, some of which he designed himself, in early 1944. Construction of the Atlantic Wall required nearly 20 million tons of poured concrete along the most narrow sections of the English Channel. Although Rommel boasted of an impregnable "zone of death" in 1944, he privately deemed Normandy's defenses to be lacking.

POISED FOR BATTLE

Anxious American soldiers aboard a Coast Guard transport ship (left) examine a model of Omaha Beach and discuss the final details for the invasion of Normandy. This scene was played out on thousands of Allied ships across the choppy waters of the English Channel. As the sailors shep-herded thier precious and fearsome cargo, it was the last chance to play cards, write a letter home, or try to find a few quiet moments of reflection.

MANNING THE WALL
Hitler's hero, Frederick the Great, once said, "He who defends everything, defends nothing." By 1944 the Wehrmacht was spread thinly over 6,000 kilometers of western European coastline. And in France one out of every six infantry soldiers was a conscripted foreign "volunteer" from German-occupied territories. The average age of a German defender was 36; his U.S. Army counterpart was more than ten years younger. Many old men and young boys defended the Normandy beaches, and with no substantial air or naval defense they, like the lone sentry above, could only watch and wait.

WADING TO HELL

When the first waves of the 116th Infantry Regiment hit Omaha Beach without the direct-fire support of their amphibious tanks, many of which had foundered or sunk, the unchecked fury of the German Reich poured down upon them. One Higgins boat (like the model at left) instantly became a floating morgue when all 30 of its occupants died in a hail of fire as soon as its doors opened. Within 10 minutes of the landings only one officer of the 116th's A Company was alive; only a few dozen of the unit's 200 men would survive D-Day, nearly all of them wounded.

PINNED DOWN

In this classic Robert Capa photograph (above), a GI makes the horrific journey through landing obstacles, hugging the surf to increase his chances of making it to the beach. Although they were meticulously planned to the second, almost all of Omaha's initial attack waves were soon off target or off schedule. Many soldiers drowned under heavy equipment when their landing crafts came under fire and were forced to unload their crews in deeper waters.

THE STRUGGLE FORWARD

Two GIs (left) help the occupant of a life raft ashore. For many soldiers, just reaching the beach was a monumental task, but a thousand isolated actions slowly brought order to Omaha as D-Day morning turned to afternoon. Impromptu platoons were formed, and little by little, assault teams began to scale the bluffs. As one officer described the heroics in Ernie Pyle's column, "The only way to take the beach is to face it and keep going. . . If the men are pinned down,. . . dug in and out of action, they might as well not be there at all. . . . We did it with every advantage on the enemy's side and every disadvantage on ours."

USAW-4062301-S
LST 1009

THE BRITISH SWORD

Compared to Omaha, the assault at Sword Beach (above) progressed more according to plan. Aided by heavy-armor support from Sherman and Churchill tanks, and covered by the thick haze of smoke grenades, British forces swarmed ashore. Despite German gun batteries, which engaged the H.M.S. *Warspite,* and pillbox machine-guns trained on the beach, all fighting had progressed inland by 8:00 a.m., only 35 minutes after landing. Lord Lovat, head of the commando brigade, strode among his men at the assembly point and told them, "Come on, get a move on, this is no different than an exercise." Some 29,000 British troops landed on Sword that day, suffering only 630 casualties.

POSITIVE REINFORCEMENT

American soldiers (left) drive inland after successfully landing on the Normandy beaches on June 6. Eisenhower knew he needed to reinforce the inital assaults with equipment and artillery before the Germans could mount a serious counterattack. Despite the continued dangers of submerged pressure mines and delays in getting the artificial harbors operational (one of them was destroyed by a storm on June 19), more than 850,000 men, almost 150,000 vehicles, and more than a half-million tons of Allied supplies landed in northern France in the three weeks after D-Day.

A STEALTHY APPROACH

Three British infantrymen (above), their rifles at the ready, creep through a field near Caen. In theory Caen was to be in British hands by nightfall on D-Day. However, the inland advance was delayed long enough for the Germans to marshal their available armored divisions and protect the strategically-located city—the logical linkup between German forces in Normandy and Calais. Additionally, the Germans wanted to defend the 18-mile plain that led south from Caen, ideal terrain for armored operations or airfield locations.

ADVANCE INTO RUINS

British soldiers (right) survey the aftermath of the battle for Caen. In the end, the only path to this critical stronghold was straight through it: Having been stymied in two attempts to outflank German positions, General Montgomery decided to storm the city from three sides. On July 7 Allied bombers kicked off Operation Charnwood by dropping over 2,000 tons of explosives in support of the main assault. The resulting destruction was so thorough that it impeded British and Canadian mechanized units as much as the desperate German resistance. Finally, on July 8, a brigade of the Canadian Third Division captured the center of the city.

PUNISHING FIRE

Its spent shells discarded, an American M-10 tank destroyer (above) belches fire as German forces retreat from the heavily-fortified city of St. Lô. The campaign for St. Lô dragged on for two weeks and cost General Bradley 40,000 casualties. But when the dust settled, he and his men had finally punched a critical hole in the Wehrmacht's defenses.

PATTON'S PURSUIT

Soldiers from the U.S. Eighth Corps (right) painstakingly clear the French coastal town of St. Malo on August 8. The remaining forces of General Patton's newly-activated Third Army, meanwhile, made a sweeping left hook to the southeast and began the sprint for Paris. Patton's involvement in the Normandy campaign had been kept secret up to this point to complete the deception of Operation Fortitude. On August 15, however, Allied command told the world that it was, in fact, the controversial general who was leading the Allied charge toward Paris and the German border.

HITLER'S YOUTH

The face of the typical German soldier in France in 1944 was either unusually old or, like these members of the Waffen-SS (above), unusually young. By the end of 1943 Germany had suffered nearly three million casualties in the war against the Soviet Union, and Hitler had been forced to call up those born in 1925 and 1926 for active service.

HELLISH HEDGEROWS

The hedgerows—impenetrable thickets and earthern mounds—that bordered Normandy's fields were perfect defensive positions for German snipers (right). A single German defender, if properly positioned in or behind a hedgerow, could paralyze an entire Allied platoon. The hedgerows were one of the main reasons that Allied progress inland on D-Day was initially measured in yards instead of miles.

POCKET-ED

Rommel was correct when he predicted that the battle would be won or lost on the beaches. Once the Allies progessed inland, outmanned and outgunned German forces—like these at right from the Falaise "pocket"—surrendered in droves. On June 17, Rommel met with Hitler and urged the Führer to negotiate a peace with the western Allies. Hitler adamantly refused and the war continued.

TEMPORARY TRIUMPH

Soldiers of the U.S. 28th Infantry Division (above) sweep down the Champs Elysées on August 29, displaying a heavy Allied presence to an anxious French populace. Although the spectacular drive from the beaches to Paris had been completed, battlefields on the Hurtgen, in the Ardennes, and in the Colmar Pocket awaited.

LIBERTÉ

Joyful Parisians, delivered at last on August 25 from more than 1,500 days of German occupation, cheer soldiers from General Leclerc's French Second Armored Division (right). By noon the French flag fluttered atop the Eiffel Tower.

Dwight Eisenhower

The Supreme Commander of the Allied Expeditionary Force was universally liked both by the soldiers who served under him and by the leaders who sent him to deliver a continent.

RALLYING THE TROOPS
Paratroopers from the 101st Airborne (top) receive a pep talk from their supreme commander on June 5. Eisenhower had made the difficult decision to drop these troops on the western flank of the D-Day invasion against the advice of his air commander, Sir Trafford Leigh-Mallory, who predicted 70 percent casualties. Less than half of the 6,600 paratroopers in the outfit would still be fighting at the end of June 6. The flaming-sword insignia (left) was Ike's special emblem for SHAEF, Supreme Headquarters of the Allied Expeditionary Force.

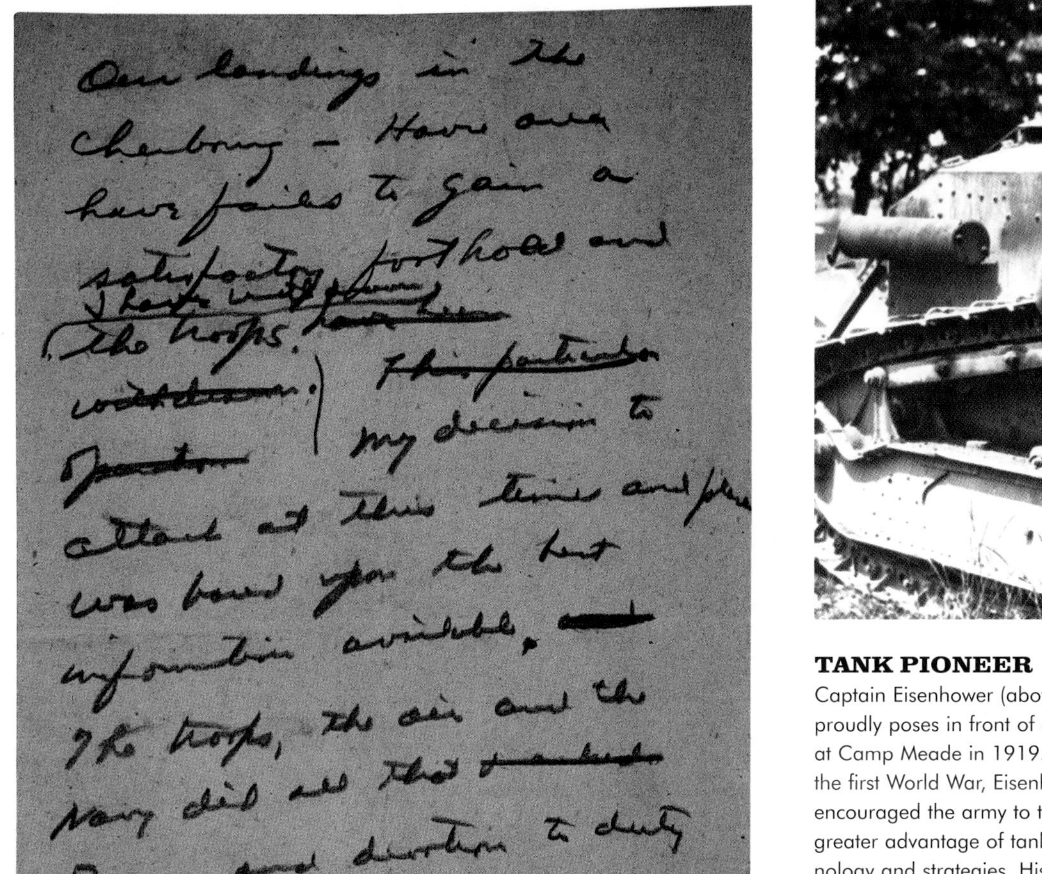

Our landings in the Cherbourg – Havre area have failed to gain a satisfactory foothold and I have withdrawn the troops. My decision to attack at this time and place was based upon the best information available. The troops, the air and the Navy did all that Bravery and devotion to duty could do. If any blame or fault attaches to the attempt it is mine alone.

July 5

FOR THE RECORD

In a hastily-scrawled—and misdated—note written just before D-Day (above) , Eisenhower prepared to assume full responsibility if the Normandy invasion failed. Fortunately, Overlord's success made the delivery of his note unnecessary.

TANK PIONEER

Captain Eisenhower (above) proudly poses in front of a tank at Camp Meade in 1919. After the first World War, Eisenhower encouraged the army to take greater advantage of tank technology and strategies. His suggestions were unfortunately ignored by the dismantled army.

AMERICAN CAESARS

Eisenhower stands deferentially next to Chief of Staff General Douglas MacArthur (above) during maneuvers in 1932. Ike spent a decade working for MacArthur and the demanding general predicted greatness for his hard-working aide. "This is the best officer in the Army," MacArthur wrote in one fitness report. "When the next war comes, he should go right to the top."

DRESSING DOWN

Eisenhower's sparsely decorated jacket belied the magnitude of the general's responsibilities. It was his keen talent for military strategy, combined with his savvy political skills and immense likability, that distinguished him as a leader of men.

UNCOMMON BRAVERY
It took a special brand of courage to leap into the heat of battle shooting film and not bullets. Yet the men of the U.S. Army Signal Corps (left) were charged with just that task—an especially dangerous venture that accounted, perhaps, for their casual swagger and sense of élan. Army photographers (below) also covered a wide range of events off the battlefield, from the summit at Yalta to the traveling shows of the USO.

Photo Journalists

Much of society would be blind to the harsh realities of war without the efforts of combat photographers. It is through their eyes and lenses that we witness and remember the war.

TOOLS OF THE TRADE
The Graflex Speed Graphic camera (left)—the C-4 in military parlance and standard equipment for Allied photographers—was as ubiquitous for the Signal Corps photographer as the M-1 carbine was for the infantry soldier. This model captured some of the most compelling images of the war, including the iconic raising of the American flag at Iwo Jima.

STARING DOWN DEATH
Robert Capa (above, left, with photographer George Rodger) was hailed as the greatest American war photographer. His "ruined" images of Omaha Beach captured the essence of D-Day's surreal horror.

CROSSING BOUNDARIES
Margaret Bourke-White (right) was the first woman photographer to travel with U.S. armed forces. She was with Patton's Third Army when it entered Germany, and her shots of concentration camp atrocities shocked the world.

AN ARMY OF CAMERAS
Photographer Hanns Hubmann (above) was part of Hitler's *Propaganda Kompanie*, a Wehrmacht division 12,000 strong at its zenith. Hubmann shot film for the military magazine *Signal*—Germany's best-selling journal during the war.

PRESS PASS
Everything shot by war photojournalists (insignia inset) was assessed for its propaganda value. General Eisenhower's opinion on the subject was clear: "Correspondents have a job in war as essential as the military personnel. . . Fundamentally, public opinion wins wars."

LAST RESORT
Although they were focused on recording the story rather than making it, the Signal Corps and their foreign counterparts were not immune to the realities of the battlefields. The German photographer above keeps a Luger nestled in his right boot, a subtle indication that the line between documentary-maker and combatant was not always clear.

The Fall of the Third Reich

Soviet soldiers (left) march victoriously past a fallen Nazi flag on their way to Vienna in April 1945. With many Germans having already abandoned the city, the Austrian city fell peacefully on April 13. Heroes of the Soviet Union's great victory received the Order of Lenin medal (below).

The room was somber as General Dwight Eisenhower entered to meet his top commanders on December 18, 1944. Two days earlier, Germany had launched a massive offensive in the Ardennes, smashing the lines of the overconfident Allies. Intelligence had estimated that the Germans had only four divisions in the area, but 25 divisions had ripped through the Allied front. Adolf Hitler's desperate gamble was as successful as it was improbable, but Eisenhower didn't panic. "The present situation is to be regarded as one of opportunity for us and not of disaster," he told his men. "There will be only cheerful faces at this conference table." Eisenhower understood that after six months of calculated retreat on the western front, the Wehrmacht had stuck its neck into an Allied noose by exposing itself in the Ardennes. As he had written the day after the German attack, "If things go well, we should not only stop the thrust, but be able to profit from it."

Eisenhower's confidence was based on the desperation implicit in Hitler's do-or-die offensive. The Wehrmacht—so superior in the early days of the war—was retreating on every front. In Italy, the Allies had captured Rome and were slowly climbing the Italian peninsula. In France, Operation Overlord had exploded beyond the beaches of Normandy, and Allied armies raced through Belgium and northern France, toward the German border. On the eastern front, the rejuvenated Soviet army, which had suffered horrific losses early in the war, exacted revenge on a beaten German foe, laying waste to

Hitler's health mirrored the demise of his Reich. In December 1944, General Hasso von Manteuffel described him as "a stooped figure with a pale and puffy face, hunched in his chair, his hands trembling."

Hitler (right) barely survived the July 20, 1944, bomb that injured his right arm and left him deaf in one ear. Colonel Claus von Stauffenberg, the German officer who had planted the bomb, was quickly captured and executed. In the weeks that followed, the Gestapo arrested 7,000 conspiracy suspects and condemned nearly 5,000 of them to death.

German prisoners retrieve the body of an American soldier (above) who was killed in the Ardennes. The Battle of the Bulge lasted six weeks and resulted in more than 180,000 American and German casualties.

cities and villages on its way west. Not all threats to Hitler, however, wore enemy uniforms. The sinking fortunes of the German Reich challenged the Führer's authority even at home. In July he narrowly escaped with his life when a bomb exploded during a conference in Rastenburg. A faction of the army had determined that the war was no longer winnable after the successful Allied landings in France and hoped to negotiate a peace with the Allies after Hitler's death. But Hitler was spared from the bomb's blast by a sturdy oak table, and the conspirators—led by Colonel Claus von Stauffenberg—were quickly captured and executed. Germany's most revered officer, Erwin Rommel, was also implicated and committed suicide to protect his family and his reputation.

His enemies purged, Hitler surrounded himself with men who shared his ludicrous enthusiasm. Their optimism had little basis in reality. By August, 30 Allied divisions were either at or across the Seine River. Paris was liberated on August 25, 1944, and by mid-September the Allies had reached the Siegfried Line, Germany's western defenses. Nevertheless, Hitler began planning a counterattack. The objective of the operation—codenamed Autumn Mist—was the port city of Antwerp. Hitler decided to strike through the Ardennes, the same region of dense woodlands and hills that German panzers had rolled through on the way to France in 1940. Allied intelligence reported that the German army was depleted and demoralized, as short on supplies as it was on organization and cohesiveness. But Hitler recently had transferred panzer units from the east to the western front and activated all German men between the ages of 16 and 60 for military service. Field Marshal Gerd von Rundstedt's western army, therefore, was still a formidable fighting machine.

The Battle of the Bulge, the largest battle of the war on the western front and the largest engagement ever involving U.S. troops, began at dawn on December 16. Foggy weather neutralized Allied air superiority, and English-speaking Germans, disguised as American GIs, spread confusion behind Allied lines. The Wehrmacht bent the Allied line back in a wedge-shaped bulge and came within four miles of the Meuse River in Belgium.

Winston Churchill, Franklin Roosevelt, and Josef Stalin (left to right) chat amicably in Yalta in February 1945. Churchill and Roosevelt conceded Poland to the Soviets at the conference, but exacted a promise from Stalin that he would declare war on Japan once Germany was defeated.

But Eisenhower's steady hand negated the initial shock of the attack, and the Allies held. The German mobile assault lacked sufficient fuel, and the American 101st Airborne Division defiantly held Bastogne, a major road junction and an essential objective for German success. In early January 1945, Hitler withdrew troops from the tip of the bulge, essentially abandoning his grand counteroffensive, and by January 16 the American First and Third Armies had pinched off the bulge at Houffalize. Twelve days later, the battle was over; the Führer's last gamble had failed. The Wehrmacht had inflicted approximately 80,000 casualties on the Allied forces—predominantly American—in the Ardennes but at an irreplaceable cost of 100,000 men, 800 tanks, and 1,000 aircraft. Eisenhower had been correct: Germany's Ardennes offensive accelerated the demise of the Wehrmacht and opened the road to Berlin for the Allies.

German survivors from the Ardennes retreated or were transferred to the eastern front, where a Soviet winter offensive was in its earliest stages. The eastern front was quickly becoming a German nightmare. Since the Battle of Kursk, in July 1943, the Wehrmacht was virtually helpless to prevent the Soviets from regaining the industrial and agricultural regions of Eastern Europe. In June 1944, as Allied troops fought past the beaches in Normandy, the Red Army celebrated the third anniversary of Barbarossa by launching Operation Bagration, a giant offensive along an 800-mile front that resulted in 350,000 German casualties. One German commander labeled it a "greater catastrophe than Stalingrad." But the worst was yet to come.

On his 56th birthday, Hitler (above) encourages the newest and youngest members of the Reich's crumbling defense. In the last months of the war, German boys born in 1929 were enrolled in the armed forces. General Wilhelm Keitel (above, right) surrenders to the Soviet Union on May 8, 1945.

As the western allies regrouped in the Ardennes, the Soviet Union prepared a final assault on Germany from the east. General Heinz Guderian, chief of the German army's high command, had reported that the Soviets outnumbered his German troops on the eastern front eleven-to-one. This numerical disparity seemed so extreme to many German leaders that they assumed it to be the product of Soviet propaganda. Heinrich Himmler, head of the SS, insisted that such reports were "grossly exaggerated," and Hitler called the incredible figures part of the "greatest bluff since Genghis Khan." The rumors, however, were true. Under the command of Marshals Ivan Konev and Georgi Zhukov, 2.2 million Red Army soldiers, equipped with 6,400 tanks, and 46,000 pieces of artillery, pounced on the Reich's 400,000-man army in Poland and Hungary. The invasion began on January 12 with an earthquake of artillery fire, and the Soviet advance quickly turned into an avalanche. Once unleashed, the Red Army avenged the unspeakable horrors the Reich's soldiers had inflicted on the Soviet people in 1941 and 1942. German civilians were murdered; women were raped. "It seemed as though the devil himself had come," said one German prisoner of war.

The Wehrmacht—beaten on both fronts—gave way as the Soviets swept toward Berlin. Germany's only hope for survival was a schism between the Allied powers. Hitler had always doubted the strength of an alliance that wed the western democracies with the Soviet Union, the ultimate ideological enemy to British colonialism and American capitalism. But he underestimated the Allies' resolve. On February 4, the "Big Three"—Winston Churchill, Franklin Roosevelt, and Josef Stalin—met in the Crimean city of Yalta to discuss the war. Although the seeds of the Cold War were planted at Yalta, as Stalin used the Red Army's strong standing on the eastern front to exact several concessions from Churchill and a sickly Roosevelt, Hitler's hopes for a miracle were dashed when the coalition emerged intact.

Only the capture of Berlin remained. Allied armies raced toward the German capital from both sides. Churchill, who had sensed at Yalta that the Soviets had great designs on postwar Europe, urged Eisenhower to push for Berlin in order to "shake hands [with the Soviets] as far east as possible." Eisenhower, however, declined to get wrapped up in the political maneuvering.

As the Soviets destroyed Berlin (left), many Germans hoped that the Americans would join them in their fight against the Soviets. There was no ill will, however, when American and Soviet soldiers (above) linked up near the banks of the Elbe River during the last week of April 1945.

Berlin was well within the postwar occupation zone assigned to the Soviets at Yalta, and although the Anglo-Americans were promised a presence in the Reich's capital, Eisenhower refused to sacrifice American lives for what he now deemed a trophy city. His decision was criticized after the fact, but his reasoning and military logic were sound and responsible at the time.

The Soviets reveled in the honor of capturing the Reich's capital, and it was well-earned—the Red Army had killed eight out of every 10 German soldiers who died in the war. Hitler, who had opportunities to flee Berlin, elected to stay until the bitter end. "I must force the decision here," he said in April 1945, "or go down fighting." His spirits were lifted on April 13, when he learned that Roosevelt had died. Hitler interpreted Roosevelt's death as a harbinger of good luck, but he was mistaken. German troops hurried to the western front to surrender to the democracies, while the Soviets closed the circle around Berlin and maliciously ravaged the city—at a cost of 300,000 Soviet casualties.

The end came at a frenetic pace. In Italy, Benito Mussolini was captured and executed; his body was dismembered and dragged through the streets of Milan on April 28. Two days later, Hitler, fearing a similar fate, retired to his underground bunker with his longtime mistress—and wife of two days—Eva Braun. They both ingested lethal doses of cyanide, and Hitler ensured his death by shooting himself in the head. Acting on the Führer's last orders, aides carried the two bodies to the garden, doused them with gasoline, and set them ablaze. The source of so much hatred, horror, and destruction was finally dead.

Germany signed an unconditional surrender on May 7, 1945, and the new Führer, Grand Admiral Karl Dönitz declared, "At 11:00 p.m. the arms will be silent." The Third Reich, which Hitler had promised would endure for 1,000 years, had lasted only 12, replaced by an exhausted nation whose guilt, predicted Hans Frank, the condemned Nazi governor general of Poland, would linger for 1,000 more.

MISTAKEN IDENTITY

The Benedictine monastery at the top of Monte Cassino (right) was needlessly demolished by the Allies in early 1944. Convinced that the Germans had transformed the abbey into a fortress, the Allies bombed it mercilessly. In 1969, however, the United States acknowledged that there was no evidence that the Germans had incorporated the sacred site into their defenses.

LYING IN WAIT

A New Zealand Infantry brigade (left) scours the rubble of Cassino for enemy snipers. The bombing failed to dislodge the Germans from Cassino. In fact, the rubble and debris created by the shelling only served to improve the Germans' defensive positions as German paratroopers and snipers burrowed in the ruins and repelled the Allies for several weeks.

NARROW ESCAPE

German officers (right) assist Abbot Diamare away from the cloisters of Monte Cassino's Monastery Hill two days after Allied bombing killed approximately 300 monks and refugees in the ancient structure.

BOLD INITIATIVE
A soldier of the British Guards Armored Division (above) participates in an attempt to rescue British paratroopers captured by the Germans during Market-Garden. Led by Field Marshal Bernard Montgomery, Allied forces had hoped to surprise the Germans by landing behind enemy lines and seizing seven bridges in Holland. One staff officer prophetically warned Montgomery, "I think we might be going a bridge too far."

DAYLIGHT DROP
Members of the British First Airborne Division (left) land during the first hours of Operation Market-Garden, the Allies' audacious plan to outflank Germany's West Wall and race across the Rhine River, in September 1944. A storm of German attacks followed in which about 7,000 Allied paratroopers were killed or captured.

FAILURE AT ARNHEM
A British officer in the guise of a Dutch civilian (left) surrenders to German soldiers in Arnhem. Although the American airborne operation was largely successful, the British First Airborne Division was outgunned by two SS panzer divisions. German artillery crushed the surviving members of the British force, causing one German soldier to say, "I truly felt sorry for the British."

CROSSROADS IN ARDENNES
Members of the First SS Panzer Division (right) pause on their way to Malmédy, Belgium, where they executed 84 U.S. soldiers on December 17. When word of the massacre reached other American units, many troops vowed to take no prisoners who wore SS uniforms.

WINTER OF DISCONTENT
An American Sherman M4 tank (above) braves the icy conditions of the Ardennes Forest during the first week of battle in December 1944. General Eisenhower swiftly deployed tanks from the Third and Ninth Armies to blunt the last major German offensive of the war.

FACED WITH DEATH
One of the thousands of German prisoners captured in the Ardennes (left) languishes near the Belgian village of La Gleize. Prisoners well enough to stand were ordered to bury fallen Allied soldiers in the frozen winter ground.

dy 13 km
ith 8

A TEST OF WILLS
Soldiers of the U.S. Fourth Armored Division (right) march toward Bastogne, site of the battle's longest siege. Attuned to the town's geographic and strategic importance, both sides allocated a generous number of troops to the fight. With the Allies surrounded, German soldiers asked Bastogne's commander, General Anthony McAuliffe, to surrender. McAuliffe defiantly replied, "Nuts!" Following heavy German attacks on Christmas Day, the Allies rallied to relieve Bastogne on December 26.

DEFIANT IN DEATH
A stoic Officer Cadet Günther Billing (left) is secured to a stake by U.S. military policemen in preparation for execution by firing squad on December 18. Moments later, he called out "Heil Hiter" as the lethal fusillade was fired. He had been caught for posing as an American GI when he and two others were stopped at an American roadblack. Billing was just one of 2,000 English-speaking Germans who disguised themselves as American troops and wreaked havoc behind Allied lines.

PERILOUS CROSSING

American soldiers (above) flatten themselves against the steely walls of their amphibious transport to avoid German sniper fire while crossing the Rhine on March 26. After the riverbanks had been secured at the German town of Worms, engineers from the U.S. Seventh Army rafted more than 1,000 vehicles across the watery expanse in just 24 hours.

HELL ON WHEELS

Tanks of the Second Armored Division (left) chew up the German countryside after surging across the Rhine River. As American armor rolled through, resistance was either snuffed out or simply outflanked. General Courtney Hodges and his First Army had been the first to set foot on the Rhine's eastern bank when they crossed at Remagen on March 7, 1945.

VARSITY

An American paratrooper (left) stands waist-deep in muddy water while taking cover from German fire during Operation Varsity, the last airborne action of the war. Coordinating more than 3,000 transport planes and gliders, 3,000 escort fighters, and 21,000 troops, the Allies successfully established a bridgehead across the Rhine near Wesel.

CHILLY RECEPTION
A Soviet infantry company (left) files through the desolate streets of Krakow, Poland, on February 8, 1945. Although the Poles had suffered miserably under German occupation, they did not welcome the Soviets as liberators. Centuries of resentment and the 1939 invasion still lingered in the minds of most Poles.

SWEEPING ADVANCE
Soviet troops (left) prowl a street in Budapest, Hungary in February 1945. Soviet forces had encircled the city in December 1944, and only 800 of the 16,000 German soldiers who attempted to break out of the besieged city made it out alive.

GO WEST

Civilians (above) traverse the remains of a railroad bridge that spanned the Elbe River near Tangemunde, Germany. A security error had revealed the Allies' postwar plans for the division of Germany, and thousands of Germans—fearing a long, oppressive Soviet occupation—hurried to the designated western occupation zones.

LAST STAND

Soviet tanks (above) roll past a Berlin building with an inscription that reads "Berlin remains German." The embattled German capital faced some 2.5 million Allied troops, 6,250 armored vehicles, and 7,500 aircraft across three fronts. It was the Red Army that had the honor of taking the city, and its forces first reached Berlin's outer defenses on April 21, 1945.

WAR IN THE STREETS

Soviet soldiers (right) rush past a dead German defender of Berlin. A German general who had inspected the capital's defenses pronounced them "utterly futile, ridiculous," but the Germans made the numerically superior Red Army pay for every block and building. "Every step cost us lives," wrote Soviet general Vasily Chuikov, commander of General Zhukov's Eighth Guard.

VICTORY
On the roof of the Reichstag, a Soviet soldier (left) hoists the hammer and sickle over Berlin on May 1. The previous day, Adolf Hitler had committed suicide. The virulent fascist evil that had plagued Europe finally had been snuffed out.

Georgi Zhukov

From Leningrad to Moscow to Berlin, Georgi Zhukov became a hero to the Soviet people and a threat to his nation's dictator.

AN INDOMITABLE SURVIVOR

By the time World War II began, Zhukov (above) had lived through a peasant childhood, a bout of typhus, World War I, a civil war, and Stalin's military purges. When he graced the cover of TIME (inset) on December 14, 1942, the former furrier and one-time non-commissioned officer had risen to the post of deputy supreme commander in chief of the Red Army, second in authority only to Stalin.

HOLDING THE REINS

Zhukov (above, right), Marshal Konstantin Rokossovsky (above, left), and front commanders Ivan Konev and Rodion Malinovsky were known as "The Four Horsemen of the German Apocalypse."

ARCHITECTS OF VICTORY

Zhukov (above, center) celebrates with General Dwight Eisenhower and Field Marshal Bernard Montgomery (above, far left) in Berlin in June 1945. Zhukov impressed the American commander, who toasted the marshal by saying, "To no one man do the United Nations owe a greater debt than to Marshal Zhukov."

TWO KINGS, ONE CROWN

Although Zhukov (below, right) outlived Stalin after the war, he didn't escape the despot's psychopathic paranoia. In 1945, Stalin accused the war hero of taking too much credit for the Red Army's defeat of Germany and exiled him to insignificant commands.

MAN OF THE WORLD

Zhukov (above) was the champion of Outer Mongolia against the Japanese in 1939, the stalwart defender of Moscow in 1941, the mastermind of the Battle of Kursk in 1943, and the smasher of Berlin in 1945.

The Horrible Truth

When advancing Allied armies liberated Germany's concentration camps, they came face-to-face with the "Final Solution."

BITTERSWEET FREEDOM

When the 80th Division of the U.S. Third Army reached Buchenwald in April 1945, it was greeted by nearly 20,000 emaciated inmates (above) who had successfully revolted against their Nazi tormentors weeks earlier. Andy Rooney, staff writer for *The Stars and Stripes* and one of the first to visit Buchenwald, said, "For the first time, I knew for certain that any peace is not better than any war." Uniforms with a yellow and red star of David (inset) designated prisoners as both Jewish and communist.

PURE EVIL

An SS officer and a female guard (left) haul bodies into a mass grave at Bergen-Belsen, the first camp to be liberated on the western front, in April 1945. The advancing British were appalled to find 60,000 inmates in critical condition, 14,000 of whom died within five days.

THE HORROR

German townspeople (right), who claimed to be unaware of the atrocities committed next door, are forced to tour Buchenwald after Americans liberated the camp.

SALVATION

Prisoners (above) of Auschwitz, one of the most notorious of the German death camps, joyfully embrace their Soviet saviors after the camp was liberated in January 1945.

THE STENCH OF DEATH

An inmate of the Wöbbelin concentration camp helps a sickly prisoner (left) to the hospital after the camp was liberated by the U.S. 82d Airborne in May 1945. Wöbbelin was the final destination for many inmates who had been evacuated from other camps by the retreating Germans. "We could smell Wöbbelin before we could see it," said one soldier from the 82d.

Harry Truman (below) takes the oath of office hours after Roosevelt's death. The modest "haberdasher" from Missouri was unprepared to lead, and he told reporters, "Boys, if you ever pray, pray for me now."

The Fall of Japan

Marines (left) from the Fifth Division (patch, below) plant the U.S. flag atop Iwo Jima's Mount Suribachi. The photograph won Joe Rosenthal the 1945 Pulitzer Prize and remains one of World War II's most indelible images. Sadly, three of the six men who raised the flag died on Iwo Jima.

The sun was setting on Japan's dream of empire in the spring of 1945. Except in southern China, where the Ichi-Go offensive assured the Imperial Army's predominance, most of its island conquests in the south and central Pacific—including Guam and Saipan in the Mariana Islands—had been recaptured by September 1944, and the Philippines, which General Douglas MacArthur had breached on October 20, had fallen in early 1945. Though ground fighting would continue to rage at dozens of locations in the region, the Pacific war's climax was now in sight.

The next logical target for the United States was Okinawa, the largest of the Ryukyu Islands, 350 miles south of the Japanese home islands. Victory at Okinawa would put the Allies on Japan's doorstep and give them a strategic airbase from which to launch an invasion of the home islands. But it would not come easily. Japanese military leaders convened in early 1945 to devise a plan to shore up the most vulnerable regions of their shrunken and tattered perimeter—an area that at its high-water mark in 1942 had covered six million square miles. Codenamed Ten-Go, the scheme called for the defense of the China coast, the island of Hainan (which sits between China and Indo-China), Formosa, and the Ryukyus.

Recognizing Okinawa's strategic value as well as its vulnerability, Japan committed 4,800 aircraft to its defense. Many of these planes were no longer expected to duel with American fighters. Instead, they would be loaded with explosives for one-way missions to crash

directly onto U.S. ships. These kamikaze—or "divine wind"—strikes, which the Japanese first had employed at the end of the Battle of Leyte Gulf, would be the disintegrating Imperial Army's most effective weapon in the final stages of the war. The suicide runs had been improvised at Leyte Gulf, but at Okinawa, kamikaze missions were official tactics.

Before Ten-Go could be implemented by the Japanese, the U.S. struck at Iwo Jima, a barren, volcanic island in the Bonin Islands, 320 miles south of the Ryukyus.

The U.S.S. *Saratoga* (right), the longest-serving carrier in the U.S. arsenal, smokes after being hit by Japanese kamikazes off Iwo Jima on February 21, 1945. The attack killed 123 members of the carrier's crew, ruined her forward flight deck, punctured her starboard side, and started fires in her hangar deck. Yet, the *Saratoga* stayed afloat and made it back to the United States.

Storming the beach on February 19, troops from the Third, Fourth, and Fifth Marine Divisions immediately sank to their calves in the thick layer of volcanic ash that covered the island. Amphibious troop-transport vehicles bogged down in the black silt and had to be abandoned at the water's edge, where they were destroyed by Japanese artillery. As they battled inland, using rifles and flamethrowers to clear the island's countless pillboxes, underground tunnels, and trenches, the Marines suffered heavy casualties. Iwo Jima offered almost no cover to an invading force, and the Japanese defended it fiercely. Lieutenant General Holland Smith said the fighting was "the toughest the Marines ran across in 168 years."

Yet, after three days of fighting, a group of Marines planted the Stars and Stripes atop Mount Suribachi, Iwo Jima's primary point of defense. When it was done, Secretary of the Navy James Forrestal, who had recently arrived from Washington, turned to Smith and said, "Holland, the raising of that flag on Suribachi means a Marine Corps for the next 500 years." (Sandwiched between the Army and the Navy, the Marine Corps had always been in danger of being absorbed by one of the larger military bodies.)

Iwo Jima, which cost the Americans nearly 27,000 casualties—6,281 of them killed—served as a grim preview of what lay ahead. Japan was determined to defend its outlying islands with a desperate ferocity. Japanese general Tadamichi Kuribayashi wrote in his journal on March 15, the day before the U.S. secured the island, "Have not eaten or drunk for five days. But fighting spirit is running high. We are going to fight bravely to the last moment." The numbers bore him out: Nearly all of the 21,000 Japanese soldiers defending Iwo Jima were killed.

Despite the heavier pre-invasion bombardment that accompanied it, the attack on Okinawa would mirror the carnage of Iwo Jima—with the added lethal element of full-scale kamikaze attacks on the U.S. fleet. On April 1, the First and Sixth Marine Divisions, along with the Seventh and 96th Army Divisions, landed in the middle of the island, where its airfields lay. To their surprise,

On April 1, 1945, the first day of the U.S. invasion of Okinawa, Marines of the 29th Regiment (left) race toward the town of Ghuta. Weeks of bitter fighting would follow before safe conduct passes (below), which were written in Japanese and English and promised fair treatment to those who surrendered, would become widespread.

THE BEARER HAS CEASED RESISTANCE
TREAT HIM IN ACCORDANCE
WITH INTERNATIONAL LAW.
TAKE HIM TO THE NEAREST
COMMANDING OFFICER.
C-IN-C AMERICAN FORCES

生命を助けるビラ
此のビラの使ひ方

they met no resistance. In a tactical change, the Japanese had withdrawn inland, out of range of U.S. air and naval firepower. Led by General Mitsuru Ushijima, the Japanese forces—numbering 120,000—packed into the heavily fortified southern half of the 80-mile-long island. The U.S. landed with 50,000 troops, but they would be heavily reinforced, and Ushijima knew that he couldn't hold Okinawa for very long. But he intended to inflict as many casualties as possible on the Americans. Like Iwo Jima, Okinawa was bored through with tunnels and bristling with concealed gun installations. While the U.S. Marine divisions marched north, the Army fought toward the mountainous south. Both encountered waves of Japanese troops, and the American advances quickly ground to a halt.

On April 6, the Japanese launched their offensive against the U.S. fleet offshore. Hundreds of kamikazes zeroed in on the U.S. carriers, battleships, and destroyers. From the north, the final remains of the Imperial Fleet, led by the huge warship *Yamato*, steamed toward Okinawa. Like the kamikazes, the *Yamato* was on a one-way suicide mission. Its goal was to penetrate the U.S. naval perimeter off Okinawa and inflict as much damage as possible. She didn't even get close. U.S. radar detected the *Yamato* well before she was within firing range and Task Force 58 dispatched 280 planes to intercept her. Slightly more than two hours later, the *Yamato* slipped beneath the waves, taking most of her crew of 2,300 with her. American aircraft also sank five of her eight escort ships.

A significant Japanese threat had been eliminated, but a worse one remained: the kamikazes. Admiral William Halsey called the suicide planes "the only weapon I feared in the war," and on the first day, kamikazes sank three destroyers, two ammunition ships, and one landing craft off Okinawa. They scored hits on a battleship, a carrier, and two destroyers the following day, and before the fighting for Okinawa quieted that summer, more than 5,000 U.S. sailors had perished in kamikaze attacks—a death toll greater than the Navy had suffered at Pearl Harbor. Needless to say,

Its hands fused at 8:16 a.m., a wristwatch (above) found in the ashes provides a grim record of the moment on August 6, 1945 when Colonel Paul Tibbets (second row, center) and the crew (above, right) of the *Enola Gay* dropped the atomic bomb (top) on Hiroshima.

though, a kamikaze campaign can last only so long; Japan started running out of pilots and planes in early summer, when the ground battle for the island also inexorably turned the Americans' way. When the fighting ended in June, some 110,000 Japanese soldiers had chosen death over surrender. More than 100,000 Okinawan civilians also had been killed, and the Japanese had lost 16 ships and 7,800 planes, more than 1,000 of the planes in kamikaze attempts.

Almost 7,000 Americans lost their lives on Okinawa, and the Army and Marine divisions involved in the invasion suffered a 35 percent casualty rate. These numbers influenced U.S. decisions for the final phase of the war. An attack on the Japanese home islands would yield a similar, if not greater, casualty percentage. The U.S. expected to commit 767,000 men to the invasion of Kyushu, the southernmost of the Japanese home islands. A 35 percent casualty rate for such an operation would yield 268,000 dead or wounded, a number that roughly equaled the total U.S. casualties for the entire war up to that point. Echoing the sentiments of the American public, President Harry Truman said that he "hoped there was a possibility of preventing an Okinawa from one end of Japan to the other."

While the U.S. had planned and enacted its invasions of Iwo Jima and Okinawa, American B-29 bombers had been attacking selected targets in Japan. In February the B-29s had changed their tactics from precision strikes to saturation fire-bombing. Since Japanese cities were composed primarily of wood, the new tactic inflicted horrific damage. A March 9 raid on Tokyo had incinerated 267,000 buildings and killed 89,000 civilians. As attacks like these—with similarly appalling results—continued throughout the summer, Truman pressed Japan to surrender. A new moderate leadership in Japan had approached the Soviet Union to mediate a peace with the Allies, but the Soviets refused to negotiate anything less than the "unconditional surrender" that the Allies required. Rebuffed in their backdoor efforts for peace, the Japanese answered the West's repeated surrender demands with silence. Japan's proud government was resolved to continue the struggle.

With U.S. general Douglas MacArthur (left, at microphone) looking on, Imperial Army general Yoshijiro Umezu signs the surrender document (inset) that officially ended World War II on September 2, 1945. "Let us pray that peace be now restored to the world," MacArthur said, "and that God will preserve it always."

The U.S. prepared two battle plans for the invasion of Japan: one for the fall of 1945 and the other for March 1946. But Truman still hoped he could save both countries from a lengthy bloodbath. On July 26, he issued the Potsdam Declaration, which promised "the utter devastation of the Japanese homeland" unless the Imperial Government surrendered unconditionally. Truman's threat was bolstered by his knowledge that the U.S. had successfully detonated the first atomic bomb 10 days earlier in the New Mexico desert. Prompted by an October 1939 letter from Albert Einstein warning that the Germans might be developing their own nuclear program, President Franklin Roosevelt had commissioned a study to pursue atomic weapons. The outgrowth of that study was dubbed the Manhattan Project, which bore its terrible fruit after four years of intensive research.

After receiving no comment from Japan, Truman issued the order to drop an atomic bomb on one of four cities—Nagasaki, Kokura, Niigata or Hiroshima—as soon as weather permitted after August 3. So it was that on August 6, Colonel Paul Tibbets and his *Enola Gay* crew set out amid clear skies, bound for Hiroshima. At 8:15 a.m., "Little Boy" exploded over Hiroshima, killing at least 78,000 people in one nightmarish blast. Still, Japan's leaders remained silent. Three days later—and a day after the Soviet Union declared war on Japan—another B-29 dropped "Fat Man" on Nagasaki, killing 40,000 more people. Even in the face of otherworldly devastation, the Japanese government remained divided on the issue of surrender. Finally, Emperor Hirohito convinced his nation's ministers to capitulate. "I cannot bear to see my innocent people suffer any longer," he said. On September 2, aboard the U.S.S. *Missouri* in Tokyo Bay, Japan signed its surrender, bringing World War II to an end.

REINFORCEMENTS
Shrouded in smoke from the battle, Mount Suribachi looms behind a detachment of U.S. Marines (above) as they inch up Iwo Jima. The barren, volcanic rock of Iwo Jima, 660 miles south of Tokyo, provided minimal cover for the invading troops, who paid a terrible price to capture the strategic island and its airstrips. More than 6,000 Americans were killed during four weeks of fighting.

RELUCTANT SURRENDER
A Japanese soldier (left, hands raised) is the first of 20 Japanese troops to emerge from a cave and surrender to U.S. troops on April 5, 1945. The fighting for the island had ended nearly three weeks earlier, but many Japanese soldiers took advantage of Iwo Jima's labyrinth of underground tunnels and caves to prolong their resistance.

DEMOLITION MEN
U.S. Marines (right) take cover behind a boulder as they destroy a cave connected to a Japanese garrison. Veteran war correspondent Robert Sherrod called the fighting for Iwo Jima the worst battle he had ever seen, saying that men died "with the greatest possible violence." More than 20,000 U.S. troops were wounded in the struggle, and nearly all of the Japanese defenders were killed.

THE LESSONS OF IWO JIMA
A U.S. ship (above) fires rockets at Okinawa in advance of the 10th Army's assault on the island. With the carnage of the Iwo Jima landings still fresh in their minds, U.S. strategists decided to use naval and aerial firepower to pound the landing area with almost 30,000 shells before sending troops ashore on April 1.

LAUNCHING THE LAST BATTLE
Bolstered by an armada of 1,300 ships positioned offshore, American tanks (left) breach the island's perimeter. Since Japanese forces had withdrawn to defend inland positions, the Americans landed almost without incident.

FOXHOLE
Three American soldiers (left) take cover in a ditch during the fighting for Okinawa. The U.S. landed 60,000 troops on April 1, against 120,000 Japanese soldiers. American casualties were so high that U.S. leadership began to reconsider their plans to invade the Japanese home islands.

302
315

THE RAVAGES OF COMBAT

Weary Marines (left) file past the body of a Japanese soldier killed in the vicious fighting for Okinawa. The Japanese death rate at Okinawa was 91 percent, and all of the Imperial Army's senior officers on the island, including General Mitsuru Ushijima, committed ritual suicide rather than surrender. The civilian population was also decimated by the fighting. One estimate put the civilian death toll at 160,000.

ANTIAIRCRAFT BARRAGE

A dense latticework of American antiaircraft fire (left) lights up the Okinawa sky, while Corsair planes from the Marines' "Hell's Belles" fighter squadron sit on the ground. Japan launched more than 1,500 kamikaze attacks at Okinawa, sinking 38 Allied ships.

REFUGEE CAMPS

A "headman" doles out rice to homeless Okinawan civilians (left) at an American-run camp in the village of Toya. Appointed by American commanders, the headman—or "honcho," as U.S. enlisted men called him—was responsible for communicating orders, seeing to the maintenance of the camp, and leading work details, most of which were designed to revitalize farming on the island.

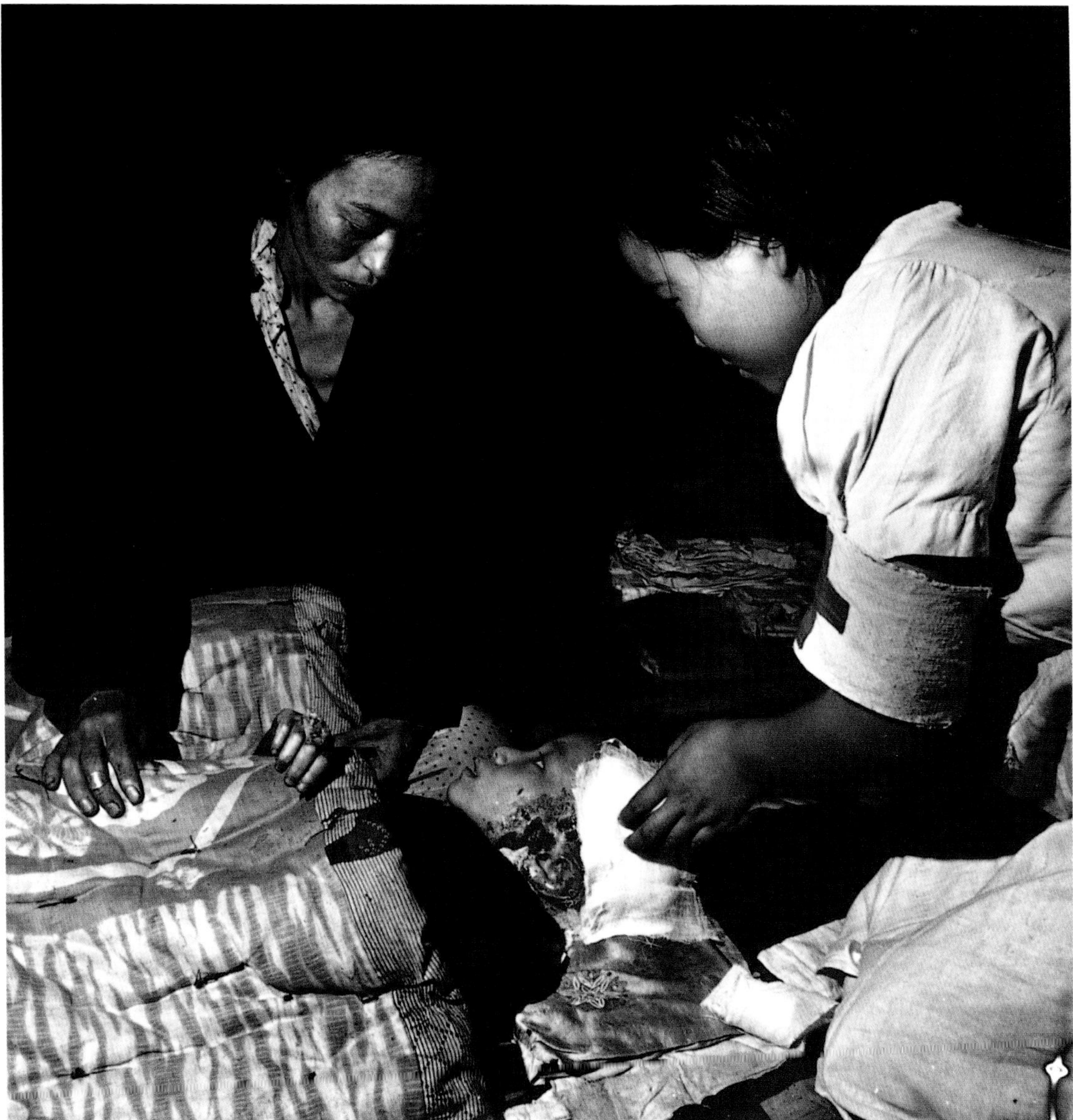

MEDICAL DISASTER

A young victim (above) of the atomic bomb receives first aid at a makeshift medical station set up in one of the city's banks. "There was not enough room for the injured in the Red Cross hospital," said one eyewitness. "They lay at the entrance asking for water." Aid stations were established throughout the city, and relief workers scurried frantically amidst what one survivor described as "an inferno of heat, sickness, and death."

GROUND ZERO

The Hiroshima bomb exploded about half a mile above the city (right), unleashing a 5,400-degree fireball that demolished four square miles. Radioactive fallout from the bomb subsequently raised the total death toll to approximately 120,000 people.

TERRIBLE TOLL

On August 10, the day after a second atomic bomb fell on Nagasaki, a woman (above) sips water from a canteen while her dazed and wounded companions try to recover. Like the citizens of Hiroshima, Nagasaki's inhabitants were perplexed by their city's good fortune in the early summer of 1945, as Americans spared their homes while levelling virtually every other industrial center in Japan. Their luck, tragically, would not last.

SPARED

Clutching balls of boiled rice provided as emergency rations by relief workers, a woman and her son (above) make their way through the streets of Nagasaki. The devastation was overwhelming. Surveying the ruined city from a hilltop, Nagasaki resident Yoshito Nagamatsu said, "All one can see are fires, fires, fires—funeral pyres burning under the night sky of August."

ATOM RUIN

The city of Nagasaki (left) smolders after Major Charles Sweeney dropped the second atomic bomb from the B-29, *Bock's Car*. Kokura, a southwestern city of 110,000 inhabitants, equidistant between Hiroshima and Nagasaki, had been Sweeney's primary target, but poor visibility forced him to proceed to the secondary target.

Harry Truman

Thrust into the presidency—an office he had never coveted—at a moment of monumental importance, the "little man from Missouri" rose to history's challenge.

GIVE 'EM HELL

In July 1945, Truman (above, middle) shakes hands with Soviet leader Josef Stalin and outgoing British prime minister Winston Churchill after the final wartime summit meeting in Potsdam, Germany. During the conference, Truman, who kept a paperweight (inset) inscribed with his motto, "The Buck Stops Here," on his desk in Washington, informed Churchill and Stalin of America's plan to use atomic weapons against Japan. Both leaders encouraged Truman to use all means to end the war as soon as possible.

RUNNING MATES

Franklin Roosevelt (above, right) shares lunch with his new running mate on the White House terrace in August 1944. Truman, who had been reluctant to accept the vice-presidential nomination, was stunned to find Roosevelt so weak and haggard. Roosevelt warned Truman not to travel by airplane during the impending campaign because it was important for one of them to stay alive.

CAPTAIN TRUMAN

Although he was 33—two years beyond the Selective Service age limit—Truman (left) enlisted during World War I. "I wouldn't be left out of the greatest history-making epoch the world has ever seen for all there is to live for," he wrote his future wife Bess.

THE BOSS

When Truman first arrived in Washington in 1935, he was derisively called the "Senator from Pendergast." Tom Pendergast (left, with hat) led the Kansas City political machine that gave Truman his start in public service.

KEEPING TABS

Truman (right, with Senators Homer Ferguson and Joseph Bell) made a name for himself by heading the committee that investigated military spending during the war. Postwar reports estimated his commission saved taxpayers $15 billion.

Manhattan Project

After four years—and more than $2 billion spent on research—science handed the American military a weapon that moved its creator to say, "I am become death, the destroyer of worlds."

THE DAY THE SUN ROSE TWICE
The Manhattan Project (special engineer shoulder badge, inset) was an endeavor of unprecedented size, importance, and secrecy. It culminated in an atomic fireball (above) that burst upon the Alamogordo Bombing Range in the New Mexico desert. The blast reverberated for hundreds of miles. "Our first feeling was one of elation," said one scientist who witnessed the blast. "Then we realized we were tired, and then we were worried."

TRINITY

Home to more than 200 soldiers and scientists in the summer of 1945, the Trinity base camp (left) lies beneath an unforgiving sun in the desolate New Mexico desert. Trinity was chosen over three other southwestern sites because of its isolation, topography, climate, and proximity to Los Alamos, which was 200 miles north. Security was of primary importance; checkpoints were set up, and employees were confined to the camp after their arrival.

FATHERS OF THE BOMB

Many of the most important scientists who contributed to the development of an atomic bomb were émigrés from Europe's fascist countries. Albert Einstein (below, left), whose theory of relativity hinted at the potential of atomic power, was a German-born Jew who had come to the United States in 1933. Enrico Fermi (below, right) fled to New York from Italy immediately after he received the 1938 Nobel prize in physics. His work at the University of Chicago yielded the first nuclear chain reaction in 1942.

BRAINS AND BRAWN

Robert Oppenheimer (far left), Los Alamos's scientific chief, and Brigadier General Leslie Groves, manager of the Manhattan Project, examine the disintegrated remains of the tower that had held the first atomic bomb. Groves, whose previous project had been to build the Pentagon, selected Oppenheimer to lead the Manhattan Project over the protests of more accomplished scientists and the FBI, who suspected the doctor was a communist.

Kamikaze

In the last months of the war, Japan's "divine wind" planes were armed with high explosives, just enough fuel, and proud—but inexperienced—young men whose last mission was to crash into the greatest sinkable American target.

FOR LOVE OF COUNTRY

Six kamikaze pilots (above), wearing national flags inscribed with patriotic slogans (inset) on their arms, proudly pose with their samurai swords prior to embarking on suicide missions in 1945. When Japan first announced plans for kamikaze units, there was no shortage of willing pilots; two or three times more men volunteered than there were planes available.

SUICIDE CEREMONIES

A kamikaze pilot (far right) fastens the unique honorary ribbon around his head before embarking on his last flight. During elaborate farewell ceremonies, kamikaze pilots (right) receive sake, rice, and special rations before taking to the air.

DEVASTATION

The U.S.S. *Bunker Hill* (below) recovers from heavy damage after a kamikaze attack on June 21, 1945. Suicide fliers usually overloaded their planes with bombs to maximize the destruction they inflicted upon impact. Several pilots from the *Bunker Hill* were killed when the explosives from this attack ripped through the pilots' ready room.

INCOMING

Antiaircraft gunners from the carrier U.S.S. *Sangamon* (above) direct sheets of fire at an incoming Japanese kamikaze plane, which has already caught fire. The plane barely missed the carrier and plunged into the sea.

PEACE
PEACE
PEACE
PEACE
PEACE
EXTRA THE STARS AND STRIPES
PEACE
PEACE

At the White House on August 14, 1945, President Truman (below) announces Japan's surrender. He called V-J Day "the day that fascism and police government ceases in the world." The Cold War, however, threatened that claim.

Aftermath

In Paris, hundreds of smiling American servicemen and servicewomen (left) celebrate Japan's surrender. For many American soldiers, the announcement meant that their next trip would take them home—not to the Pacific. TIME's cover (below) of August 20, 1945, told the story without words.

On August 15, 1945, Emperor Hirohito addressed the Japanese people in a nationwide radio broadcast. Most of his subjects had never heard him speak, and his words moved many listeners to tears. "We have ordered our government," Hirohito stated in a high-pitched, quavering voice, "to communicate to the governments of the United States, Great Britain, China, and the Soviet Union that our empire accepts the provisions of their joint declaration." Alluding to the atomic bombs dropped on Hiroshima and Nagasaki, he solemnly continued, "The enemy has begun to employ a new and most cruel bomb. . . . Should we continue to fight, it would not only result in the ultimate collapse and obliteration of the Japanese nation . . . but would lead also to the total extinction of human civilization."

Halfway around the world, President Harry Truman already had announced to the White House press corps, "I have received this afternoon a message from the Japanese government. . . . I deem this reply a full acceptance of the Potsdam Declaration, which specifies the unconditional surrender of Japan." It was not quite unconditional, in that the Allies agreed to preserve the role of the emperor, but it met all other conditions and terms for concluding a peace settlement.

After Truman's announcement, impromptu V-J Day celebrations exploded all over the world. After six long years of war, the victors and the vanquished felt an enormous sense of relief. No one was more grateful than the American servicemen who had dreaded a protracted, costly invasion of the Japanese home islands scheduled for the fall of 1945.

Later that evening, Truman stepped outside the White House to greet a crowd of revelers along Pennsylvania Avenue. "I felt deeply moved by the excitement, perhaps as much as were the crowds that were celebrating in cities and towns all over the nation," he later recalled. "The guns were silenced. The war was over."

Josef Stalin once callously said, "One death is a tragedy; one million is a statistic." Mere numbers cannot begin to measure or describe the horrible nature of war,

Emperor Hirohito (above, with Empress Nagato) was stripped of any political power but "played a major role in the spiritual regeneration of Japan," according to General MacArthur. In Dresden (right) residents went about picking up the pieces of their shattered city while hungry Germans posted ads (inset) which bartered such things as baby beds for potatoes.

but the sheer magnitude of human loss as a result of World War II is numbing. Of the approximately 110 million people from over 60 nations who served in uniform during the conflict, nearly 20 million died. As staggering as these losses are, they were exceeded by the even greater number of civilian fatalities, which may have exceeded 40 million.

The Soviet Union suffered the greatest loss of life by far, with more than 25 million civilian and military deaths. On the eastern front, where the war's largest and most pitiless campaign scorched the land for more than three years, the Soviet government estimated that the costs of damage to its cities, villages, factories, and transportation networks equaled 30 percent of the country's total wealth. China suffered almost as much; more than 11 million of its people died during its long struggle against Japanese invaders.

Both Germany and Japan, once proud nations that endured great destruction from unrelenting Allied air bombardment, lay helpless, their cities razed and their economies in utter ruin. American troops led by General Douglas MacArthur became the first foreign army to occupy the Japanese homeland. Germany and its capital city of Berlin were each partitioned into four separate occupation zones, administered by the United States, the Soviet Union, Great Britain, and France.

The U.S. emerged as the war's only unscathed beneficiary. America's industrial might was unchallenged, its territory—other than Pearl Harbor—bore no scars of battle, its armed forces had suffered the fewest casualties of all the major combatants, and the country's civilian population had experienced no great hardships.

In addition to its staggering number of casualties, World War II also produced an unparalleled flood of dis-

placed persons. In the early stages of the war, millions of European and Asian people abandoned their homes to escape German and Japanese aggression. Later, as the tide of battle turned in Europe, other refugees fled in fear of the advancing Soviet armies.

In the postwar years, many refugees resettled in the United States, Canada, and Australia. Western Germany was inundated with families who had escaped the Soviet zone of occupation. But perhaps the most pitiable victims of war were the European Jews who had escaped the Nazi death machine, but lost their homes and, in many cases, their families. Zionist leaders surreptitiously slipped boatloads of these refugees into Palestine, with the hope of establishing a Jewish homeland. Although they quickly learned that they were not welcome in Palestine, the Jewish settlers would succeed in founding the state of Israel in 1948.

The victorious Allies were understandably keen on punishing those enemies who had committed atrocities during the war. In the fall of 1945 they convened a war crimes tribunal in the German city of Nuremberg, the site of the Nazi Party's elaborate prewar rallies. Some 22 high-ranking Nazis, including Luftwaffe chief Hermann Göring, Wehrmacht chief of staff Wilhelm Keitel, Foreign Minister Joachim von Ribbentrop, and Minister of Armaments Albert Speer, were charged with crimes against humanity, the deliberate instigation of wars of aggression, and war crimes against civilians and prisoners of war, in violation of the Geneva Convention. Almost a year later the tribunal handed down its verdicts: Twelve of the defendants received death sentences, seven were sent to prison for terms ranging from 10 years to life, and three were acquitted. Those condemned to death were hanged on October 16, 1946, but Göring

Jewish refugees (above) arrive in Palestine in October 1947. Great Britain, which governed Palestine, where a Jewish homeland was to be created, promised neighboring Arab states that it would allow only 1,500 Jews per month to enter. The Jewish militia responded by smuggling as many Jews as possible into Palestine. When the British evacuated in May 1948, Arab-Israeli hostilities quickly exploded.

Truman (above, left) watches Edward Stettinius sign the United Nations Charter in June 1945. Truman challenged the organization's members "to be the architects of a better world. In your hands rests our future." The U.N. was designed to prevent men like Tojo (above, right) from instigating global hostilities. Japan's wartime prime minister, Tojo was found guilty of war crimes and executed in December 1948.

cheated the hangman by swallowing a poison capsule in his cell a few hours before his execution.

Twelve more trials indicted an additional 185 officials, including Nazi jurists, SS officers, concentration camp guards and doctors, and industrialists who had participated in slave-labor programs. The most heinous offenders were hanged, and more than 100 others were sentenced to prison.

Another war crimes trial convened in Tokyo on May 3, 1946. Of the 28 defendants named in the indictment, seven, including former prime minister Hideki Tojo, were sentenced to hang, and all but two of the remaining 21 were sentenced to life in prison. Separate trials in several Asian countries that had suffered years of brutal Japanese occupation condemned other Imperial Army officers to death or imprisonment.

With retribution exacted, the world moved into a postwar era that bore no resemblance to the political landscape of 1939. Japan's defeat left a power vacuum in the Far East that would draw the U.S. into a more active role in that region. Germany's collapse had similar repercussions and would call for a continuing American military presence in Europe. France and Great Britain, though partners in the Allied cause and in the partition of Germany, were overshadowed in victory by the military might of the United States and the Soviet Union. From 1945 onward the global influence of the two great colonial powers would wane, and their overseas empires would eventually slip away.

Peace had hardly settled across Europe before rifts began developing between victors, East and West. Josef Stalin had no intention of withdrawing the Red Army from Eastern Europe or holding free elections in those countries so recently liberated from Nazi tyranny. In 1946, Winston Churchill—no longer prime minister of Great Britain—visited the United States and somberly declared, "From Stettin in the Baltic to Trieste in the Adriatic, an iron curtain has descended across the continent." The Cold War had begun.

To curtail further Soviet expansion, the U.S. intro-

duced the Truman Doctrine, a new policy of containment which promised to support "free peoples who are resisting attempted subjugation by armed minorities or by outside pressures." The U.S. sent aid to anticommunist forces in Greece and Turkey, and also initiated a much larger plan to resuscitate war-torn Europe. General George Marshall, who became secretary of state under Truman in 1947, proposed the European Recovery Program, a $13-billion aid package to rebuild the continent's shattered economies. The largest shares of this monetary support went to Great Britain, France, and Italy, but the Marshall Plan also included substantial assistance for the western zones of Germany. Marshall felt that the continued existence of a democratic Germany would not only assuage European fears of future German aggression but would also provide a stable buffer against Soviet intrusion into central Europe. The Marshall Plan proved to be a resounding diplomatic and economic success that helped lay the foundation for a united Europe.

Even while World War II still raged, the Allied powers had taken steps to ensure that such a catastrophe would never be repeated. They had pledged to establish "at the earliest practicable date a general international organization," which President Roosevelt had dubbed the United Nations. At the Tehran Conference in 1943, Roosevelt, Churchill, and Stalin had reaffirmed "the supreme responsibility resting upon us and all the United Nations to make a peace which will . . . banish the scourge and terror of war."

Delegates from 50 nations met in San Francisco in the spring of 1945 to formulate the organization's charter. During the following half century, the United Nations would expand to include almost every country on earth. Despite its many shortcomings, this world body has played an important role in preventing Cold War tensions, political crises, and regional wars from escalating into apocalyptic superpower confrontations. Perhaps its greatest legacy is that there has not been a World War III.

The Soviet Union had grand designs on a defeated Germany, and Soviet propagandists designed posters (inset) that welcomed Germany to the communist community. After Stalin blockaded Berlin in June 1948, the U.S. countered with airlifts (top) that supplied the city for more than a year.

SQUARE DANCING
An ocean of Moscow's citizens (above) hoists a soldier in Red Square to celebrate the Allied victory against the Germans. Victory came at a high price for the Soviet Union, which lost more than 25 million people during the war.

FINEST HOUR
London police officers (left) form a human chain to push back the tide of revelers during V-E Day celebrations in Parliament Square. In the dark days of the Blitz in 1940, Great Britain seemed on the brink of collapse. British courage and leadership fueled the empire's narrow escape from defeat and subsequent victory against Germany.

HAPPY DAYS

A jubilant American sailor (left) plants a kiss on a nurse during V-J Day celebrations in New York's Times Square. These two weren't the only couple eager to put the war behind them. As America's soldiers returned home, the country experienced an unprecedented population surge—later called the Baby Boom. Between 1946 and 1964, 77 million children were born in the United States.

BLACK MARKET

Allied soldiers and German civilians (left) mingle near the ruins of the Reichstag in postwar Berlin. In the aftermath of the war, black markets for goods and services appeared throughout Germany as the conquered civilians traded and bartered what they could with the occupying Allied armies. Although the bartering process—*kompensieren* in German—was banned, black marketeering thrived in both urban and rural areas.

STARTING OVER

Before Germany could begin to rebuild its ruined cities, the rubble had to be removed. In the Soviet sector of Berlin, German women (right) form lines to clear the area of debris. This type of work was widespread in Germany and across Europe, as people began the imposing task of beginning again.

THE PRICE OF WAR

A German man (left) walks through the desolate streets of Hamburg. His country, whose ambition had sparked another world war, had suffered horribly in the final years of the conflict. Hamburg was firebombed in July 1943, and a similar fate befell almost every major German city. "The country is devastated," General Eisenhower wrote to his wife. "Whole cities are obliterated; and the German population . . . is largely homeless."

ON THE MOVE
German women (above) cart their belongings through the streets of postwar Berlin. The end of the war spurred a mass migration in Europe, as millions of civilians were dislocated to accommodate the borders of new or reestablished nations.

DISPLACED
A group of central European refugees (right) hopes for food and shelter at an Allied camp for displaced persons in Germany. The United Nations Relief and Rehabilitation Administration organized camps in abandoned German barracks or factories, housing people who were made homeless by the war.

HOMEWARD BOUND

A lone Frenchmen (left), recently liberated from a German prison camp, walks along the quiet cobblestone road leading to his village. After the war, thousands of Europeans traversed hundreds of miles to return home. They often found that their homes had been destroyed and their families were gone.

BLOCKADE BUSTERS

Trucks loaded with coal (above) await air transport to the isolated city of Berlin in 1948. Soviet efforts to force the western democracies out of Berlin failed. In 13 months of airlifts, 277,804 flights delivered more than two million tons of supplies to Berlin.

GREAT ESCAPE
In the days before the Berlin Wall, a German policeman (above) assists two women in their flight from the Soviet occupation zone. As the yoke of Soviet rule began to tighten, more and more Germans fled west before all avenues of escape were blocked.

OPERATION SANTA
Young children of Berlin (left) open Christmas gifts that were airlifted from the West in 1948. The Soviet blockade was finally lifted in May 1949—13 months after it had begun—sparking celebrations throughout the world. "I saw the spirit and soul of a people reborn," said U.S. general Lucius Clay. "This time the people of Berlin cast their lot with those who love freedom."

INDEPENDENCE DAY
Prime Minister David Ben-Gurion of Israel (left, in jacket) bids farewell to the final contingent of British troops to leave Palestine in 1948. Relations between Britain, which had governed Palestine since 1923, and the growing Jewish population soured after the British prevented thousands of Jewish refugees from entering.

NO PLACE TO GO
Disgruntled Jewish passengers (right) of the prison ship *Runnymede Park* sail for Germany after they were denied entry to Palestine aboard the *Exodus 1947*. When they reached Hamburg after a two-month journey, proud passengers refused to disembark and had to be physically removed by British soldiers.

SHIP OF SHATTERED DREAMS
The *Exodus 1947* arrives in Haifa in July 1947, after it was intercepted and rammed by British destroyers as it neared Palestine. Two Jewish refugees were killed when British Marines stormed the ship. None of the refugees was allowed to enter Palestine; instead, they were shipped by boat to Hamburg, Germany.

BENEVOLENT CONQUEROR
General Douglas MacArthur (right) arrives at Atsugi airport to receive the Imperial Army's final surrender. MacArthur's term as military governor of Japan, which lasted until 1951, witnessed the birth of a new era of Japanese-American cooperation and friendship.

ASHES OF TOKYO
During the war, the Japanese capital (above) was repeatedly incinerated by American bombers. In all of Japan, more than two million buildings were destroyed and more than 40 percent of the nation's cities lay in ruins.

POSTWAR POVERTY
Japanese children (right) orphaned by the war hunt for food in Tokyo garbage cans. Postwar Japan was plagued by food shortages. When the Americans arrived there were fears that 10 million Japanese might die from starvation. The Allies set up soup kitchens and food warehouses to feed the population and prevent a catastrophe.

FRATRICIDE

Chinese Nationalists (above) execute five political prisoners in Shanghai in May 1949. As soon as the Japanese were defeated, Chiang Kai-shek's Nationalist forces and Mao Tse-tung's Communist armies resumed the civil war that had been waged since 1927. In December 1949, Chiang's defeated Kuomintang Army fled to the island of Formosa.

VICTORY PARADE

After several weeks of siege, the victorious Communist Eighth Route Army (right) sweeps into Peking in February 1949. Mao's armies were bolstered by the theft of hundreds of pieces of American military equipment—ranging from rifles to heavy vehicles—that had been intended for Chiang's Kuomintang Army.

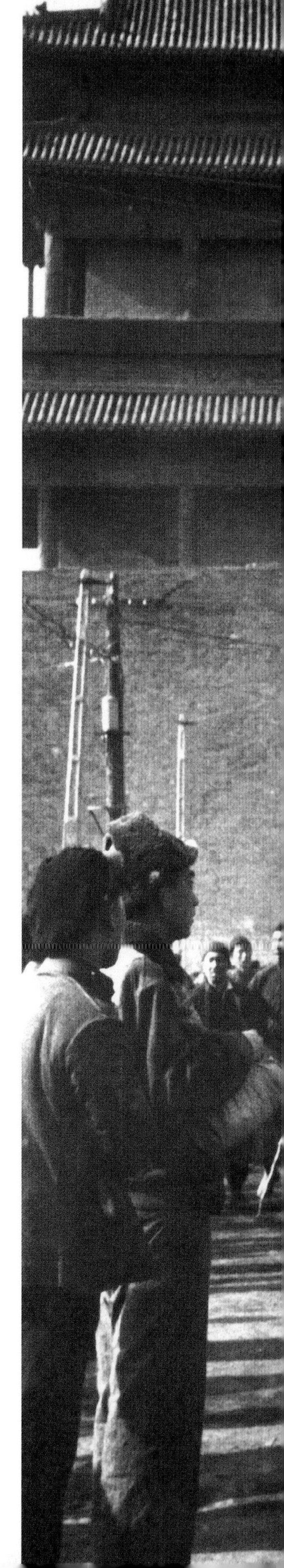

REVOLUTION

A young Chinese communist (left) boldly declares his allegiance to the movement and its leaders. When Mao began his Long March in 1934—a 6,000-mile journey from Juichin to Yenan to escape Chiang's armies—his supporters numbered only 100,000. On October 1, 1949, Mao stood outside Peking's Forbidden City and proclaimed the People's Republic of China.

38046

CONDEMNED
Hermann Göring (far left) and Rudolf Hess hang their heads in despair as their sentences are handed down from the Allied military tribunal (see seating pass, inset). Göring was one of 12 Nazi officials sentenced to death, and Hess joined six others who received prison terms. Despite his verdict, Göring predicted that he would be celebrated as a German hero and martyr. "I am determined to go down in history as a great man," the Reich Marshal said.

Nuremberg

The city best known for its fanatical Nazi rallies before the war became the site of National Socialism's final judgment, as the Allies tried 22 leaders of the Third Reich for their crimes against humanity.

SUICIDE WATCH

American soldiers (left) stand watch to prevent the Nuremberg defendants from taking their own lives. Despite these efforts, Göring committed suicide by swallowing poison.

SUPREME JURIST

Robert Jackson (below), the lead American prosecutor, made it clear that the tribunal was trying the German regime, not the German people.

JUSTICE

Julius Streicher (above), the editor of the anti-Semitic *Der Stürmer*, condemned the mass killings of the Jews, but Göring (left) joked that someone must have slipped up if there were still any Jews alive in Hungary.

NO REGRET

Master Sergeant John Woods (left) makes final preparations for the hangings of the Nazi criminals on October 16, 1946. After the executions, he said, "I hanged those 10 Nazis and I am proud of it."

The Marshall Plan

As the Soviet Union stood poised to exploit a devastated Europe, the United States helped the continent get back on its feet with an unprecedented financial assistance program.

THE MAN WITH THE PLAN
When he became the first career soldier to be appointed secretary of state in 1947, George Marshall (above, middle) immediately addressed the growing crises in Greece and Turkey—two nations threatened by civil strife. At a commencement address at Harvard University, Marshall proposed a program whose "purpose should be the revival of a working economy in the world so as to permit the emergence of political and social conditions in which free institutions can exist."

DUTCH TREAT

A Dutchman (left) leans against the most recent American shipments to the port of Rotterdam. Sixteen nations, and the western occupation zones of Germany, applied for a total of $13-billion worth of American aid. The Soviet Union predictably declined American offers of assistance, labeling the plan "a retail purchase of several European countries."

FIAT FEAT

Italian workers in a Fiat factory (above) assemble a car nicknamed the "Marshall Plan Baby," to honor the program that financed new automobile equipment and machinery. When the Marshall Plan formally ended in 1952 it was praised as "the most straightforward, generous thing that any country has ever done for others."

SOLDIER STATESMEN

Dwight Eisenhower (above, left) and Marshall (above, right) shared the burdens of the burgeoning Cold War. In 1950, Ike was named commander of the North Atlantic Treaty Organization, a coalition forged to check Soviet aggression.

CHINESE QUAGMIRE

After the war, Truman sent Marshall (right, second from left) to broker a peace between Chiang Kai-shek and Mao Tse-tung (far right), but both sides undermined Marshall's efforts.

Europe in 1939
Fascist
Communist
SWEDEN
FINLAND
NORWAY
Helsinki
Oslo
Talinn
Stockholm
ESTONIA
North Sea
Riga
LATVIA
Moscow
IRELAND
DENMARK
Baltic Sea
LITHUANIA
Dublin
Kaunas
GREAT BRITAIN
Danzig
EAST PRUSSIA (GER)
U S S R
HOLLAND
Berlin
London
Amsterdam
Warsaw
Atlantic Ocean
GERMANY
POLAND
Brussels
BELGIUM
RHINELAND
Prague
Paris
LUXEMBOURG
CZECHOSLOVAKIA
Vienna
Bay of Biscay
FRANCE
Bern
Budapest
AUSTRIA
SWITZERLAND
HUNGARY
ROMANIA
Belgrade
Bucharest
Black Sea
PORTUGAL
YUGOSLAVIA
Madrid
ITALY
BULGARIA
Lisbon
Sofia
Corsica
SPAIN
Rome
ALBANIA (ITA)
Balearic Islands
Sardinia
GREECE
Mediterranean Sea
TURKEY
Sicily
Athens
Rhodes
MOROCCO
ALGERIA
TUNISIA

Europe in December 1941
Greater Germany and Occupied Territories
Axis Nations and Satellites
Neutral
Allies
SWEDEN
FINLAND
NORWAY
Helsinki
Oslo
Talinn
Stockholm
North Sea
Riga
Moscow
IRELAND
DENMARK
Baltic Sea
OSTLAND
Dublin
Kaunas
GREAT BRITAIN
Danzig
EAST PRUSSIA
U S S R
HOLLAND
Berlin
London
Amsterdam
Warsaw
Atlantic Ocean
GERMANY
POLAND
Brussels
BELGIUM
RHINELAND
UKRAINE
Paris
Prague
LUXEMBOURG
SLOVAKIA
Vienna
Bay of Biscay
FRANCE
Bern
Budapest
AUSTRIA
SWITZERLAND
HUNGARY
ROMANIA
Bucharest
YUGOSLAVIA
Belgrade
Black Sea
PORTUGAL
SERBIA
Madrid
ITALY
BULGARIA
Lisbon
Sofia
Corsica
SPAIN
Rome
ALBANIA
Balearic Islands
Sardinia
GREECE
TURKEY
Mediterranean Sea
Sicily
Athens
Rhodes
MOROCCO
ALGERIA
TUNISIA

Postwar Europe
Soviet-imposed Communism
Communist
SWEDEN
FINLAND
NORWAY
Helsinki
Oslo
Stockholm
North Sea
Moscow
IRELAND
DENMARK
Baltic Sea
Dublin
GREAT BRITAIN
Danzig
U S S R
HOLLAND
Berlin
Warsaw
London
Amsterdam
Atlantic Ocean
EAST GERMANY
POLAND
Brussels
Bonn
BELGIUM
WEST GERMANY
Prague
Paris
LUXEMBOURG
CZECHOSLOVAKIA
Vienna
Bay of Biscay
FRANCE
Bern
Budapest
AUSTRIA
SWITZERLAND
HUNGARY
ROMANIA
Bucharest
Belgrade
Black Sea
PORTUGAL
YUGOSLAVIA
Madrid
ITALY
BULGARIA
Lisbon
Sofia
Corsica
SPAIN
Rome
ALBANIA
Balearic Islands
Tirana
Sardinia
GREECE
TURKEY
Mediterranean Sea
Sicily
Athens
Rhodes
MOROCCO
ALGERIA
TUNISIA

The Eastern Front
June 22, 1941 Front
NORWAY
FINLAND
Karelian Isthmus
USSR
Leningrad
SWEDEN
ESTONIA
Volga River
Demyansk
Moscow Military District
Oka River
Basic Military District
LATVIA
Moscow
Baltic Sea
LITHUANIA
Smolensk
EAST PRUSSIA
Minsk
Berlin
BELORUSSIA
Don River
Kursk
Warsaw
Bug River
Desna River
GERMANY
Pripyat Marshes
Kharkov
POLAND
Kiev
Donets River
Stalingrad
Prague
Dnieper River
CZECHOSLOVAKIA
UKRAINE
Rostov
Vienna
Budapest
HUNGARY
Odessa
Sea of Azov
CRIMEA
ROMANIA
Sevastopol
Belgrade
CAUCASUS
YUGOSLAVIA
Black Sea
Sofia
Adriatic Sea
ALBANIA
BULGARIA
TURKEY
GREECE

The Western Front
ENGLISH CHANNEL
Le Havre
Ste.-Mere-Eglise
Bay of the Seine
Colleville
Carentan
Aure R.
Bayeux
Caen Canal
Dives
Merville
Troarn
Dives R.
Caen
Vire R.
St-Lo
Bourgueous
North Sea
Baltic Sea
Kiel
Lubeck
Wilhemshaven
Hamburg
Bremen
NETHERLANDS
The Hague
Amsterdam
Rotterdam
Hanover
Braunschweig
Berlin
GERMAN REICH
Dunkirk
Calais
Antwerp
Brussels
Dusseldorf
Cologne
Kassel
Leipzig
Dresden
Erfurt
English Channel
BELGIUM
Remagen
Koblenz
Frankfurt am Main
Prague
Cherbourg
Dieppe
Le Havre
Bastogne
Schweinfurt
Caen
Rouen
Periers
St. Lo
Lisieux
Soissons
Mainz
Luxembourg
Furth
Brest
St.-Malo
Mantes
Rheims
Nuremberg
Falaise
Mortain
Snarbrud
Paris
Metz
Rennes
Alencon
Stuttgart
Regensburg
Lorient
Le Mans
Orleans
Ulm
Munich
St. Barthelemy
St.-Nazaire
Nantes
Salzburg
Berchtesgaden
Dijon
Zurich
FRANCE
SWITZERLAND
Bay of Biscay
Lyons
Milan
Venice
Bordeaux
Turin
CROATIA
Montelimar
Bayonne
Toulouse
Avignon
Nice
Marseilles
Cannes
ITALY
Toulon
SPAIN
Mediterraneann Sea
Corsica

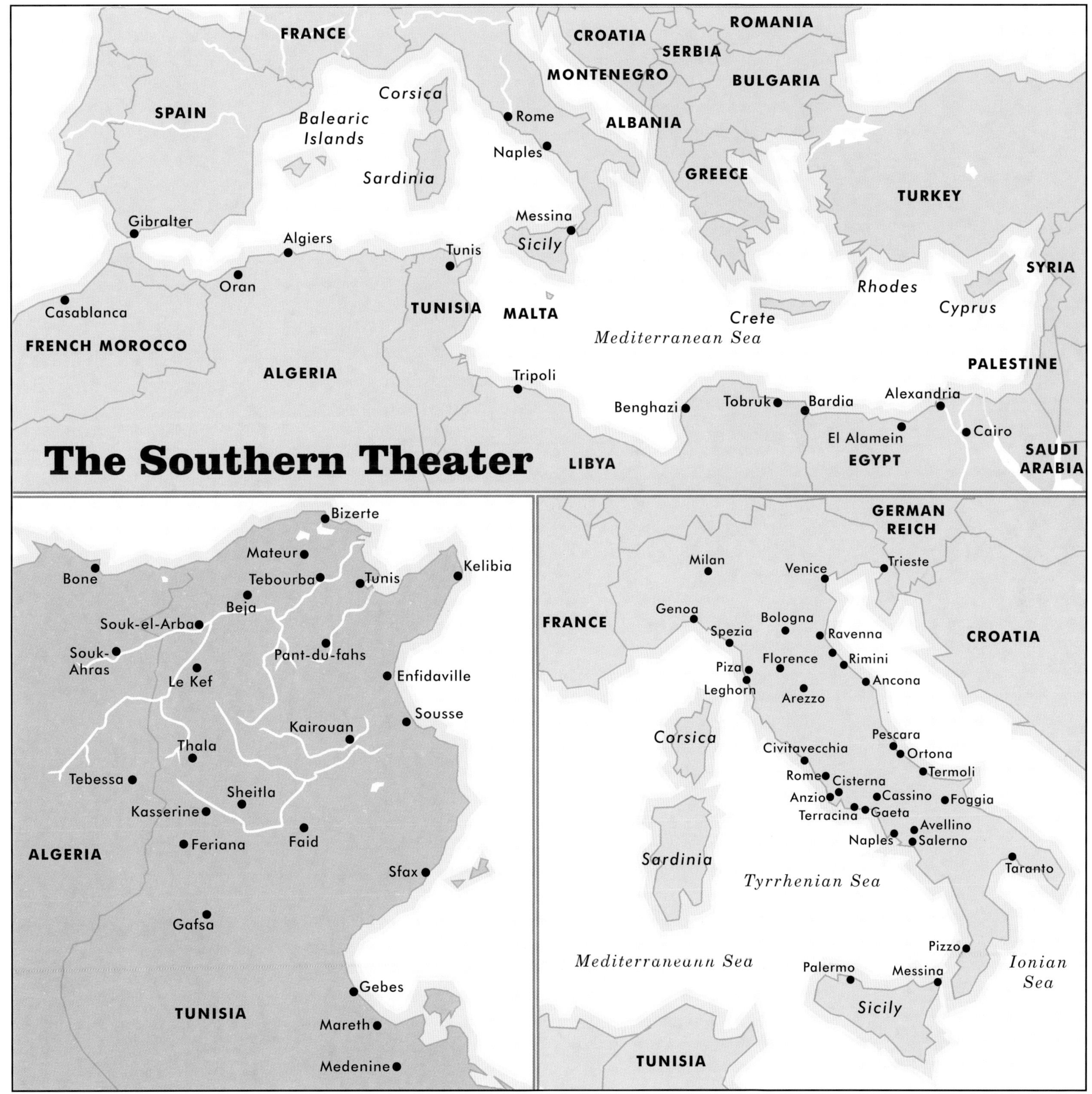
The Southern Theater
FRANCE
CROATIA
ROMANIA
SERBIA
MONTENEGRO
BULGARIA
SPAIN
Corsica
Balearic Islands
Rome
ALBANIA
Naples
Sardinia
GREECE
TURKEY
Gibralter
Messina
Algiers
Sicily
Tunis
Oran
SYRIA
Rhodes
Casablanca
TUNISIA
MALTA
Crete
Cyprus
FRENCH MOROCCO
Mediterranean Sea
ALGERIA
PALESTINE
Tripoli
Alexandria
Benghazi
Tobruk
Bardia
El Alamein
Cairo
EGYPT
LIBYA
SAUDI ARABIA
Bizerte
Mateur
Kelibia
Bone
Tebourba
Tunis
Beja
Souk-el-Arba
Souk-Ahras
Pant-du-fahs
Le Kef
Enfidaville
Sousse
Kairouan
Thala
Tebessa
Sheitla
Kasserine
Faid
Feriana
ALGERIA
Sfax
Gafsa
Gebes
TUNISIA
Mareth
Medenine
GERMAN REICH
Milan
Trieste
Venice
FRANCE
Genoa
Bologna
Ravenna
CROATIA
Spezia
Florence
Rimini
Piza
Ancona
Leghorn
Arezzo
Corsica
Pescara
Civitavecchia
Ortona
Termoli
Rome
Cisterna
Anzio
Cassino
Foggia
Terracina
Gaeta
Avellino
Naples
Salerno
Taranto
Sardinia
Tyrrhenian Sea
Pizzo
Mediterraneann Sea
Ionian Sea
Palermo
Messina
Sicily
TUNISIA

The Asian Mainland
USSR
OUTER MONGOLIA
MANCHURIA
(Manchukuo)
INNER MONGOLIA
CHINA
HOKKAIDO
Sapporo
Peking
KOREA
Sea of Japan
Seoul
Yellow Sea
Yellow River
HONSHU
Tokyo
Hiroshima
Kyoto
Tungshan
Nagasaki
SHIKOKU
KYUSHU
Nanking
Chengtu
Hankow
Shanghai
Pacific Ocean
Chungking
Yangtze River
East China Sea
Ledo
INDIA
OKINAWA
Imphal
Irrawaddy River
Kunming
Canton
FORMOSA
Lashio
Mandalay
Hanoi
Macao
Hong Kong
BURMA
FRENCH INDOCHINA
HAINAN
Rangoon
THAILAND
Manila
Bangkok
South China Sea
PHILIPPINE ISLANDS
Saigon
MALAYA
BRITISH NORTH BORNEO
PHILIPPINE ISLANDS
LUZON
Clark Field
Manila
MINDORO
SAMAR
PANAY
CEBU
LEYTE
NEGROS
BOHOI
MINDANAO
Sulu Sea

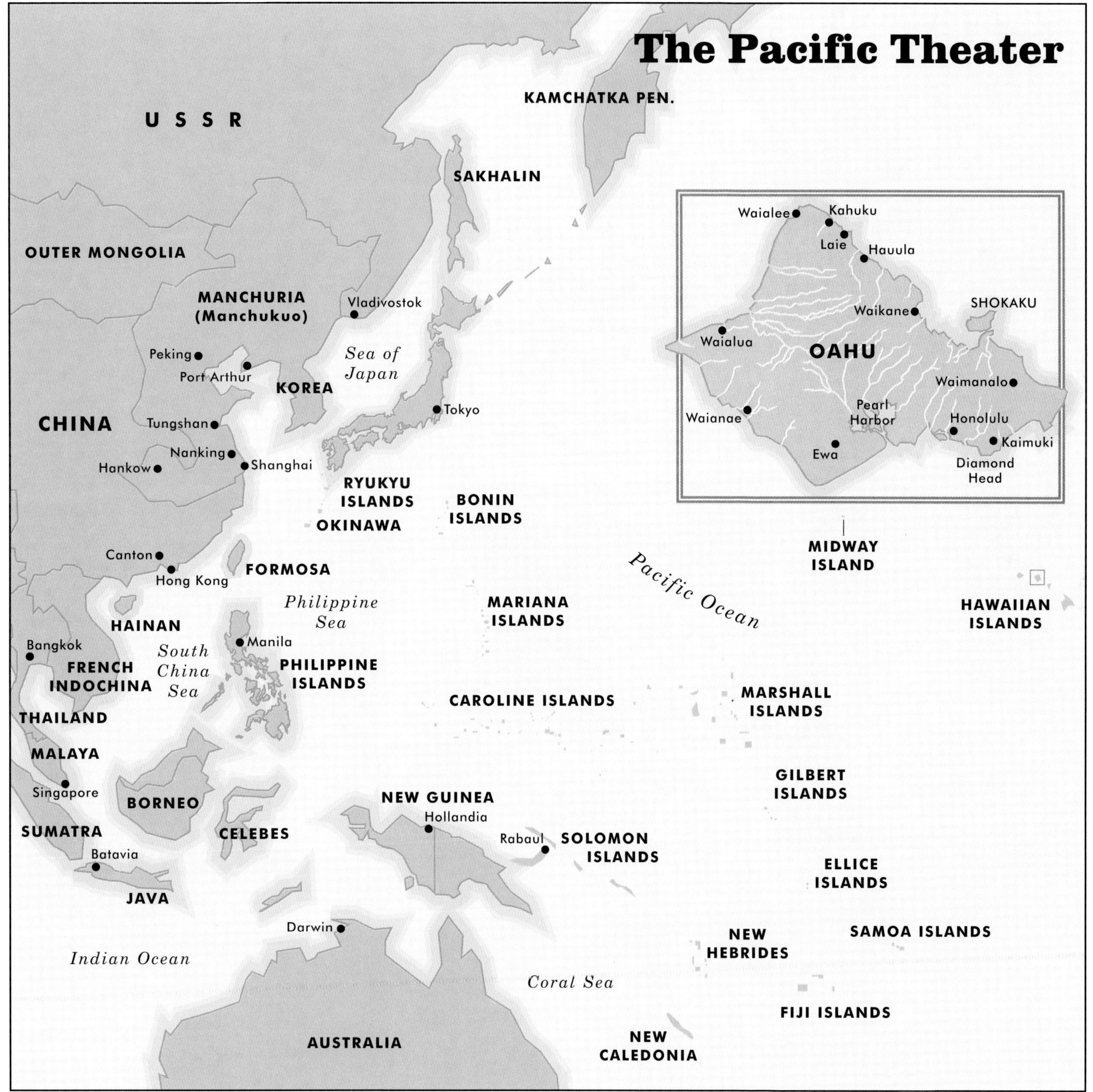
The Pacific Theater
KAMCHATKA PEN.
U S S R
SAKHALIN
OUTER MONGOLIA
MANCHURIA
(Manchukuo)
Vladivostok
Sea of
Japan
Peking
Port Arthur
KOREA
Tokyo
CHINA
Tungshan
Nanking
Shanghai
Hankow
RYUKYU
ISLANDS
BONIN
ISLANDS
OKINAWA
Canton
Hong Kong
FORMOSA
Philippine
Sea
MARIANA
ISLANDS
Pacific Ocean
MIDWAY
ISLAND
HAWAIIAN
ISLANDS
HAINAN
Bangkok
Manila
South
China
Sea
FRENCH
INDOCHINA
PHILIPPINE
ISLANDS
CAROLINE ISLANDS
MARSHALL
ISLANDS
THAILAND
MALAYA
GILBERT
ISLANDS
Singapore
BORNEO
NEW GUINEA
Hollandia
SUMATRA
CELEBES
Rabaul
SOLOMON
ISLANDS
Batavia
ELLICE
ISLANDS
JAVA
Darwin
NEW
HEBRIDES
SAMOA ISLANDS
Indian Ocean
Coral Sea
FIJI ISLANDS
AUSTRALIA
NEW
CALEDONIA
Waialee
Kahuku
Laie
Hauula
Waikane
SHOKAKU
Waialua
OAHU
Waimanalo
Pearl
Harbor
Waianae
Honolulu
Kaimuki
Ewa
Diamond
Head

Photo Credits

Credits from left to right are separated by semicolons; from top to bottom by dashes.

Cover: both, TimePix
Back Cover: Alfred Eisenstaedt/TimePix
Spine: Chrysalis Picture Library
Endpapers: National Archives/Neg. #III-SC-174523

2: TimePix. 7: Leonard McCombe/TimePix. 9: Robert Capa/Magnum Photos. 10-11: Hans Hubmann/Bildarchiv Preussischer Kulturbesitz. 12: Corbis; TimePix; Corbis. 13: courtesy of Franklin D. Roosevelt Library; Theodor Eisenhart/Bildarchiv Preussischer Kulturbesitz; Hulton-Deutsch Collection/Corbis. 14: Bettmann/Corbis; Hulton/Archive by Getty Images. 15: Mary Evans Picture Library; Bundesarchiv Koblenz/Neg. #ABC 14469; Hulton-Deutsch Collection/Corbis. 16: Hulton/Archive by Getty Images. 17: Christopher Ailsby Historical Archive; Roger Viollet/Getty Images. 18: Hulton/Archive by Getty Images; Hulton/Archive by Getty Images. 19: Ullstein Bilderdienst—Larry Scherer/High Impact Photography. 20: Süddeutscher Verlag Bilderdienst. 21: Robert Capa/Magnum Photos—Hulton/Archive by Getty Images—Robert Capa/Magnum Photos. 22: Roger Viollet/Getty Images. 23: Ullstein Bilderdienst. 24: Süddeutscher Verlag Bilderdienst—Corbis. 25: Hulton/Archive by Getty Images. 26: Bundesarchiv Koblenz/Neg. #102/14599—National Archives/Neg. #306-NJ-804. 27: Bundesarchiv Koblenz. 28: Bettmann/Corbis. 29: Hulton/Archive by Getty Images. 30: AP/Wide World Photos—Hulton/Archive by Getty Images. 31: AP/Wide World Photos. 32: Bundesarchiv Koblenz/Neg. #183/R47/312. 33: Corbis—Bettmann/Corbis. 34: Robert Capa/Magnum Photos—TimePix. 35: David Seymour/Magnum Photos. 36: Hulton/Archive by Getty Images. 37: clockwise from top left, TimePix; Corbis; TimePix; Deutsches Historiches Museum, Berlin Museum/Bildarchiv; Imperial War Museum/Dorling Kindersley. 38: Stadtarchiv Neustadt, courtesy of United States Holocaust Memorial Museum (USHMM)—Virginius Dabney, courtesy of USHMM. 39: clockwise from top left, Bundesarchiv Koblenz/Neg. #183/N 0827/322; Bundesarchiv Koblenz/Neg. #183/Z/1223/307; Bettmann/Corbis; courtesy of USHMM. 40: Süddeutscher Verlag Bilderdienst. 41: Christopher Ailsby Historical Archives; Popperfoto. 42: Bettmann/Corbis; Bundesarchiv Koblenz; Hulton-Deutsch Collection/Corbis. 43: Ullstein Bilderdienst. 44: Heinrich Hoffmann/TimePix. 45: Hulton/Corbis; Mary Evans Picture Library—Dorling Kindersley. 46: National Archives/Neg. #208-AA-175-QQ-1. 47: Ullstein Bilderdienst—Bildarchiv Preussischer Kulturbesitz. 48: Hulton/Archive by Getty Images—Bildarchiv Preussischer Kulturbesitz. 49: Bundesarchiv Koblenz/Neg. #101/318/71/11A. 50: Bettmann/Corbis. 51: Bundesarchiv Koblenz/Neg. #101/13/60/20—Bundesarchiv Koblenz/Neg. #146/85/75/29. 52: Bildarchiv Preussischer Kulturbesitz—Bettmann/Corbis. 53: Corbis. 54: Julien Bryan, courtesy of Sam Bryan—Bildarchiv Preussischer Kulturbesitz. 55: Bundesarchiv Koblenz. 56: Finnish Defense Force. 57: Sovfoto—Sovfoto. 58: Hugo Jaeger/TimePix; USHMM. 59: clockwise from top, Bildarchiv Preussischer Kulturbesitz; USHMM; USHMM/George Kaddish; Bundesarchiv Koblenz. 60-61: Imperial War Museum. 62, Bundesarchiv Koblenz; TimePix. 63: Bettmann/Corbis; Dorling Kindersley/Eden Camp Collection; Hulton/Archive by Getty Images. 64: National Museum of American History/Smithsonian Institution; Christopher Ailsby Historical Archive; Hulton/Archive. 65: Deutsches Historisches Museum, Berlin; Henry Groskinsky/TimePix. 66: Corbis. 67: Chrysalis Image Library; AP/Wide World Photos. 68: Bundesarchiv Koblenz. 69: AP/Wide World Photos; Mandeville Special Collections Library/University of California, San Diego—Imperial War Museum/Dorling Kindersley. 70: Cabinet War Rooms; Imperial War Museum. 71: Hulton/Archive by Getty Images; Imperial War Museum—Imperial War Museum. 72: Bildarchiv Preussischer Kulturbesitz. 73: Hulton/Archive by Getty Images. 74: Hugo Jaeger/TimePix—Bundesarchiv Koblenz/Neg. #146/72/59/12. 75: Bettmann/Corbis. 76: Bildarchiv Preussischer Kulturbesitz—Süddeutscher Verlag Bilderdienst. 77: Bundesarchiv Koblenz/Neg. #183/L 6187. 78: Bayerische Staatsbibliothek Munchen, Fotoarchiv Hoffman. 79: Bildarchiv Preussischer Kulturbesitz. 80: TimePix. 81: Corbis—Hulton/Archive by Getty Images. 82: Hulton/Archive by Getty Images. 83: William Vandivert/TimePix. 84: Hulton/Archive by Getty Images—Hulton/Archive by Getty Images. 85: Imperial War Museum. 86: Hulton/Archive by Getty Images; Imperial War Museum/Neg. #PC0243. 87: clockwise from top left, Arthur Rothstein/Corbis; Corbis; Archive Photos/Getty Images; Archive Photos/Getty Images. 88: Bettmann/Corbis—Smithsonian Institution/National Museum of American History. 89: clockwise from top left, Bettmann/Corbis; Bettmann/Corbis; Stan Cohen/Missoula, Montana; TimePix; Photofest. 90: Bildarchiv Preussischer Kulturbesitz. 91: Imperial War Museum; Bundesarchiv Koblenz/Neg. #146/77/18/114. 92: Associated Newspapers, courtesy of General Research Division, New York Public Library; Hulton/Archive by Getty Images. 93: Ullstein Bilderdienst; Christopher Ailsby Historical Archive—George Peterson Collection/High Impact Photography. 94: Bundesarchiv Koblenz/Neg. #78z/18/8a; Bildarchiv Preussischer Kulturbesitz—Christopher Ailsby Historical Archive. 95: Imperial War Museum/Neg. #E1636—Dorling Kindersley/Imperial War Museum/Neg. #DK-smf-11. 96: Bildarchiv Preussischer Kulturbesitz. 97: Ullstein Bilderdienst. 98: Imperial War Museum/Neg. #E 1636—Ullstein Bilderdienst. 99: AP/Wide World Photos. 100: Imperial War Museum/Neg. #A4143. 101: Dever/Black Star—Ullstein Bilderdienst. 102: Bildarchiv Preussischer Kulturbesitz—Imperial War Museum/Neg. #E1599. 103: Imperial War Museum/Neg. #E1579. 104: Bundesarchiv, Koblenz/Neg. #101/784/208/32A—IPOL, Inc. 105: Bildarchiv Preussischer Kulturbesitz. 106: Bildarchiv Preussischer Kulturbesitz. 107: Hulton/Archive by Getty Images—Imperial War Museum/Neg. #E1770. 108: Corbis; courtesy Herr Manfred Rommel/Lyndon Baines Johnson Library. 109: clockwise from top left, Imperial War Museum/RML 342; Courtesy Herr Manfred Rommel; Patton Museum of Cavalry and Armour; Mary Evans Picture Library. 110: Hulton/Archive by Getty Images; Peter Stackpole/TimePix. 111: clockwise from top left, Underwood & Underwood/Corbis; PIX INC./TimePix; Tommy Lavergne/Rice University; Hugo Jaeger/TimePix. 112: Museum Berlin Karlshorst, Arkadij Shaikhet Collection. 113: Christopher Ailsby Historical Archive; Ullstein Bilderdienst. 114: Süddeutscher Verlag Bilderdienst—Süddeutscher Verlag Bilderdienst. 115: Hulton-Deutsch Collection/Corbis; Sovfoto—Deutsches Historisches Museum, Berlin. 116: Ullstein Bilderdienst; Bildarchiv Preussischer Kulturbesitz—Dorling Kindersley/Imperial War Museum. 117: Bundesarchiv Koblenz/Neg. #146/91/39/2; Dorling Kindersley/Imperial War Museum. 118: A. Grimm/Bildarchiv Preussischer Kulturbesitz—Robert Hunt Library. 119: Süddeutscher Verlag Bilderdienst. 120: Ullstein Bilderdienst. 121: Bildarchiv Preussischer Kulturbesitz—Bundesarchiv Koblenz/Neg. #748836. 122: Tass/Bildarchiv Preussischer Kulturbesitz. 123: Sovfoto. 124: Hans Hubmann/Bildarchiv Preussischer Kulturbesitz. 125: PK-Schmidt-Schaumberg/Bildarchiv Preussischer Kulturbesitz—Bundesarchiv Koblenz. 126: Dmitri Baltermants/Magnum Photos. 127: Hulton/Archive by Getty Images. 128: Corbis—Dorling Kindersley/Imperial War Museum. 129: clockwise from top left, Sovfoto; Corbis; Hulton/Archive by Getty Images; Hulton/Archive by Getty Images. 130: Bildarchiv Preussischer Kulturbesitz—Christopher Ailsby Historical Archive. 131: clockwise from top left, Robert Hunt Library; Bildarchiv Preussischer Kulturbesitz; Bildarchiv Preussischer Kulturbesitz; Heinrich Hoffmann/TimePix. 132: National Archives/Neg. #NH 30549. 133: Chrysalis Picture Library; Corbis. 134: Corbis/Bettmann; Corbis/Bettmann—Al Freni/TimePix. 135: National Archives/Neg. #80-G-19930; John Frost Historical Newspaper Service—Henry Groskinsky/TimePix. 136: Corbis/Bettmann; TimePix—Imperial War Museum. 137: Special Collections, U.S. Military Academy Library/Courtesy Lyndon Baines Johnson Library; Corbis. 138: U.S. Naval Historical Center/Neg. #NH 50930. 139: National Archives/Neg. #80-G-19948. 140: National Archives/Neg. #80-G-182248—TimePix. 141: National Archives/Neg. #NH32420. 142: National Archives/Neg. #III-SC-282334. 143: Hulton/Archive by Getty Images. 144: Imperial War Museum/Neg. #HU31329—Imperial War Museum/Neg. #HU2777/V107. 145: Imperial War Museum/Neg. #HU2675. 146: Bettmann/Corbis; courtesy of Franklin D. Roosevelt Library. 147: clockwise from left, courtesy of Franklin D. Roosevelt Library; Bettmann/Corbis; Bettmann/Corbis; courtesy of Franklin D. Roosevelt Library. 148: Bettmann/Corbis; National Archives/Neg. #RG338/290/38/22/4. 149: clockwise from top left, National Archives/Neg. #210-CC-S-26C; Library of Congress/Neg. #LC-USE 618-D-5074; Stan Cohen, Missoula, Montana; Stan Cohen, Missoula, Montana. 150: Culver Pictures—Imperial War Museum. 151: clockwise from top left, National Archives/Neg. #III-SC-282345; Archive Photos/Getty Images; Imperial War Museum/Neg. #A30559; Chrysalis Picture Library; Milwaukee Public Museum. 152-153: Margaret Bourke-White/TimePix. 154: Myron Davis/TimePix. 155: Mary Evans Picture Library; courtesy of Franklin D. Roosevelt Library; Ullstein Bilderdienst. 156: AKG, London; USHMM; Imperial War Museum/Neg. #NA894. 157: Christopher Ailsby Historical Archive; Corbis; Corbis. 158: Arthur Grimm/Bildarchiv Preussischer Kulturbesitz. 159: Christopher Ailsby Historical Archive; Bundesarchiv Koblenz/Neg. #146/96/38/3. 160: Public Record Office; Imperial War Museum/Neg. #A24871. 161: Bundesarchiv Koblenz/Neg. #146/2001. 162: Imperial War Museum/Neg. #ZZZ3130C; Hulton/Archive by Getty Images. 163: Imperial War Museum/Neg. #HU2256. 164: Imperial War Museum/Neg. #A19726. 165: Imperial War Museum/Neg. #FX4000. 166: Lothar-Gunther Buchheim. 167: Arthur Grimm/Bildarchiv Preussischer Kulturbesitz. 168: Lothar-Gunther Buchheim—Bundesarchiv Koblenz/Neg. #146/97/17/2. 169: Bundesarchiv Koblenz/Neg. #87/88/78. 170: Imperial War Museum/Neg. #NY1248. 171: National Archives/Neg. #26-G-1517. 172: Anne Frank Fonds, Basel/Anne Frank House, Amsterdam—USHMM. 173: clockwise from top left, Anne Frank Fonds, Basel/Anne Frank House, Amsterdam; Anne Frank Fonds, Basel/Anne Frank House, Amsterdam; Anne Frank Fonds, Basel/Anne Frank House, Amsterdam; Anne Frank Fonds, Basel/Anne Frank House, Amsterdam/Archive Photos; Anne Frank Fonds,

Basel/Anne Frank House, Amsterdam/Archive Photos. 174: Corbis/Bettmann—National Museum of American History/Smithsonian Institution. 175: clockwise from top left, AP/Wide World Photos; Public Record Office Image Library; Royal Air Force Museum, Hendon; Dorling Kindersley/Imperial War Museum; Dorling Kindersley/courtesy H. Keith Melton Collection; Dorling Kindersley/Imperial War Museum. 176: National Archives/Neg. #80-G-640553. 177: Bishop Books Collection; National Archives/Neg. #80-G-16511. 178: National Archives/Neg. #342-FH-3A2972—Bettmann/Corbis. 179: Hulton-Deutsch Collection/Corbis. 180: National Archives/Neg. #127-GR-HI-109148—National Archives/Neg. #80-G-17054. 181: National Archives/Neg. #80-G-312064—courtesy of Franklin D. Roosevelt Library. 182: National Archives/Neg. #80-G-41194—Ralph Morse/TimePix. 183: Corbis/Bettmann-UPI. 184: National Archives/Neg. #80-G-16569—Corbis. 185: National Archives/Neg. #80-G-13106. 186: National Archives/Neg. #80-G-7413—National Archives/Neg. #80-G-17422. 187: National Archives/Neg. #80-G-7397. 188: National Archives. 189: National Archives/Neg. #80-G-41686—National Archives/Neg. #80-G-414422. 190: National Archives/Neg. #80-G-182252—National Archives/Neg. #80-G-14384. 191: National Archives/Neg. #80-G-414423. 192: National/Archives/Neg. #80-G-14384. 193: National Archives/Neg. #80-G-17061—Library of Congress/Neg. #MI-10-11060. 194: National Archives/Neg. #179-WP-1563—TimePix. 195: Library of Congress/Neg. #LC-USW3-24739-d; Library of Congress/Neg. #LC-USW33-25833-zc—Library of Congress. 196: Bletchley Park Trust/Science & Society Picture Library. 197: clockwise from top left, Bildarchiv Preussischer Kulturbesitz; National Crypotological Museum/NSA; National Archives/Neg. #127-mn-57875; Science and Society Picture Library; National Cryptological Museum/Larry Scherer. 198: Hulton/Archive by Getty Images. 199: Imperial War Museum; Imperial War Museum. 200: Chrysalis Picture Library; George Rodger/Magnum Photos. 201: Hulton/Archive by Getty Images; Imperial War Museum; Corbis. 202: Popperfoto/Archive Photos: Imperial War Museum/Neg. #SE 2138. 203: Imperial War Museum. 204: Bettmann/Corbis. 205: George Rodger/TimePix—Hulton/Archive by Getty Images. 206: Corbis. 207: William Vandivert/TimePix. 208: William Vandivert/TimePix; Imperial War Museum. 209: Imperial War Museum. 210: Hulton/Archive by Getty Images. 211: National Archives/Neg. #III-SC-197483—Imperial War Museum. 212: Hulton/Archive by Getty Images. 213: Imperial War Museum. 214: Imperial War Museum. 215: Imperial War Museum. 216: Imperial War Museum; courtesy of Franklin D. Roosevelt Library. 217: National Archives/Neg. #III-SC-134627; courtesy of *New York Times*—Corbis. 218: Bundesarchiv Koblenz/Neg. #Z18-510-22. 219: Christopher Ailsby Historical Archive; Ullstein Bilderdienst. 220: AKG London—Christopher Ailsby Historical Archive. 221: Ullstein Bilderdienst/Frentz. 222: Itar-Tass/Sovfoto—Sovfoto; Itar-Tass/Sovfoto. 223: Sovfoto. 224: Ullstein Bilderdienst. 225: Ullstein Bilderdienst—Süddeutscher Verlag Bilderdienst. 226: Süddeutscher Verlag Bilderdienst—Bildarchiv Preussischer Kulturbesitz. 227: Bundesarchiv Koblenz. 228: Sovfoto. 229: Sovfoto—AKG London. 230: Bildarchiv Preussischer Kulturbesitz—Ullstein Bilderdienst. 231: Sovfoto/Eastfoto. 232: AKG London. 233: AKG London (2). 234: Sovfoto. 235: Itar-Tass/Sovfoto—Bundesarchiv Koblenz/Neg. #73/80/38. 236: Bildarchiv Preussischer Kulturbesitz—USHMM. 237: clockwise from top left, USHMM; USHMM; USHMM; Sovfoto. 238: Bundesarchiv Koblenz/Neg. #2498A—Christopher Ailsby Historical Archive. 239: clockwise from top left, Bettmann/Corbis; Bundesarchiv Koblenz/Neg. #102/14381; AKG London; Ullstein Bilderdienst; Christopher Ailsby Historical Archive. 240: Imperial War Museum. 241: courtesy of Franklin D. Roosevelt Library; TimePix. 242: Imperial War Museum/Neg. #A12661; TimePix. 243: Imperial War Museum/Neg. #NA894; John Frost Historical Newspaper Service. 244: courtesy of Franklin D. Roosevelt Library. 245: Corbis; Imperial War Museum/Neg. #K5287—John Frost Historical Newspaper Service. 246: Bildarchiv Preussischer Kulturbesitz (2). 247: Imperial War Museum/Neg. #E18832. 248: Imperial War Museum/Neg. #E19353. 249: Imperial War Museum/Neg. #NA1165—Imperial War Museum/Neg. #NA2003. 250: Archive Photos/Getty Images—Eliot Elisofon/TimePix. 251: Eliot Elisofon/TimePix. 252: Hulton/Archive by Getty Images. 253: Imperial War Museum/Neg. #NA5388—Hulton/Archive by Getty Images. 254: Imperial War Museum/Neg. #NA6630. 255: Library of Congress/Neg. #LC-USZ62-67839—Imperial War Museum. 256: Imperial War Museum/Neg. #NA7273. 257: Robert Capa/Magnum Photos—Imperial War Museum/Neg. #NA6999. 258: Imperial War Museum/Neg. #E18980—courtesy D-Day Museum, Portsmouth. 259: clockwise from top left, Corbis; Imperial War Museum/Neg. #Q112044; Corbis; Imperial War Museum/Neg. #E15788. 260: Bettmann/Corbis—National Archives/Neg. #NWDNS-44-PA-370. 261: clockwise from top left, Schomburg Center for Research in Black Culture, New York Public Library; Schomburg Center for Research in Black Culture, New York Public Library; Schomburg Center for Research in Black Culture, New York Public Library; National Archives/Neg. #NWDNS44-PA-87. 262: Library of Congress/Neg. #LC-USZ62-98194. 263: courtesy of Franklin D. Roosevelt Library; National Archives/Neg. #NWDNS-127-N-64363. 264: Frank Schershel/TimePix; TimePix—Lyndon Baines Johnson Library and Museum. 265: Corbis—Chrysalis Picture Library. 266: Chrysalis Picture Library; George Strock/TimePix. 267: Australian War Memorial; George Silk/Australian War Memorial. 268: George Silk/Australian War Memorial (2). 269: TimePix. 270: US Navy/Archive Photos/Getty Images—TimePix. 271: AP/Wide World Photos. 272: Corbis. 273: TimePix. 274: Library of Congress—TimePix. 275: Library of Congress/Neg. #LC-USZ62-92427. 276: National Archives/Neg. #III-SC-174164. 277: AP/Wide World Photos—National Archives/Neg. #III-SC-174525. 278: AP/Wide World Photos. 279: clockwise from top left, courtesy Mainichi Newspapers; Bettmann/Corbis; Natori/Black Star/TimePix; Berliner Zeitung. 280: Corbis—Photofest. 281: clockwise from top left, Photofest; Hulton/Archive by Getty Images; Photofest; Photofest; AP/Wide World Photos. 282: National Archives/Neg. #NWDNS-208-YE-7. 283: courtesy of Franklin D. Roosevelt Library; Imperial War Museum/Neg. #CH11647. 284: Imperial War Museum/Neg. #TR1156; Bildarchiv Preussischer Kulturbesitz/E.Gnilka. 285: Hulton/Getty by Getty Images—Public Record Office, Key Surrey/INF 3/184. 286: Margaret Bourke-White/TimePix. 287: Imperial War Museum/Neg. #HU44474; West Point Museum/Chrysalis Picture Library. 288: Imperial War Museum/Neg. #HU42331—Imperial War Museum/Neg. #CH10712. 289: Imperial War Museum/Neg. #C3371. 290: Bundesarchiv Koblenz. 291: Imperial War Museum/Neg. #HU12143—Bundesarchiv Koblenz/Neg. #183/J7449. 292: Imperial War Museum/Neg. #C3186. 293: Ullstein Bilderdienst. 294: Margaret Bourke-White/TimePix. 295: Imperial War Museum/Neg. #CH11641. 296: Süddeutscher Verlag Bilderdienst. 297: Süddeutscher Verlag Bilderdienst. 298: Archive France/Tallandier/Archive Photos/Getty Images—Erich Lessing/Art Resource, NY; courtesy of Franklin D. Roosevelt Library. 299: clockwise from top left, Juen Wang/Museum of Danish Reisistance; Public Record Office, Surrey; Polish Underground Movement Study Trust, London; Roger Viollet/Getty Images. 300: Globe Photos; Mary Evans Picture Library. 301: clockwise from left, Deutsches Historiches Museum, Berlin; Corbis; Deutsches Filminsitut-DIF; Deutsches Filminsitut-DIF. 302-303: TimePix. 304: courtesy of Franklin D. Roosevelt Library; John Frost Historical Newspaper Service; Bettmann/Corbis; Carl Mydans/TimePix. 305: Imperial War Museum/Neg. #EA48001; AP/Wide World Photos. 306: courtesy of Franklin D. Roosevelt Library; Sovfoto/Eastfoto. 307: Tass/Bildarchiv Preussischer Kulturbesitz; courtesy Hiroshima Peace Memorial Museum; Bettmann/Corbis. 308: Library of Congress/Neg. #USZ62-93535. 309: courtesy of Franklin D. Roosevelt Library; AP/Wide World Photos. 310:Warren M. Bodie Collection; Imperial War Museum/Neg. #NYP21768—courtesy of Franklin D. Roosevelt Library. 311: Museum of Flight/Corbis. 312: Hulton/Archive by Getty Images; AKG London—Dorling-Kindersley/Imperial War Museum. 313: Bernard Hoffman/TimePix. 314: National Archives/Neg. #342-FH-3-A5385-53959 A.C.—National Archives/Neg. #342-K 2785. 315: National Archives/Neg. #342-FH-3A-16140-52895 A.C. 316: J.R. Eyerman/TimePix—Bernard Hoffman/TimePix. 317: J. R. Eyerman/Timepix. 318: TimePix—courtesy Mainichi Newspapers. 319: Corbis. 320: TimePix—Bettmann/Corbis. 321: National Archives/Neg. #80-G-334769. 322: The Illustrated London News Picture Library. 323: clockwise from left, U.S. Army/TimePix; Bettmann/Corbis; Ullstein Bilderdienst; Imperial War Museum/Neg. #HU44273. 324: Bundesarchiv Koblenz/Neg. #0827/318N—USHMM/National Archives. 325: clockwise from top left, Bundesarchiv Koblenz/Neg. #79022/IN; TimePix; USHMM; Corbis. 326: Imperial War Museum/Neg. #NYF 36579. 327: courtesy of Franklin D. Roosevelt Library; Corbis. 328: TimePix. 329: Corbis; J. R. Eyerman/TimePix—courtesy of Franklin D. Roosevelt Library. 330: TimePix. 331: TimePix; courtesy of Franklin D. Roosevelt Library; courtesy of Franklin D. Roosevelt Library. 332: Imperial War Museum/Neg. #NYF14749. 333: TimePix. 334: William Shrout/TimePix. 335: National Archives/Neg. #111-SC-190036—National Archives/Neg. #80-G-284948. 336: Corbis. 337: National Archives/Neg. #127-GR-135-70532. 338: W. Eugene Smith/TimePix—Imperial War Museum. 339: W. Eugene Smith/TimePix. 340: National Archives/Neg. #80-G-238363. 341: J. R. Eyerman/Timepix. 342: TimePix—National Archives/Neg. #111-SC-260631. 343: Corbis. 344: National Archives/Neg. #80-G-273413—Corbis. 345: TimePix. 346: TimePix—Salamander Books. 347: clockwise from top left, Imperial War Museum/Neg. #A30426; Corbis; Chrysalis Picture Library; Hulton/Archive by Getty Images; Hulton-Deutsch Collection/Corbis. 348: Robert Capa/Magnum Photos. 349: courtesy of Franklin D. Roosevelt Library; TimePix. 350: TimePix. 351: Public Record Office, Key Surrey/ADM234-366; John Frost Historical Newspaper Service. 352: Bundesarchiv Koblenz/Neg. #146/89/26/18A. 353: Bundesarchiv Koblenz/Neg. #101/721/359/35; Chysalis Picture Library/Memorial Museum, Bayeaux—Chysalis Picture Library/Memorial Museum, Bayeaux. 354: Robert Hunt Library—Robert Capa/Magnum Photos. 355: Bildarchiv Preussischer Kulturbesitz. 356: TimePix. 357: Robert Capa/Magnum Photos—TimePix. 358: Imperial War Museum/Neg. #MH25274. 359: Imperial War Museum/Neg. #B5114. 360: Imperial War Museum/Neg. #B-6184. 361: Imperial War Museum/Neg. #B-6782. 362: National Archives/Neg. #III-SC-191876. 363: Corbis. 364: Bundesarchiv Koblenz/Neg. #146/84/35/9a—Bundesarchiv Koblenz/Neg. #101/738/293 I/1A. 365: AP/Wide World Photos. 366: Bettmann/Corbis. 367: Roger Viollet/Getty Images.

368: Imperial War Museum/Neg. #EA25491—courtesy of Franklin D. Roosevelt Library. 369: clockwise from left, Dwight D. Eisenhower Library; Corbis; Bettmann/Corbis; Dwight D. Eisenhower Library. 370: clockwise from left, Bettmann/Corbis; Alan Gottlieb Collection; George Eastman House. 371: clockwise from top left, Magnum Photos; Hans Hubmann/Bildarchiv Preussischer Kulturbesitz; Hans Hubmann/Bildarchiv Preussischer Kulturbesitz; Margaret Bourke-White/TimePix; courtesy of Franklin D. Roosevelt Library. 372: Yevgeny Khaldei/Corbis. 373: Dorling Kindersley/Imperial War Museum; Ullstein Bilderdienst. 374: Bayerische Staatsbibliotheque, Munchen (Fotoarchiv Hoffmann S.116:4601)—TimePix. 375: Hulton-Deutsch Collection/Corbis. 376: Heinrich Hoffman/Bildarchiv Preussischer Kulturbesitz; Tass/Bildarchiv Preussischer Kulturbesitz. 377: Yevgeny Khaldei/Corbis; Archive Photos by Getty Images. 378: TimePix—Bildarchiv Preussischer Kulturbesitz. 379: Imperial War Museum/Neg. #EA17886. 380: Corbis. 381: George Silk/TimePix— Süddeutscher Verlag Bilderdienst. 382: TimePix—TimePix. 383: Imperial War Museum/Neg. #EA47958. 384: Imperial War Museum/Neg. #EA 68789. 385: Imperial War Museum/Neg. #EA 48582. 386: George Silk/TimePix. 387: Bildarchiv Preussischer Kulturbesitz—Robert Capa/ Magnum Photos. 388: Sovfoto—Yevgeny Khaldei/Corbis. 389: Imperial War Museum/Neg. #KY12151F. 390: Sovfoto—Ivan Shagin/Magnum Photos. 391: Sovfoto/Eastfoto. 392: Sovfoto—TimePix. 393: clockwise from top left, Sovfoto; TimePix; Sovfoto/Eastfoto; TimePix. 394: TimePix—USHMM. 395: clockwise from top left, George Rodger/TimePix; Margaret Bourke-White/TimePix; USHMM; TimePix. 396: AP/Wide World Photos. 397: courtesy of Franklin D. Roosevelt Library; Bettmann/Corbis. 398: Imperial War Museum. 399: National Archives/Neg. #127-N-117054; Chrysalis Picture Library. 400: TimePix; John Frost Historical Newspaper Service—Yuichiro Sasaki/courtesy Hiroshima Peace Memorial Museum. 401: Carl Mydans/TimePix; Chrysalis Picture Library. 402: National Archives/Neg. #127-GR-90-111688—AP/Wide World Photos. 403: W. Eugene Smith/TimePix. 404: Corbis. 405: Hulton/Archive by Getty Images—W. Eugene Smith/TimePix. 406: National Archives/Neg. #127-G-118775. 407: National Archives/Neg. #127-N-119485—J.R. Eyerman/TimePix. 408: Wayne Miller/Magnum Photos. 409: Bernard Hoffman/TimePix. 410: Yosuke Yamahata/G.T. Sun Co., Tokyo. 411: Yosuke Yamahata/G.T. Sun Co., Tokyo; Yosuke Yamahata/Magnum Photos. 412: Imperial War Museum—courtesy of Harry S. Truman Library. 413: clockwise from top left, Bettman/Corbis, courtesy Harry S. Truman Library; TimePix, courtesy Harry S. Truman Library; Bettmann/Corbis, courtesy of Harry S. Truman Library; Bettmann/Corbis, courtesy of Harry S. Truman Library. 414: courtesy Los Alamos National Laboratory—courtesy of Franklin D. Roosevelt Library. 415: clockwise from top left, National Archives/Neg. #434-OR-42-MED-325; Corbis; Underwood & Underwood/Corbis; Bettmann/Corbis; 416, Hulton/Archive by Getty Images—Chrysalis Picture Library. 417: clockwise from top left, NHK, Japan; Hulton/Archive by Getty Images; Bettmann/Corbis; AP. 418: TimePix. 419: TimePix; Corbis. 420: Bettmann/Corbis; Bildarchiv Preussischer Kulturbesitz—Deutsches Historiches Museum, Berlin. 421: Hulton/Archive by Getty Images. 422: Corbis; Carl Mydans/TimePix. 423: Corbis—Deutsches Historiches Museum, Berlin. 424: Sovfoto/Eastfoto—Bob Landry/TimePix. 425: Alfred Eisenstaedt/TimePix. 426: Bettmann/Corbis. 427: Hulton/Archive by Getty Images—Hulton-Deutsch Collection/Corbis. 428: Hulton/Archive by Getty Images—Hulton/Archive by Getty Images. 429: Ralph Morse/TimePix. 430: Walter Sanders/TimePix. 431: Corbis—Bettmann/Corbis. 432: Bettmann/Corbis—AP/Wide World Photos. 433: Ruth Gruber/TimePix. 434: George Silk/TimePix—John Florea/TimePix. 435: Bettmann/Corbis. 436: Bettmann/Corbis—Henri Cartier-Bresson/Magnum Photos. 437: Jim Burke/TimePix. 438: AP/Wide World Photos—Deutches Historiches Museum. 439: clockwise from top left, National Archives/USHMM; Ralph Morse/TimePix; Hulton/Archive by Getty Images; National Archives/USHMM; Ralph Morse/TimePix. 440: Frank Schershel/TimePix—Bildarchiv Preussischer Kulturbesitz. 441: clockwise from top left, Nat Farbman/TimePix; National Archive/Neg. #NWDNS-286-ME-9(18); AP/Wide World Photos; Corbis.

Bibliography

Ambrose, Stephen E., *American Heritage New History of World War II*. Viking Penguin, 1970.

——— *Band of Brothers*. Simon & Schuster, 1992

——— *D-Day*. Simon & Schuster, 1994.

——— *Eisenhower: Soldier and President*. Simon & Schuster, 1990.

Barnett, Correlli, *Hitler's Generals*. Quill/William Morrow, 1989.

Bickers, Richard Townshend, *The Battle of Britain*. Salamander, 1990.

Binns, Stewart, and Adrian Wood, *The Second World War in Color*. Contemporary Books, 1999.

Boyle, David, *World War II: A Photographic History*. Metro Books, 2000.

Boyne, Walter J., *Clash of Wings: Airpower in World War II*. Simon & Schuster, 1994.

Boatner, Mark, III, *The Biographical Dictionary of World War II*. Presidio, 1996.

Bradley, Omar, *A Soldier's Story*. Henry Holt, 1951.

Cannon, M. Hamlin, *Leyte: The Return to the Philippines*. Department of the Army, 1954.

Coffey, Thomas M., *Lion by the Tail*. Viking Press, 1974.

Cohen, Stan, *V for Victory*. Pictorial Histories, 1991.

Cray, Ed, *General of the Army*. Cooper Square Press, 1990.

Cruikshank, Charles, *Greece, 1940-1941*. University of Delaware Press, 1976.

DeNevi, Donald, *The West Coast Goes to War*. Pictorial Histories, 1998.

Dugan, James, and Laurence Lafore, *Days of Emperor and Clown*. Doubleday, 1973.

Dunnigan, James F., and Albert A. Nofi, *The Pacific War Encyclopedia*. Checkmark Books, 1998.

Eisenhower, Dwight, *Crusade in Europe*. Doubleday, 1948.

Flaherty, Thomas H., and John Newton, *World War II, vols. 1-39*. Time-Life Books, 1982.

Fest, Joachim, *Hitler*. Harcourt, 1971.

The German Campaigns in the Balkans. Center for Military History, U.S. Army, 1986.

Gilbert, Martin, *The Second World War*. Henry Holt, 1989.

Goldstein, Donald M., Katherin V. Dillon, and J. Michael Wenger, *Rain of Ruin*. Brassey's, 1995.

Hall, Tony, ed., *D-Day: Operation Overlord*. Salamander, 1993.

Harriman, W. Averell, and Elie Abel, *Special Envoy to Churchill and Stalin, 1941-1946*. Random House, 1975.

Hastings, Max, *Victory in Europe*. Little, Brown, 1985.

Hitler, Adolf, *Mein Kampf*, trans. Ralph Manheim, Houghton Mifflin, 1971.

Holmes, Richard, *The World Atlas of Warfare*. Viking, 1988.

——— *World War II in Photographs*. Carlton Books, 2000.

Horne, Alistair, *To Lose a Battle: France 1940*. Little, Brown, 1969.

Jäckel, Eberhard, *Hitler's World View*. Harvard, 1981.

Jenkins, Rupert, ed., *Nagasaki Journey*. Pomegranate Artbooks, 1995.

Jones, James, *WWII*. Ballantine, 1975.

Jordan, Killian, ed., *Our Finest Hour*. Time Inc., 2000.

Keegan, John, *The Second World War*. Penguin Books, 1989.

Macintyre, Donald, *The Battle of the Atlantic*. B. T. Batsford, 1961.

Mallmann-Showell, Jak P., *The German Navy in World War II*. Naval Institute Press, 1979.

McCullough, David, *Truman*. Simon & Schuster, 1992.

Morrison, Samuel Elliot, *The Battle of the Atlantic*. Little, Brown, 1950.

——— *The Two Ocean War: A Short History of the United States Navy in World War II*. Little Brown, 1963.

Murray, Williamson and Allan R. Millett, *A War to Be Won: Fighting the Second World War*. Harvard, 2000.

Nalty, Bernard C., ed., *War in the Pacific: Pearl Harbor to Tokyo Bay*. University of Oklahoma, 1991.

Overy, Richard, *Why the Allies Won*. Norton, 1995.

Overy, Richard, with Andrew Wheatcroft, *The Road to War*. Penguin, 1989.

Padfield, Peter, *War Beneath the Sea: Submarine Conflict During World War II*. John Wiley & Sons, 1995.

Potter, E. B., *Nimitz*. Naval Institute Press, 1976.

Rees, Laurence, *War of the Century: When Hitler Fought Stalin*. The New Press, 1999.

Rhodes, Richard, *The Making of the Atomic Bomb*. Simon & Schuster, 1986.

Rooney, Andy, *My War*. Public Affairs, 1995.

Scherman, David E., ed., *LIFE Goes to War*. Little, Brown, 1977.

Slamaggi, Cesare, and Alredo Pallavisini, *2194 Days of War*. Barnes & Noble, 1977.

Schlesinger, Arthur M., Jr., *A Life in the 20th Century, 1917-1950*. Houghton Mifflin Company, 2000.

Sherwood, Robert E., *The White House Papers of Harry L. Hopkins*. Eyre & Spottiswoode, 1949.

Shirer, William, *The Rise and Fall of the Third Reich*. Simon & Schuster, 1960.

Snyder, Louis L., *Encyclopedia of the Third Reich*. McGraw Hill, 1976.

Speer, Albert, *Inside the Third Reich*. Macmillan Company, 1970.

Swift, Michael, and Michael Sharpe, *Historical Maps of World War II Europe*. PRC, 2000.

Taylor, Telford, *Munich: The Price of Peace*. Doubleday, 1979.

Toland, John, *The Rising Sun*. Random House, 1970.

Watt, Donald Cameron, *How War Came: The Immediate Origins of the Second World War, 1938-1939*. Pantheon Books, 1989.

Weinberg, Gerhard L., *A World at Arms*. Cambridge University Press, 1994.

Woodhead, Henry, ed., *The Third Reich, vols. 1-21*. Time-Life Books, 1992.

Index